Garfield throws his weight around

BY: JIM DAVIS

Ballantine Books • New York

A Ballantine Book
Published by The Ballantine Publishing Group

Copyright © 1998 by PAWS, Incorporated.

All rights reserved under International and Pan-American Copyright
Conventions. Published in the United States by The Ballantine Publishing
Group, a division of Random House, Inc., New York, and simultaneously in
Canada by Random House of Canada Limited, Toronto.

http://www.randomhouse.com

Library of Congress Catalog Card Number: 98-96144

ISBN: 0-345-42749-1

Manufactured in the United States of America

First Edition: October 1999

10 9 8 7 6 5 4 3 2 1

ODIE'S PAST LIVES

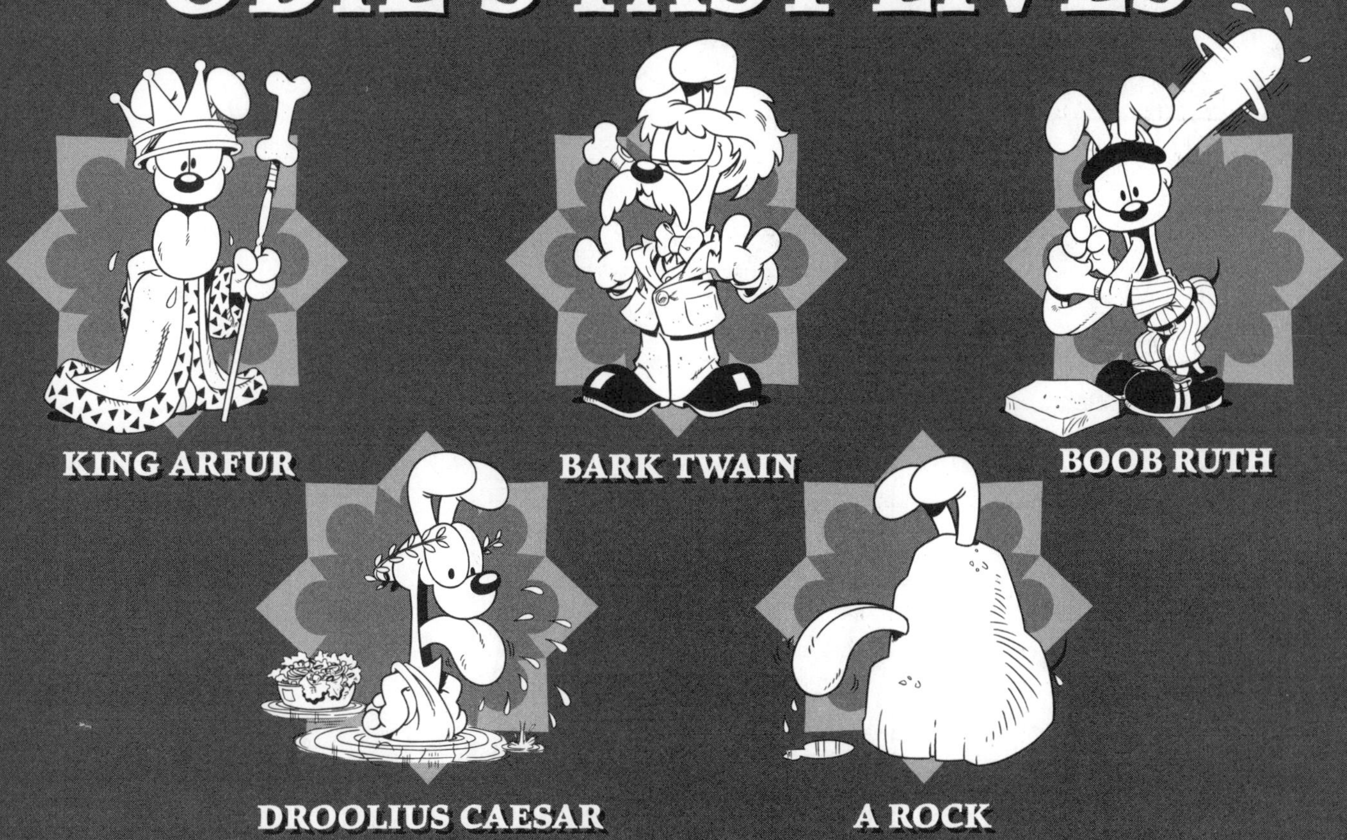
KING ARFUR
BARK TWAIN
BOOB RUTH
DROOLIUS CAESAR
A ROCK

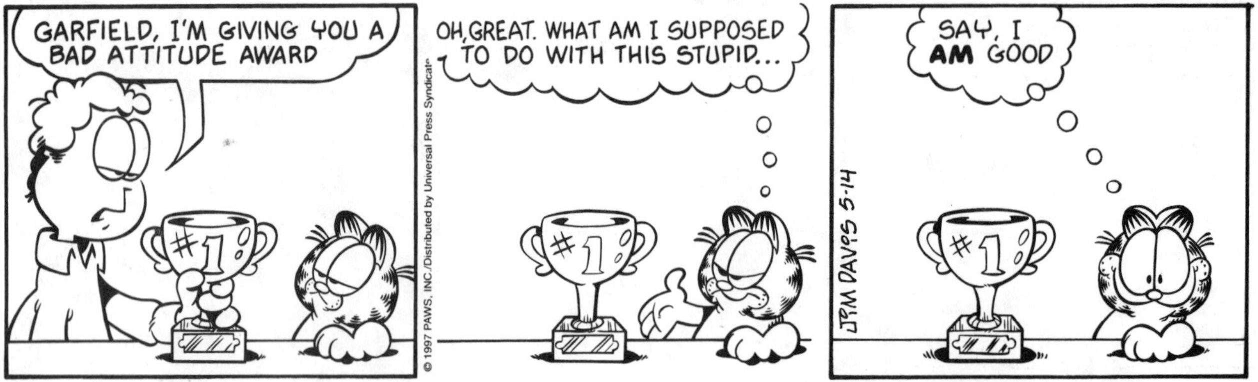
GARFIELD, I'M GIVING YOU A BAD ATTITUDE AWARD
© 1997 PAWS, INC./Distributed by Universal Press Syndicate
OH, GREAT. WHAT AM I SUPPOSED TO DO WITH THIS STUPID...
JIM DAVIS 5-14
SAY, I **AM** GOOD

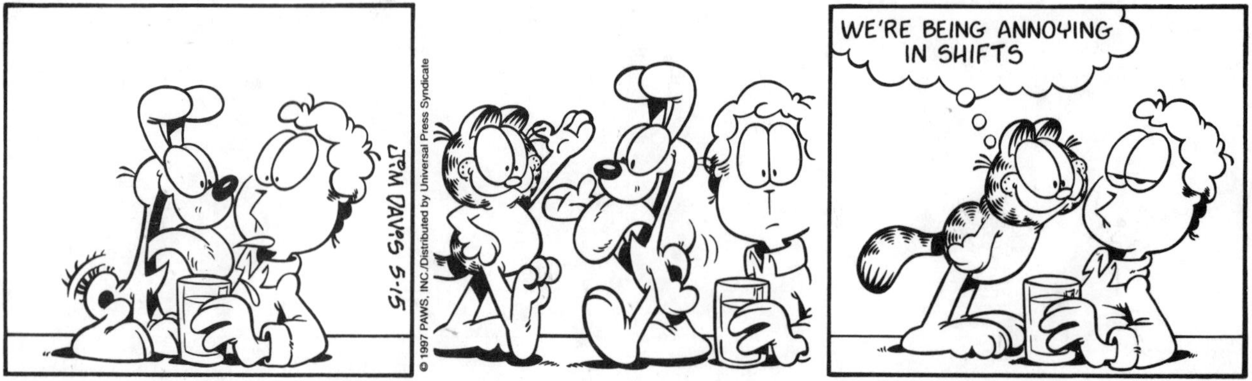
JIM DAVIS 5-15
© 1997 PAWS, INC./Distributed by Universal Press Syndicate
WE'RE BEING ANNOYING IN SHIFTS

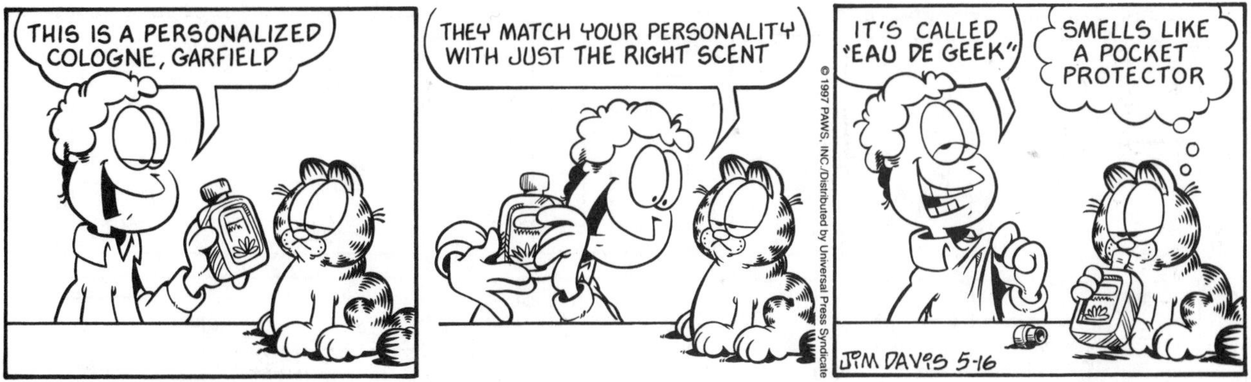
THIS IS A PERSONALIZED COLOGNE, GARFIELD
THEY MATCH YOUR PERSONALITY WITH JUST THE RIGHT SCENT
IT'S CALLED "EAU DE GEEK"
SMELLS LIKE A POCKET PROTECTOR
© 1997 PAWS, INC./Distributed by Universal Press Syndicate
JIM DAVIS 5-16

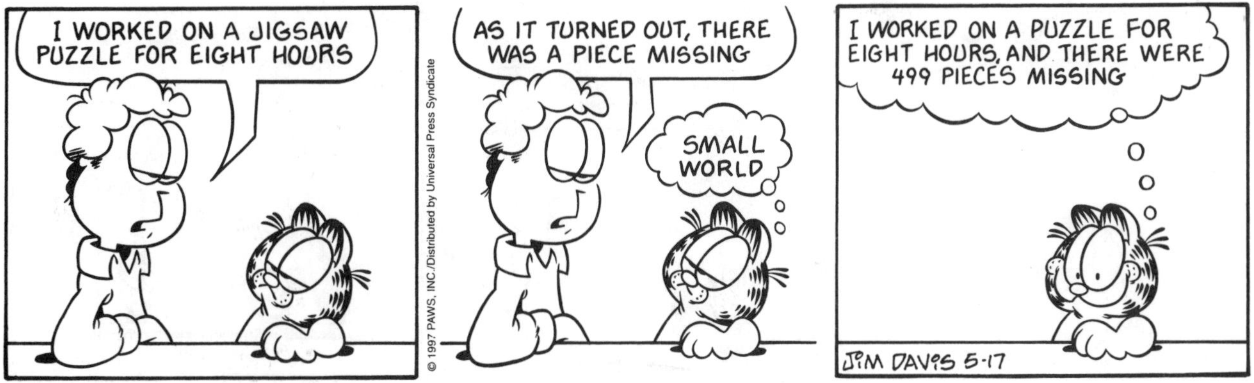
I WORKED ON A JIGSAW PUZZLE FOR EIGHT HOURS
AS IT TURNED OUT, THERE WAS A PIECE MISSING
SMALL WORLD
I WORKED ON A PUZZLE FOR EIGHT HOURS, AND THERE WERE 499 PIECES MISSING
© 1997 PAWS, INC./Distributed by Universal Press Syndicate
JIM DAVIS 5-17

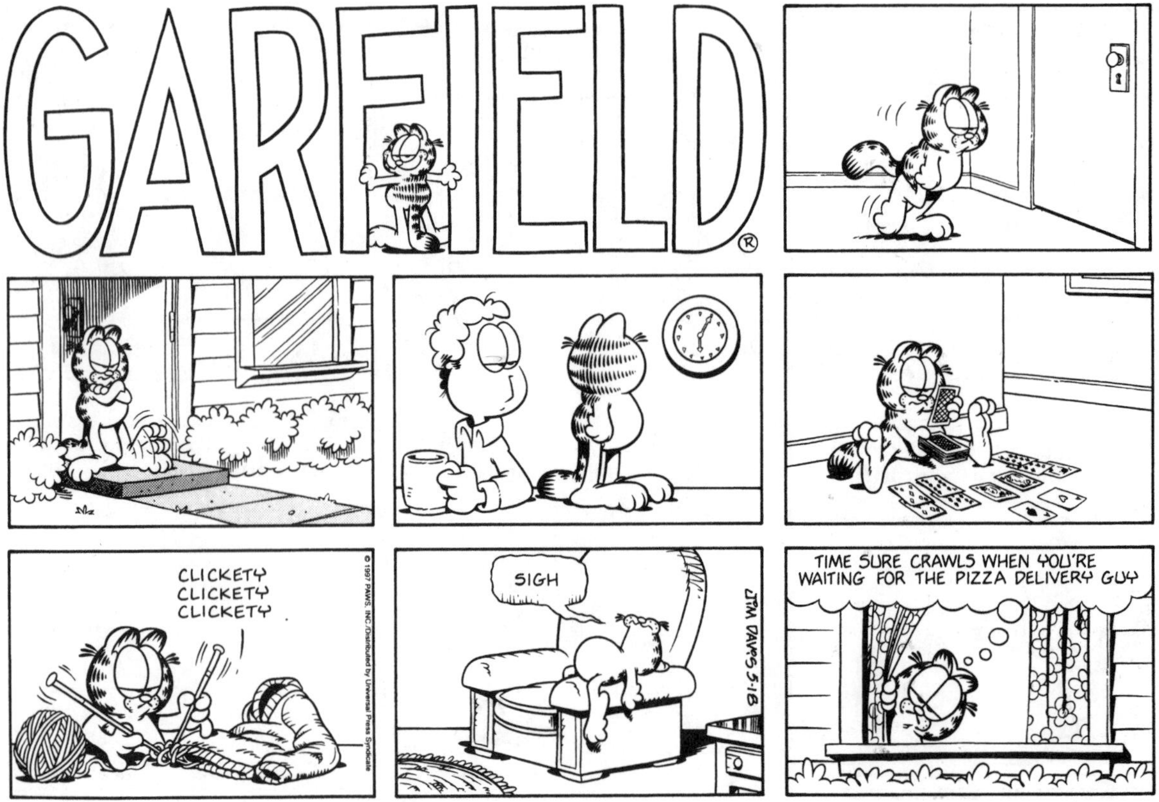
GARFIELD
© 1997 PAWS, INC./Distributed by Universal Press Syndicate
CLICKETY
CLICKETY
CLICKETY
SIGH
JIM DAVIS 5-18
TIME SURE CRAWLS WHEN YOU'RE WAITING FOR THE PIZZA DELIVERY GUY

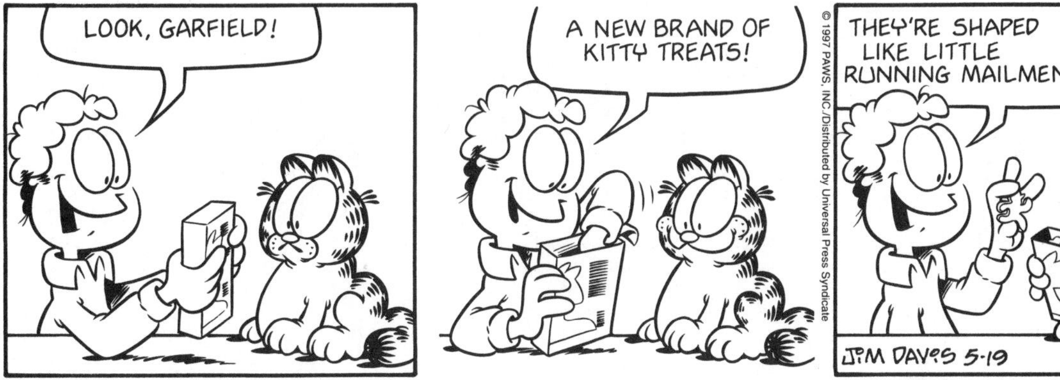
LOOK, GARFIELD!
A NEW BRAND OF KITTY TREATS!
THEY'RE SHAPED LIKE LITTLE RUNNING MAILMEN
"SUGAR SWEETENED CIVIL SERVANTS," I LIKE IT!
JIM DAVIS 5-19

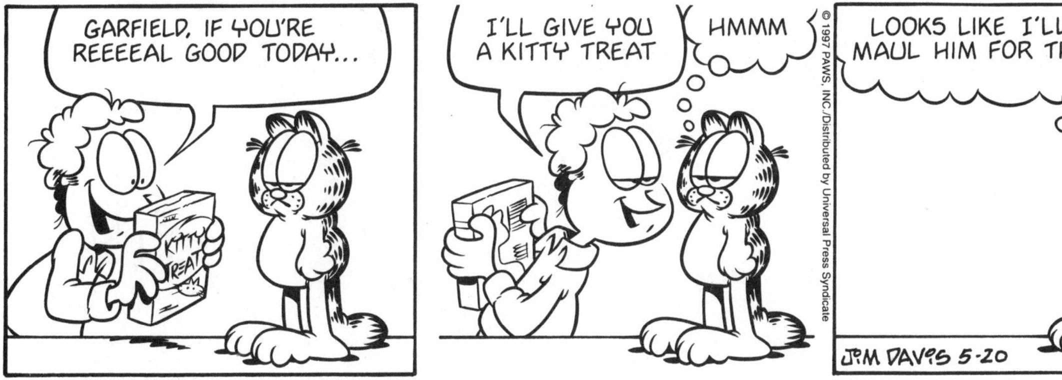
GARFIELD, IF YOU'RE REEEEAL GOOD TODAY...
I'LL GIVE YOU A KITTY TREAT
HMMM
LOOKS LIKE I'LL HAVE TO MAUL HIM FOR THE BOX AGAIN
JIM DAVIS 5-20

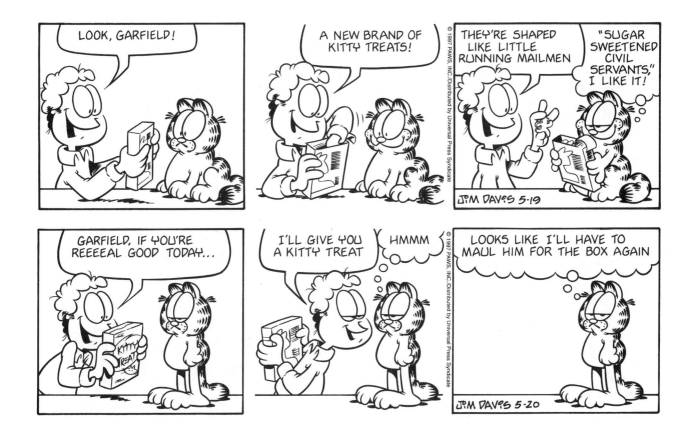

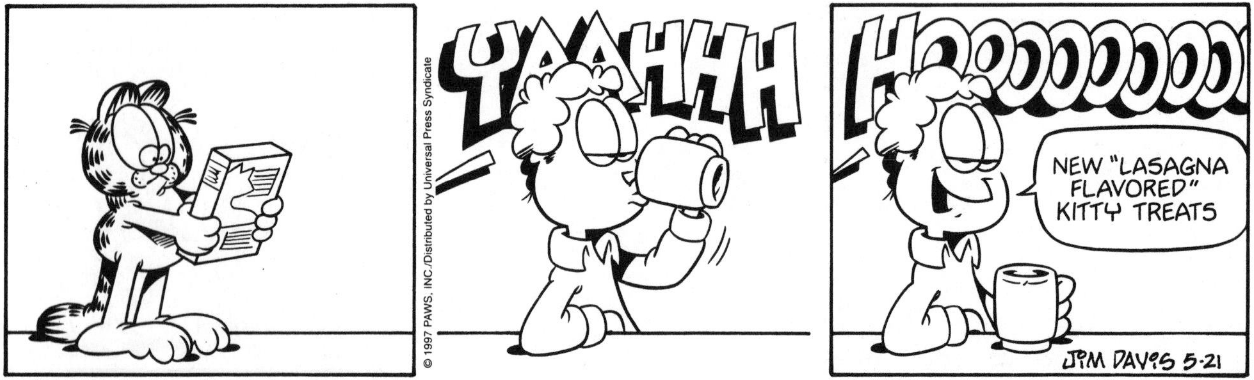
YAAHHH
HOOOOOOOO
NEW "LASAGNA FLAVORED" KITTY TREATS
JIM DAVIS 5-21
© 1997 PAWS, INC./Distributed by Universal Press Syndicate

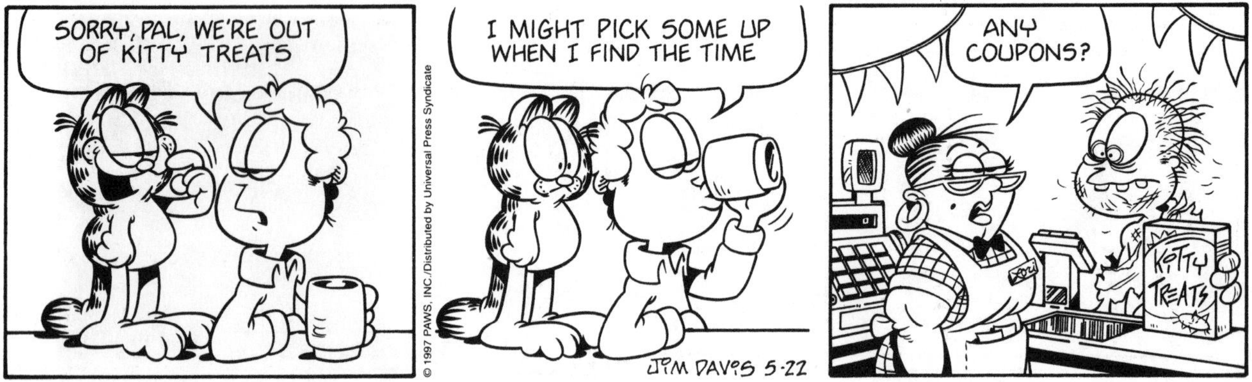
SORRY, PAL, WE'RE OUT OF KITTY TREATS
I MIGHT PICK SOME UP WHEN I FIND THE TIME
JIM DAVIS 5-22
ANY COUPONS?
KITTY TREATS
© 1997 PAWS, INC./Distributed by Universal Press Syndicate

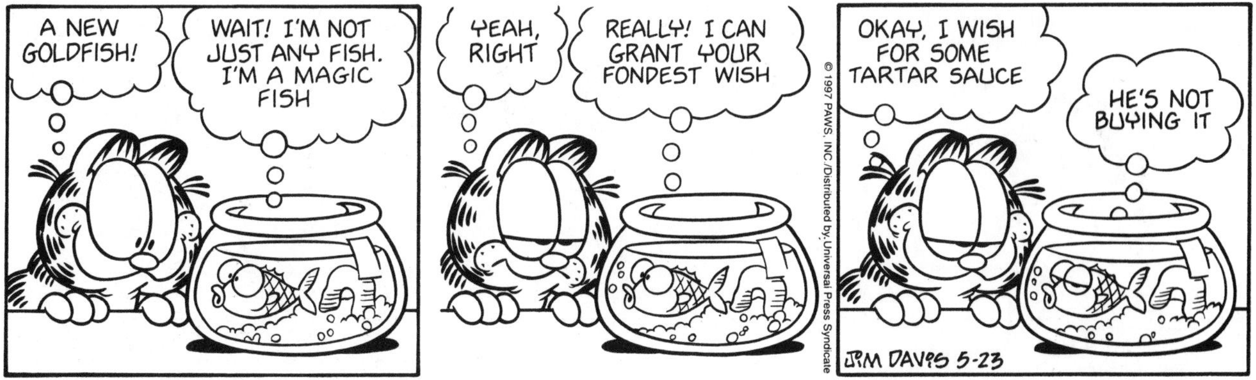
A NEW GOLDFISH!
WAIT! I'M NOT JUST ANY FISH. I'M A MAGIC FISH
YEAH, RIGHT
REALLY! I CAN GRANT YOUR FONDEST WISH
OKAY, I WISH FOR SOME TARTAR SAUCE
HE'S NOT BUYING IT
JIM DAVIS 5-23

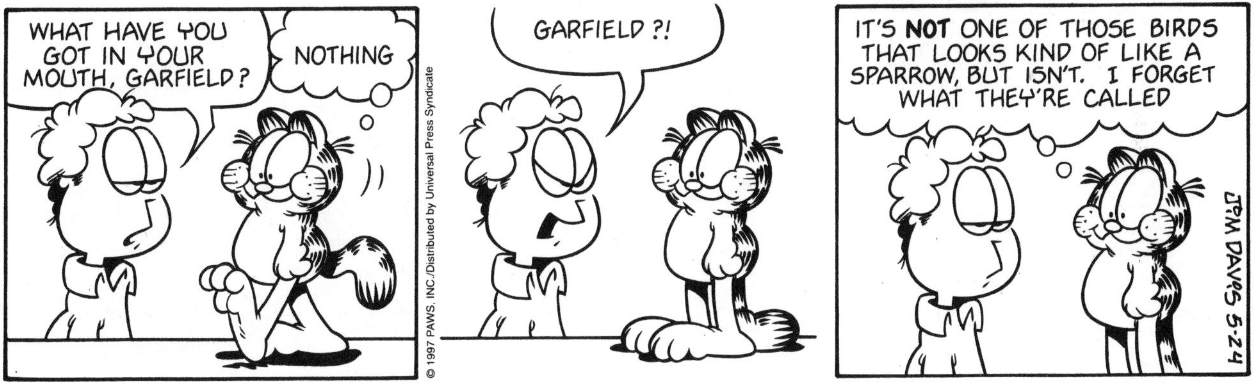
WHAT HAVE YOU GOT IN YOUR MOUTH, GARFIELD?
NOTHING
GARFIELD?!
IT'S **NOT** ONE OF THOSE BIRDS THAT LOOKS KIND OF LIKE A SPARROW, BUT ISN'T. I FORGET WHAT THEY'RE CALLED
JIM DAVIS 5-24

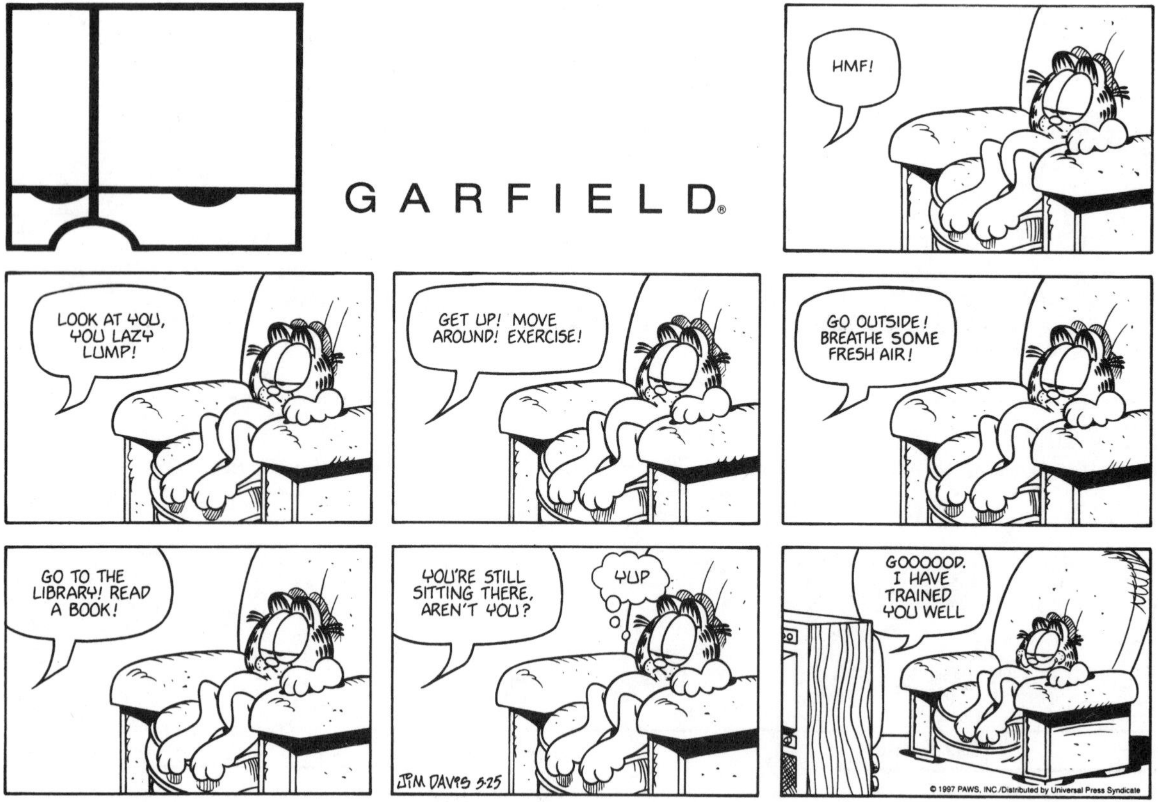
GARFIELD®
HMF!
LOOK AT YOU, YOU LAZY LUMP!
GET UP! MOVE AROUND! EXERCISE!
GO OUTSIDE! BREATHE SOME FRESH AIR!
GO TO THE LIBRARY! READ A BOOK!
YOU'RE STILL SITTING THERE, AREN'T YOU?
YUP
JIM DAVIS 5-25
GOOOOOD. I HAVE TRAINED YOU WELL
© 1997 PAWS, INC./Distributed by Universal Press Syndicate

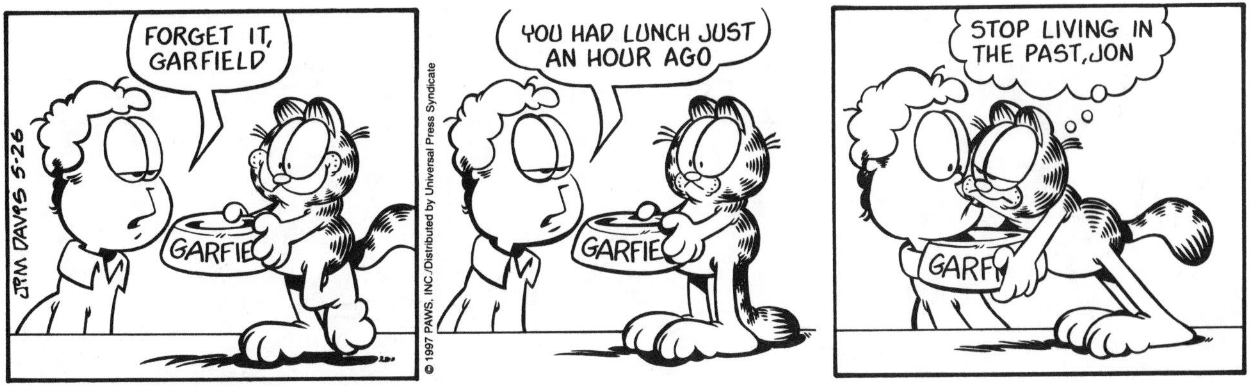
FORGET IT, GARFIELD
YOU HAD LUNCH JUST AN HOUR AGO
STOP LIVING IN THE PAST, JON
GARFIE
GARFIE
GARF
JIM DAVIS 5-26

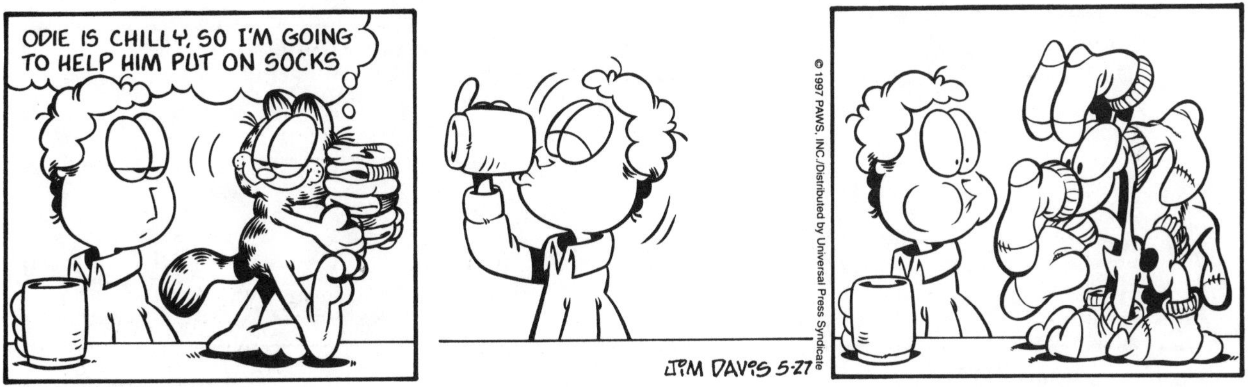
ODIE IS CHILLY, SO I'M GOING TO HELP HIM PUT ON SOCKS
JIM DAVIS 5-27

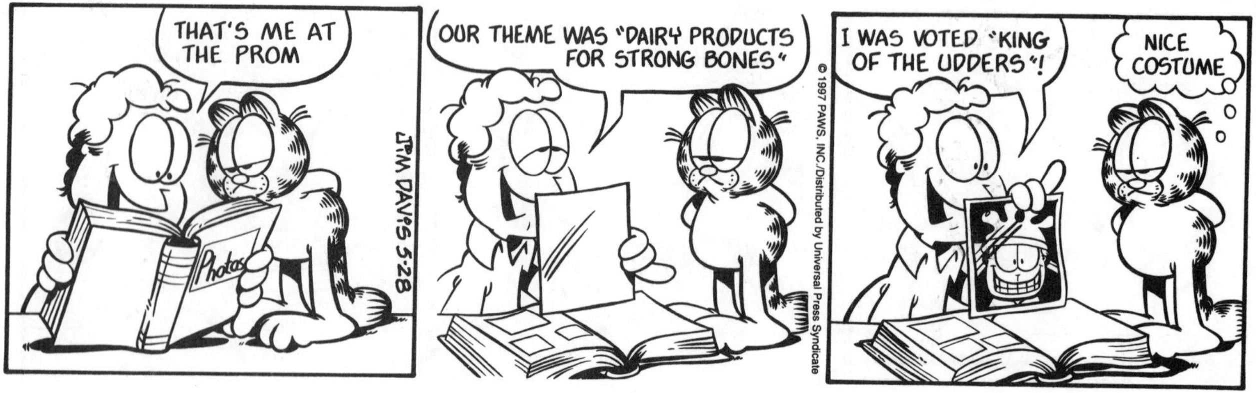
THAT'S ME AT THE PROM
Photos
JIM DAVIS 5-28
OUR THEME WAS "DAIRY PRODUCTS FOR STRONG BONES"
© 1997 PAWS, INC./Distributed by Universal Press Syndicate
I WAS VOTED "KING OF THE UDDERS"!
NICE COSTUME

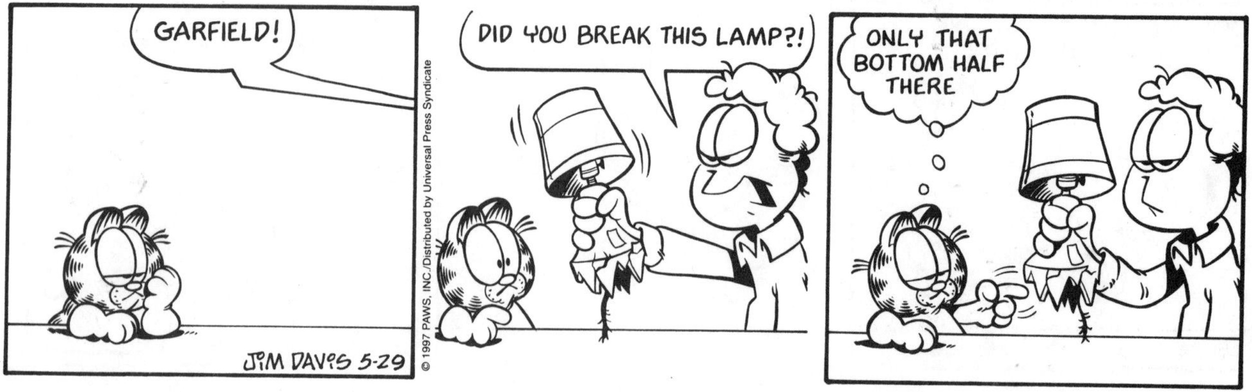
GARFIELD!
JIM DAVIS 5-29
© 1997 PAWS, INC./Distributed by Universal Press Syndicate
DID YOU BREAK THIS LAMP?!
ONLY THAT BOTTOM HALF THERE

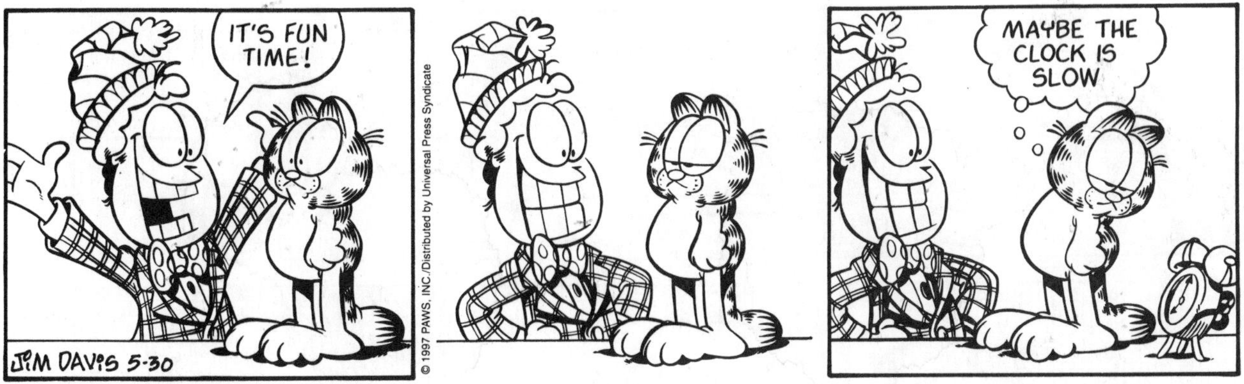
IT'S FUN TIME!
MAYBE THE CLOCK IS SLOW
JIM DAVIS 5-30
© 1997 PAWS, INC./Distributed by Universal Press Syndicate

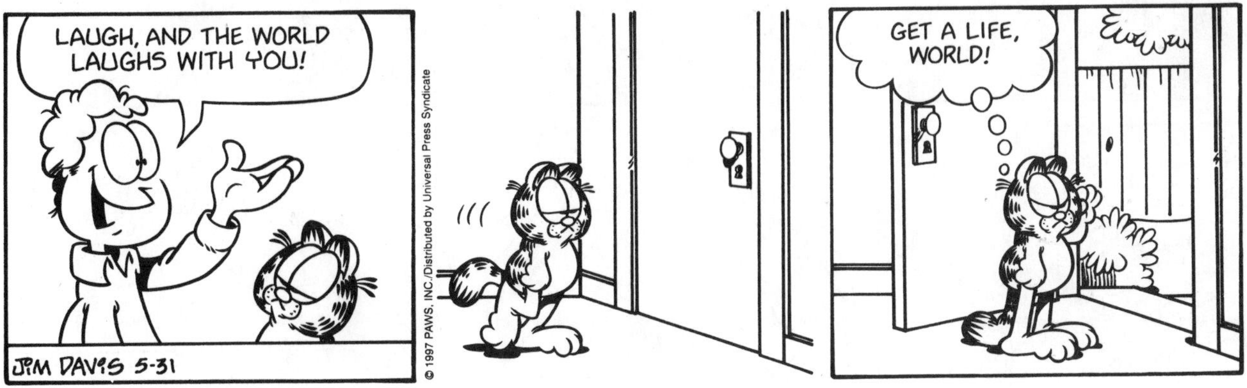
LAUGH, AND THE WORLD LAUGHS WITH YOU!
GET A LIFE, WORLD!
JIM DAVIS 5-31
© 1997 PAWS, INC./Distributed by Universal Press Syndicate

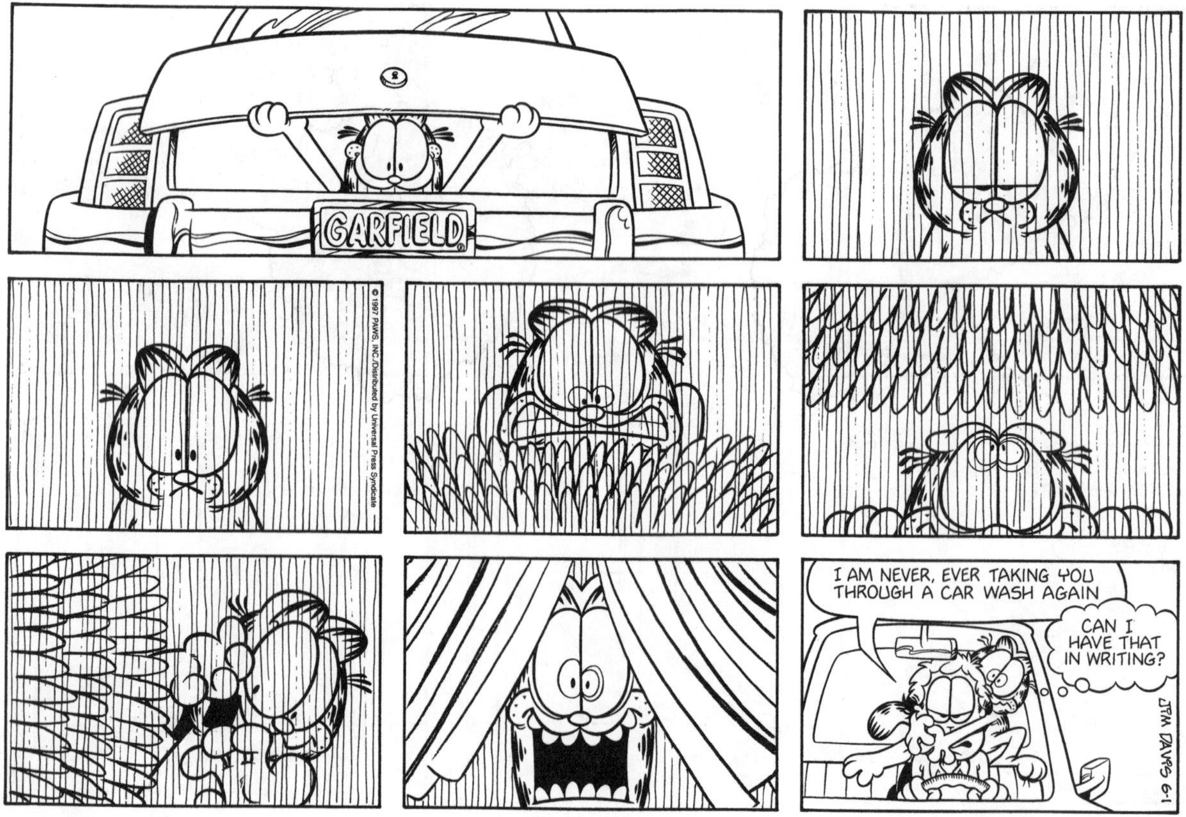
GARFIELD®
© 1997 PAWS, INC./Distributed by Universal Press Syndicate
I AM NEVER, EVER TAKING YOU THROUGH A CAR WASH AGAIN
CAN I HAVE THAT IN WRITING?
JIM DAVIS 6-1

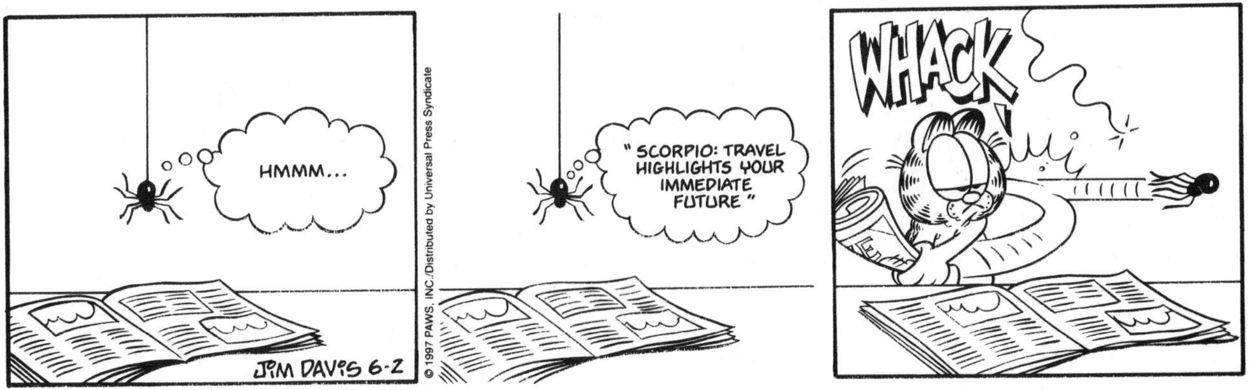
HMMM...
JIM DAVIS 6-2
" SCORPIO: TRAVEL HIGHLIGHTS YOUR IMMEDIATE FUTURE "
WHACK

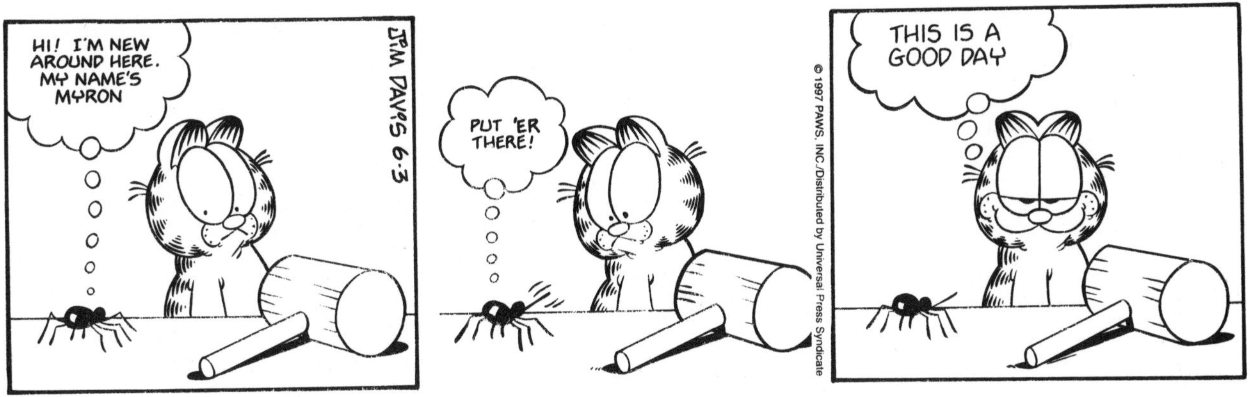
HI! I'M NEW AROUND HERE. MY NAME'S MYRON
JIM DAVIS 6-3
PUT 'ER THERE!
THIS IS A GOOD DAY

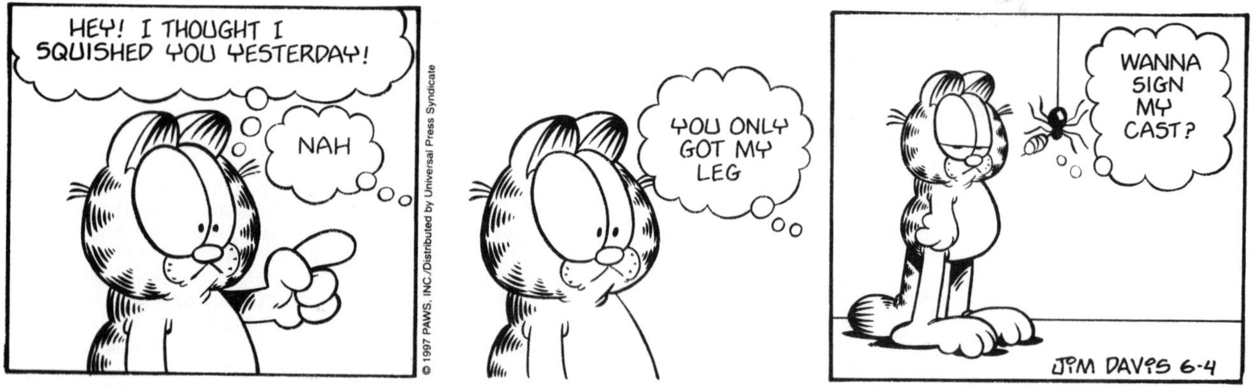
HEY! I THOUGHT I SQUISHED YOU YESTERDAY!
NAH
YOU ONLY GOT MY LEG
WANNA SIGN MY CAST?
JIM DAVIS 6-4

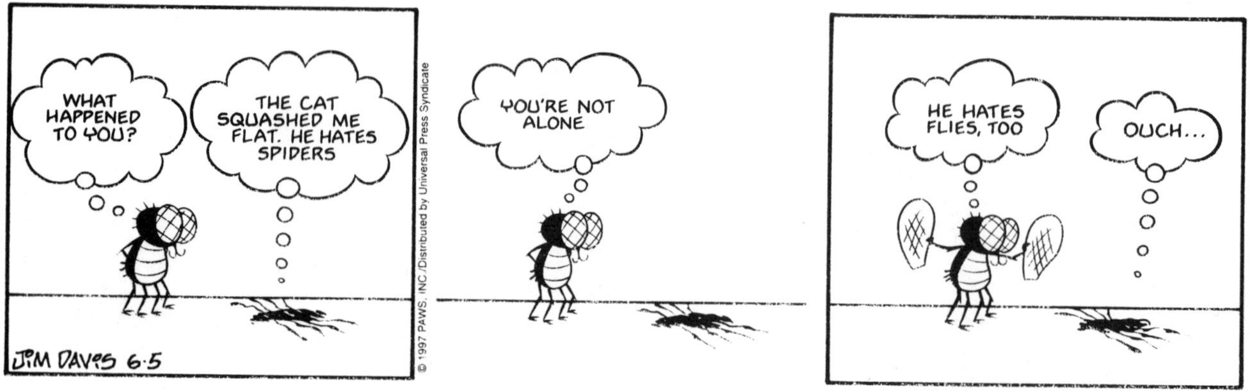
WHAT HAPPENED TO YOU?
THE CAT SQUASHED ME FLAT. HE HATES SPIDERS
YOU'RE NOT ALONE
HE HATES FLIES, TOO
OUCH...
JIM DAVIS 6-5

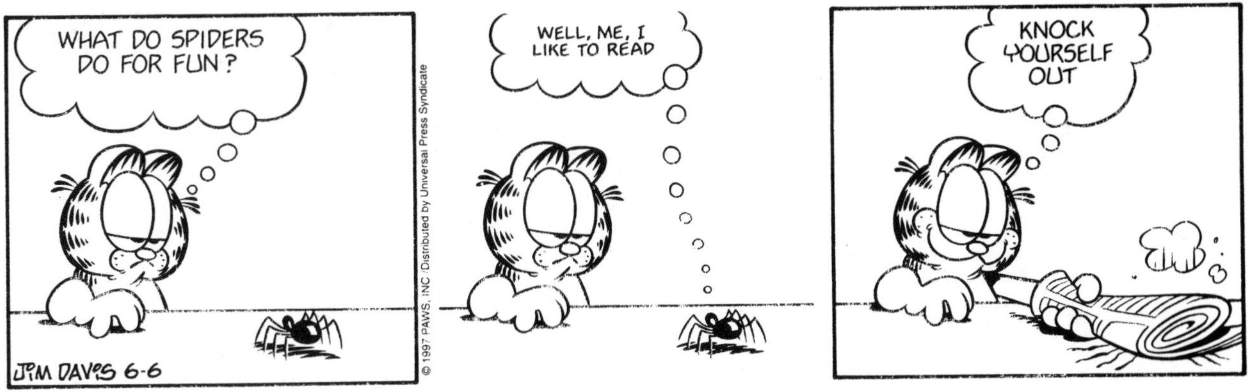
WHAT DO SPIDERS DO FOR FUN?
JIM DAVIS 6-6
© 1997 PAWS, INC./Distributed by Universal Press Syndicate
WELL, ME, I LIKE TO READ
KNOCK YOURSELF OUT

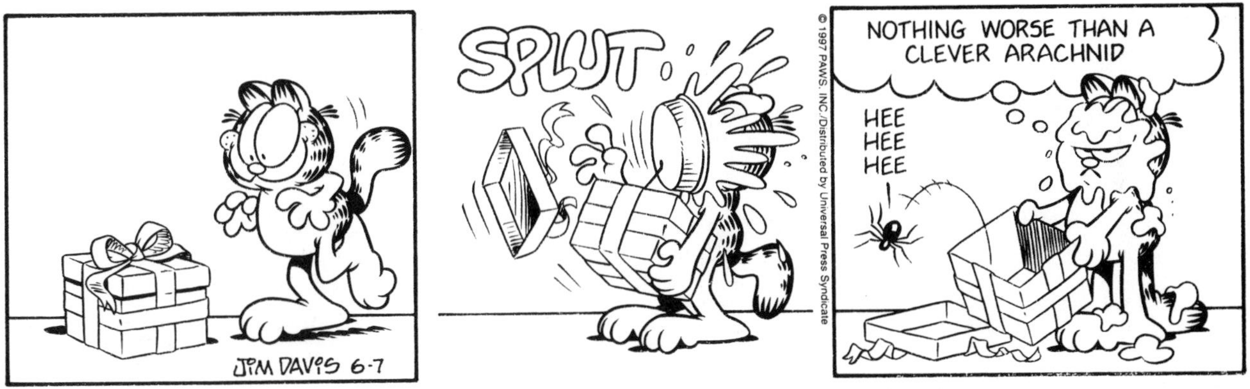
JIM DAVIS 6-7
SPLUT
© 1997 PAWS, INC./Distributed by Universal Press Syndicate
NOTHING WORSE THAN A CLEVER ARACHNID
HEE HEE HEE

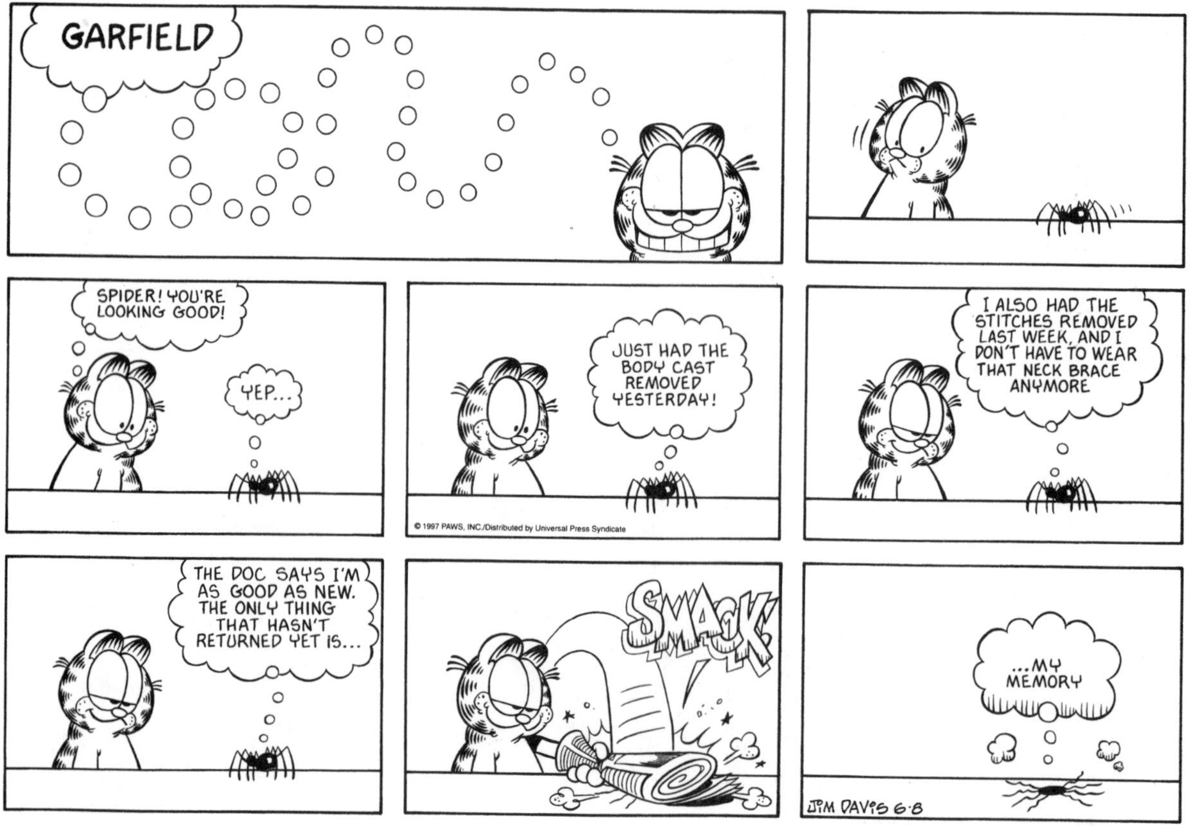
GARFIELD
SPIDER! YOU'RE LOOKING GOOD!
YEP...
JUST HAD THE BODY CAST REMOVED YESTERDAY!
I ALSO HAD THE STITCHES REMOVED LAST WEEK, AND I DON'T HAVE TO WEAR THAT NECK BRACE ANYMORE
THE DOC SAYS I'M AS GOOD AS NEW. THE ONLY THING THAT HASN'T RETURNED YET IS...
SMACK!
...MY MEMORY
JIM DAVIS 6-8
© 1997 PAWS, INC./Distributed by Universal Press Syndicate

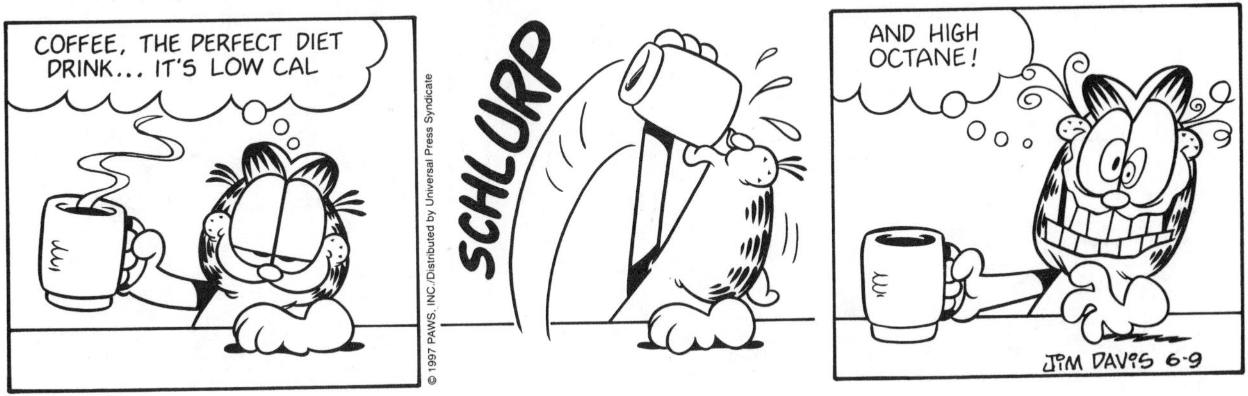
COFFEE, THE PERFECT DIET DRINK... IT'S LOW CAL
© 1997 PAWS, INC./Distributed by Universal Press Syndicate
SCHLURP
AND HIGH OCTANE!
JIM DAVIS 6-9

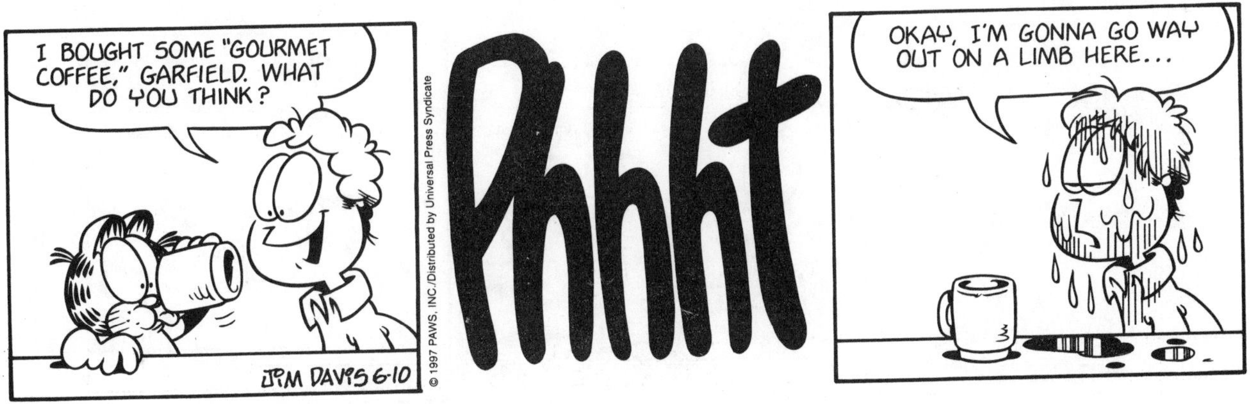
I BOUGHT SOME "GOURMET COFFEE," GARFIELD. WHAT DO YOU THINK?
JIM DAVIS 6-10
© 1997 PAWS, INC./Distributed by Universal Press Syndicate
Phhht
OKAY, I'M GONNA GO WAY OUT ON A LIMB HERE...

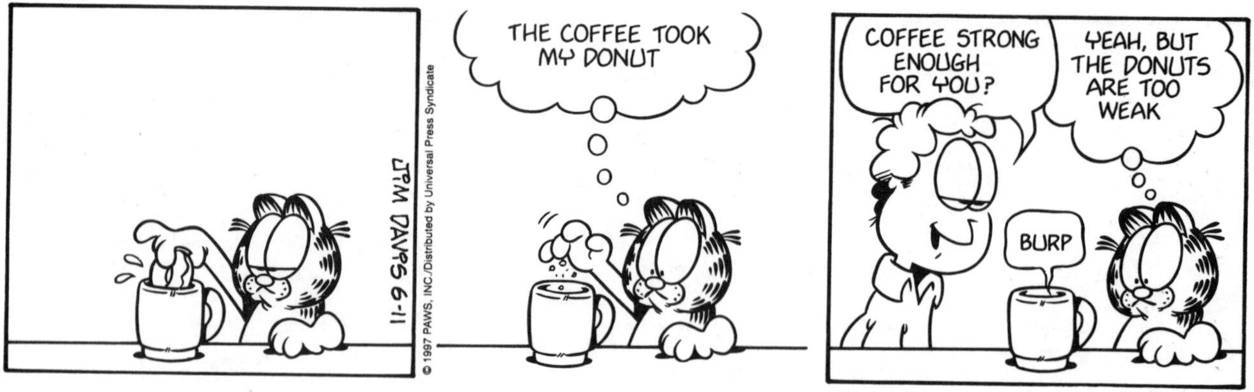
JIM DAVIS 6-11
© 1997 PAWS, INC./Distributed by Universal Press Syndicate
THE COFFEE TOOK MY DONUT
COFFEE STRONG ENOUGH FOR YOU?
YEAH, BUT THE DONUTS ARE TOO WEAK
BURP

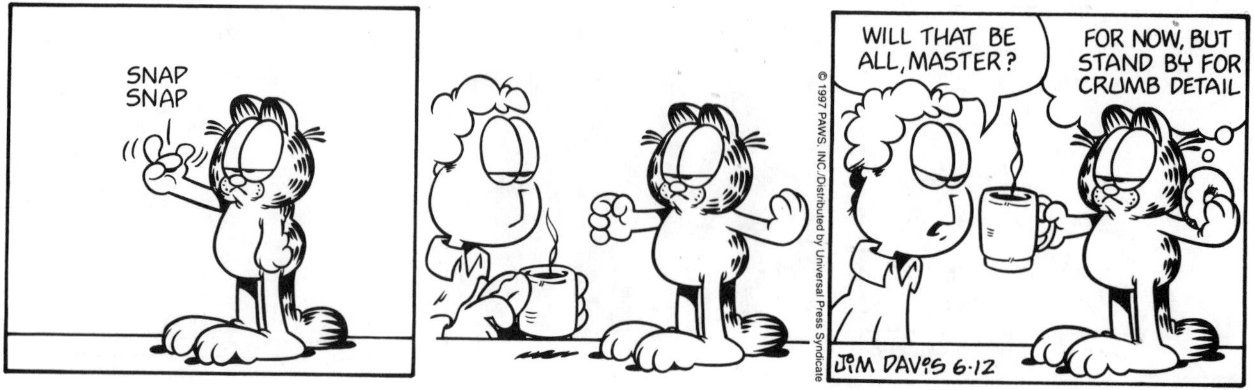
SNAP SNAP
© 1997 PAWS, INC./Distributed by Universal Press Syndicate
WILL THAT BE ALL, MASTER?
FOR NOW, BUT STAND BY FOR CRUMB DETAIL
JIM DAVIS 6-12

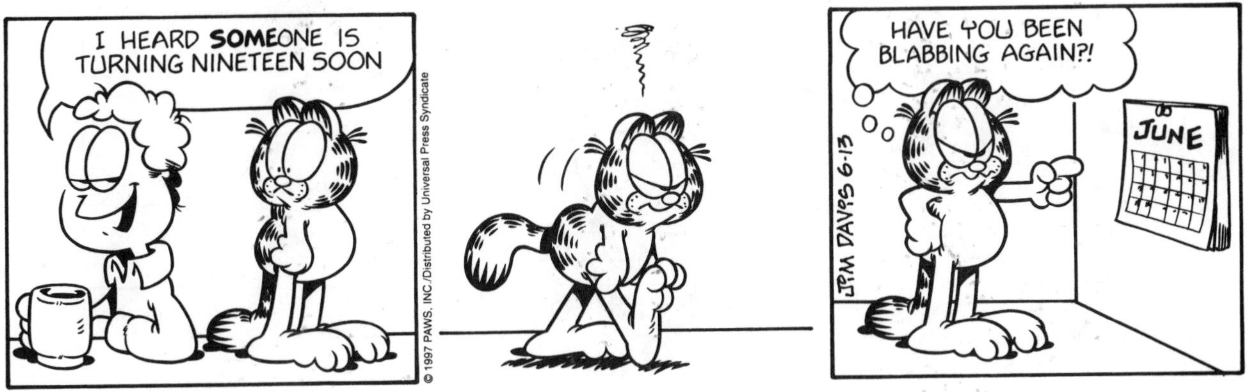
I HEARD SOMEONE IS TURNING NINETEEN SOON
HAVE YOU BEEN BLABBING AGAIN?!
JUNE
JIM DAVIS 6-13
© 1997 PAWS, INC./Distributed by Universal Press Syndicate

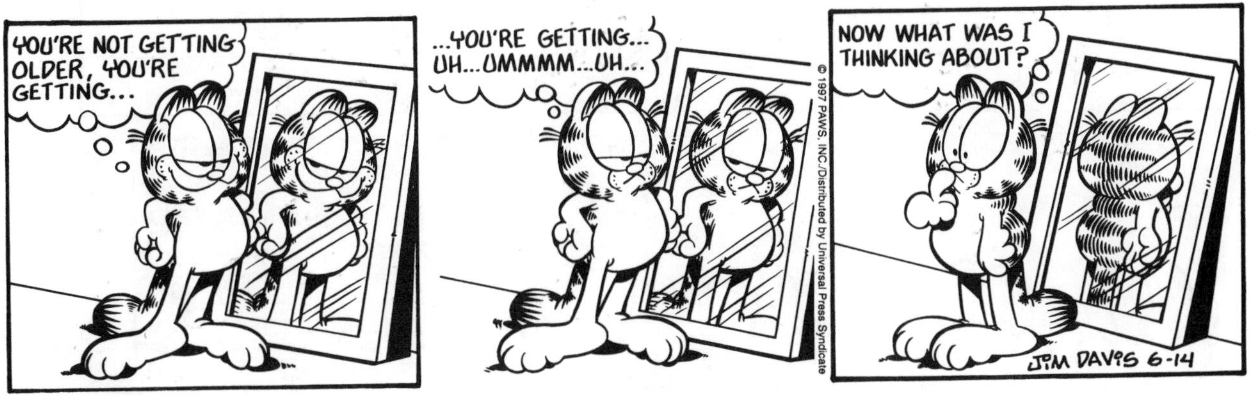
YOU'RE NOT GETTING OLDER, YOU'RE GETTING...
...YOU'RE GETTING... UH...UMMMM...UH...
NOW WHAT WAS I THINKING ABOUT?
JIM DAVIS 6-14
© 1997 PAWS, INC./Distributed by Universal Press Syndicate

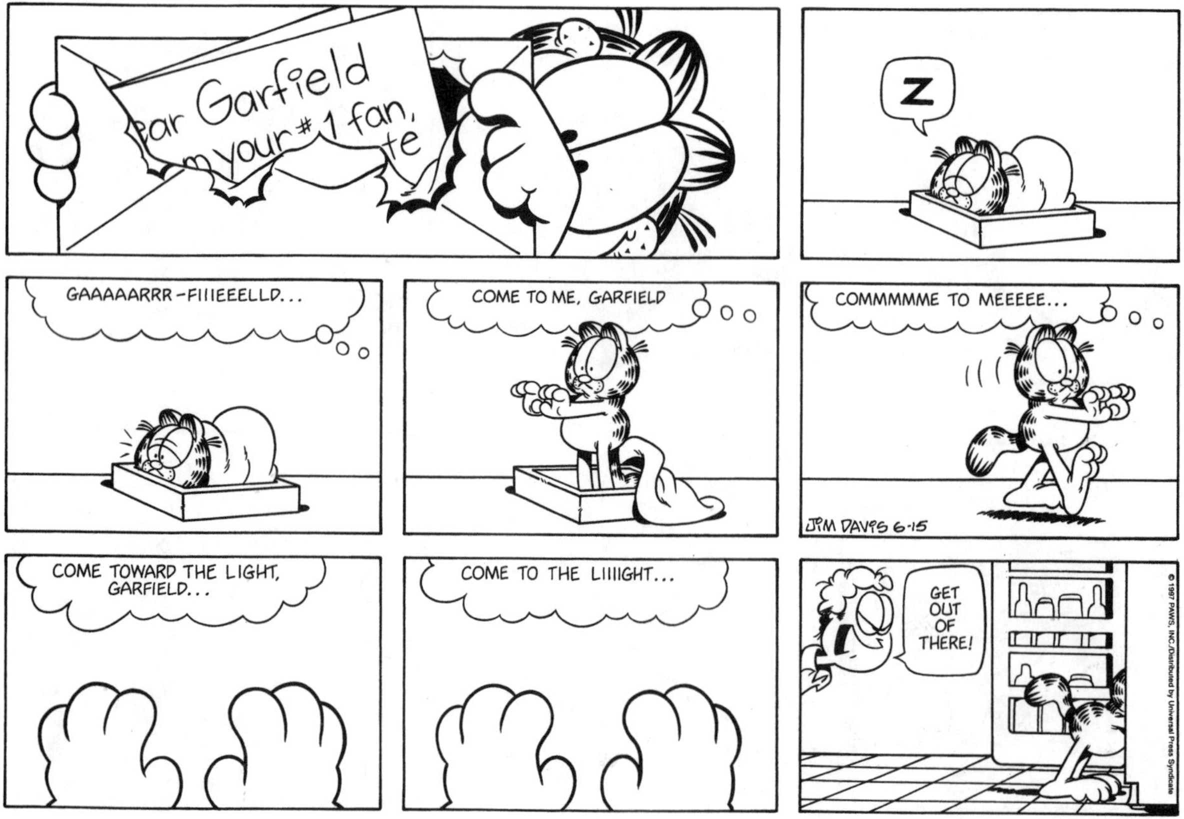
ear Garfield
m your # 1 fan,
te
Z
GAAAAARRR-FIIIEEELLD...
COME TO ME, GARFIELD
COMMMMME TO MEEEEE...
JIM DAVIS 6-15
COME TOWARD THE LIGHT, GARFIELD...
COME TO THE LIIIIGHT...
GET OUT OF THERE!
© 1997 PAWS, INC./Distributed by Universal Press Syndicate

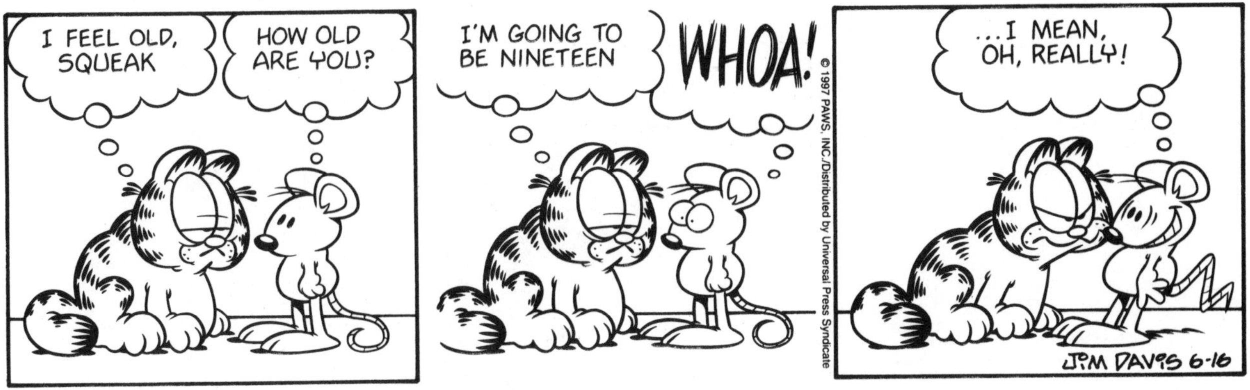
I FEEL OLD, SQUEAK
HOW OLD ARE YOU?
I'M GOING TO BE NINETEEN
WHOA!
...I MEAN, OH, REALLY!
JIM DAVIS 6-16
© 1997 PAWS, INC./Distributed by Universal Press Syndicate

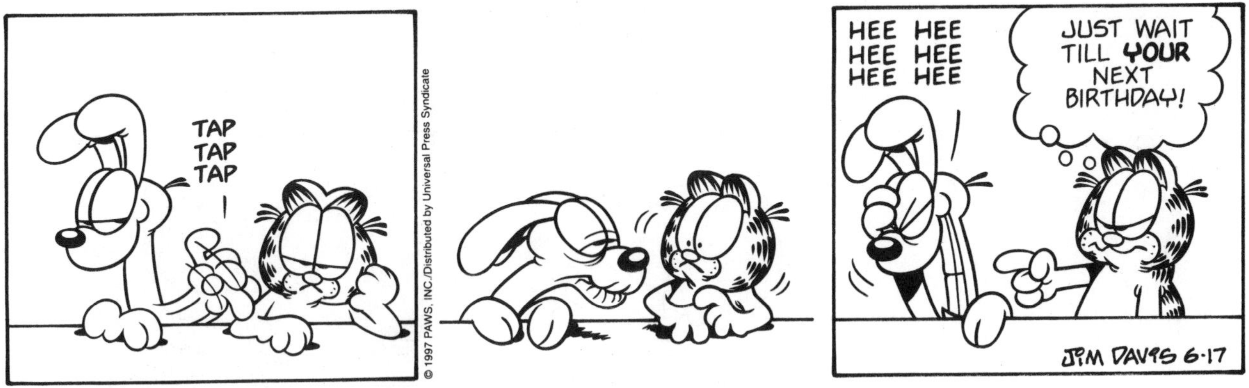
TAP TAP TAP
HEE HEE HEE HEE HEE HEE
JUST WAIT TILL **YOUR** NEXT BIRTHDAY!
JIM DAVIS 6-17
© 1997 PAWS, INC./Distributed by Universal Press Syndicate

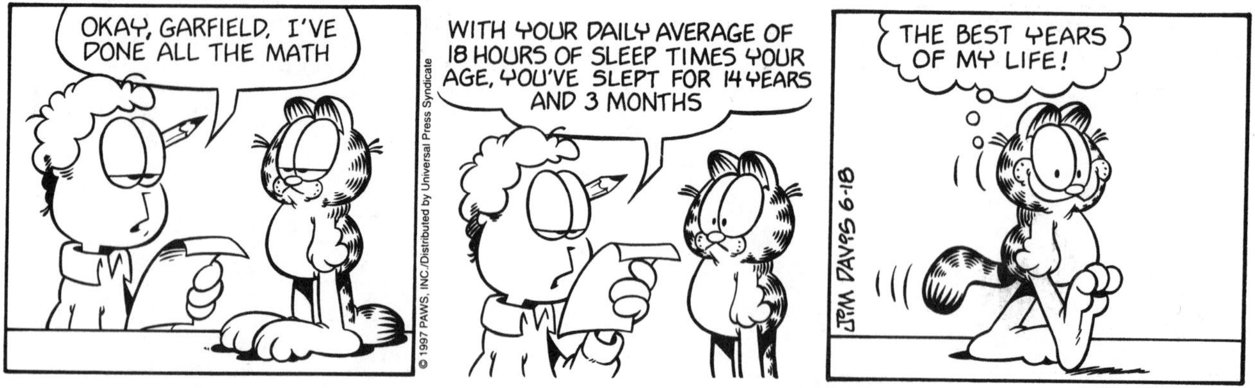
OKAY, GARFIELD, I'VE DONE ALL THE MATH
WITH YOUR DAILY AVERAGE OF 18 HOURS OF SLEEP TIMES YOUR AGE, YOU'VE SLEPT FOR 14 YEARS AND 3 MONTHS
THE BEST YEARS OF MY LIFE!
JIM DAVIS 6-18
© 1997 PAWS, INC./Distributed by Universal Press Syndicate

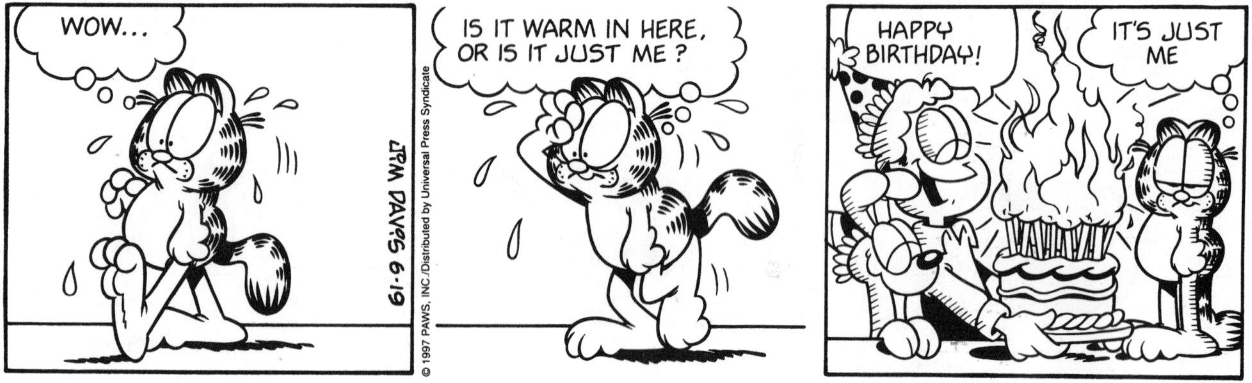
WOW...
JIM DAVIS 6-19
© 1997 PAWS, INC./Distributed by Universal Press Syndicate
IS IT WARM IN HERE, OR IS IT JUST ME ?
HAPPY BIRTHDAY!
IT'S JUST ME

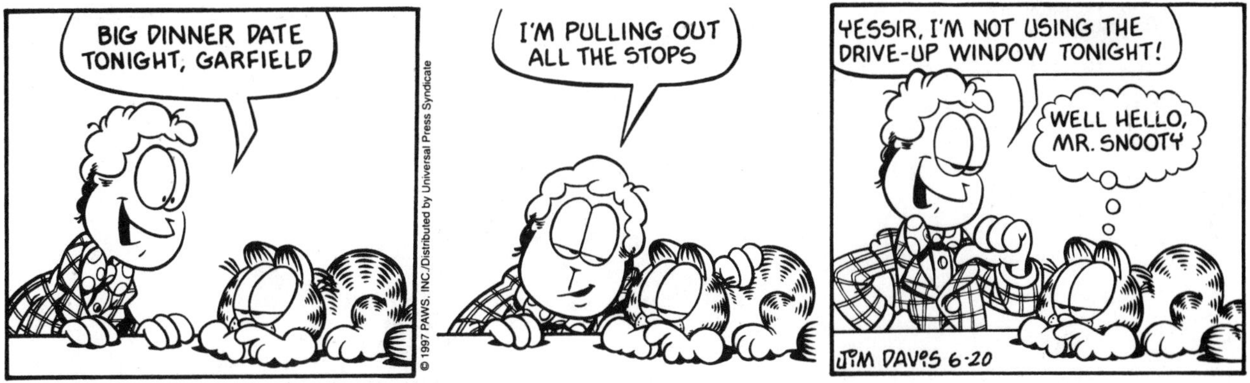

BIG DINNER DATE TONIGHT, GARFIELD
I'M PULLING OUT ALL THE STOPS
YESSIR, I'M NOT USING THE DRIVE-UP WINDOW TONIGHT!
WELL HELLO, MR. SNOOTY
JIM DAVIS 6-20
© 1997 PAWS, INC./Distributed by Universal Press Syndicate

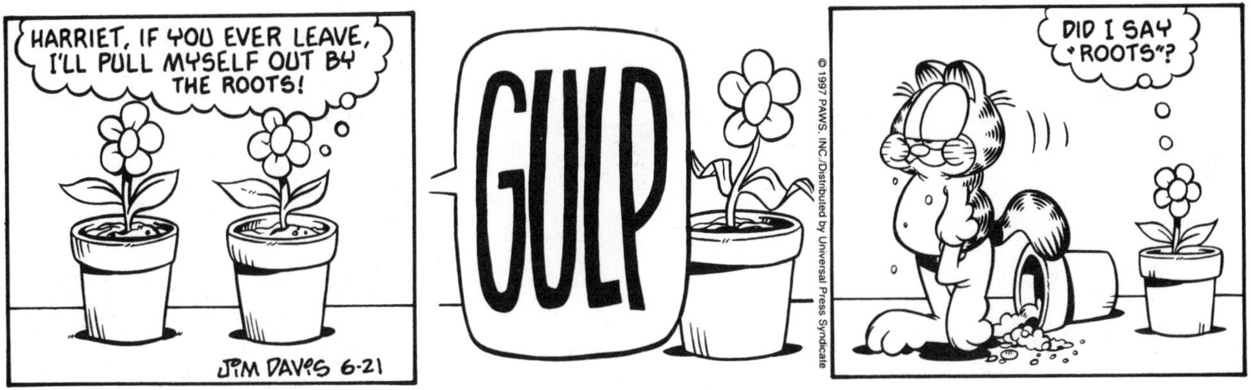

HARRIET, IF YOU EVER LEAVE, I'LL PULL MYSELF OUT BY THE ROOTS!
JIM DAVIS 6-21
GULP
DID I SAY "ROOTS"?
© 1997 PAWS, INC./Distributed by Universal Press Syndicate

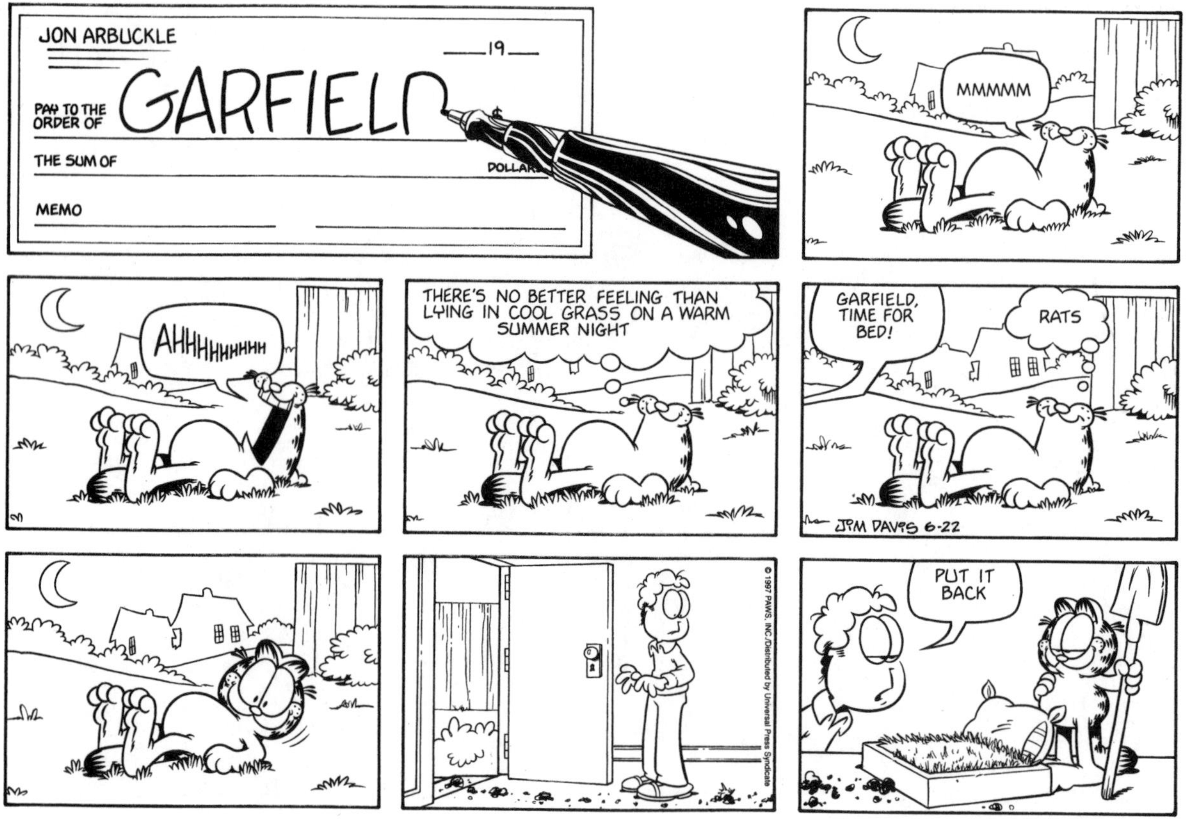
JON ARBUCKLE
19
PAY TO THE ORDER OF
GARFIELD
$
THE SUM OF
DOLLAR
MEMO
MMMMM
AHHHHHHHH
THERE'S NO BETTER FEELING THAN LYING IN COOL GRASS ON A WARM SUMMER NIGHT
GARFIELD, TIME FOR BED!
RATS
JIM DAVIS 6-22
© 1997 PAWS, INC./Distributed by Universal Press Syndicate
PUT IT BACK

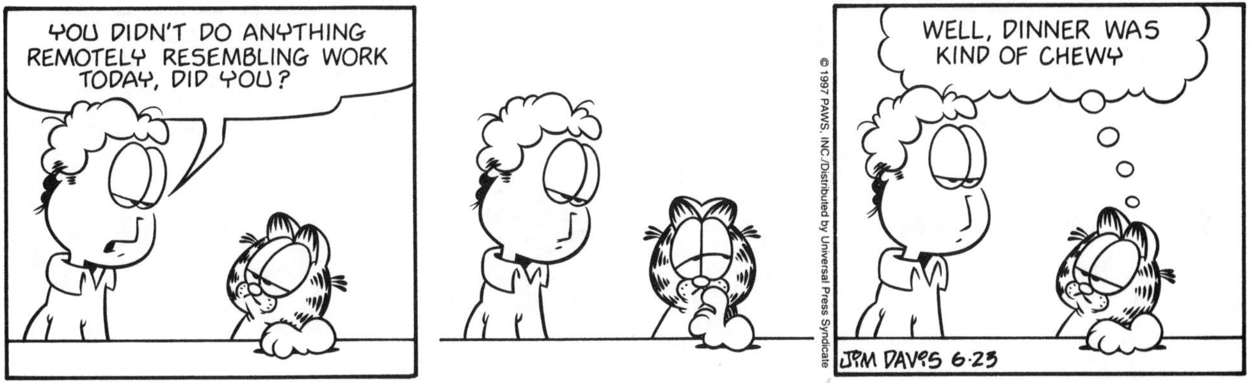
YOU DIDN'T DO ANYTHING REMOTELY RESEMBLING WORK TODAY, DID YOU?
WELL, DINNER WAS KIND OF CHEWY
© 1997 PAWS, INC./Distributed by Universal Press Syndicate
JIM DAVIS 6·23

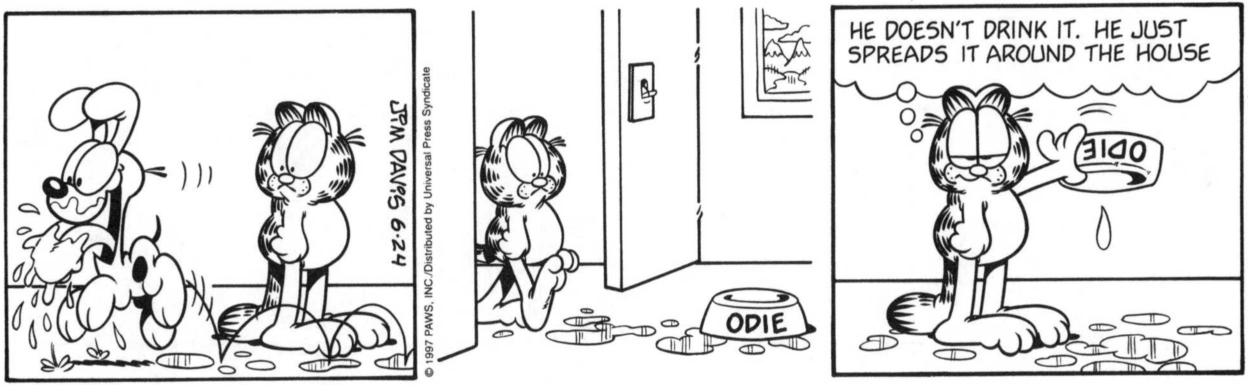
JIM DAVIS 6·24
© 1997 PAWS, INC./Distributed by Universal Press Syndicate
ODIE
HE DOESN'T DRINK IT. HE JUST SPREADS IT AROUND THE HOUSE
ODIE

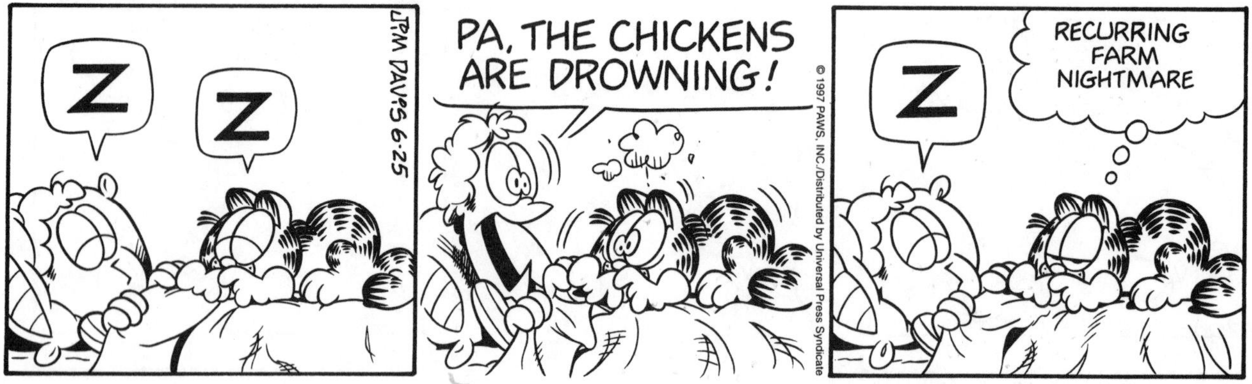
Z
Z
JIM DAVIS 6-25
PA, THE CHICKENS ARE DROWNING!
© 1997 PAWS, INC./Distributed by Universal Press Syndicate
Z
RECURRING FARM NIGHTMARE

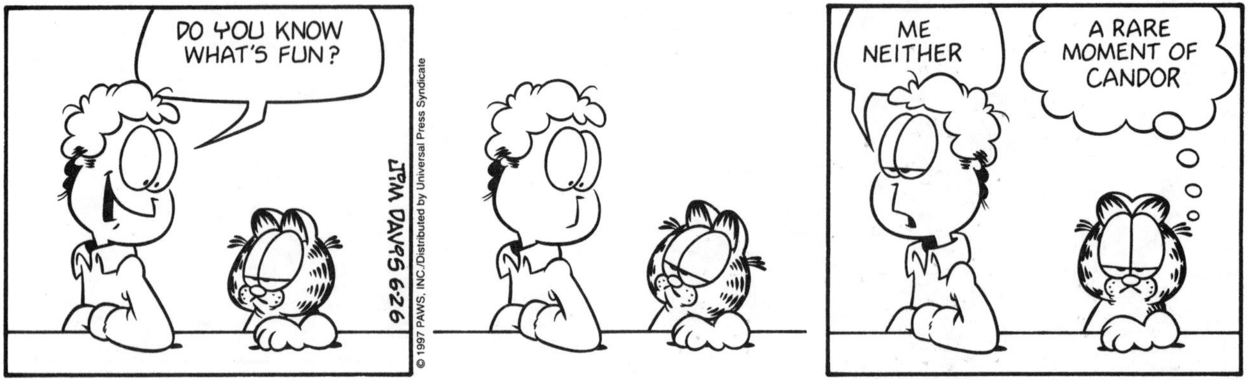
DO YOU KNOW WHAT'S FUN?
JIM DAVIS 6-26
© 1997 PAWS, INC./Distributed by Universal Press Syndicate
ME NEITHER
A RARE MOMENT OF CANDOR

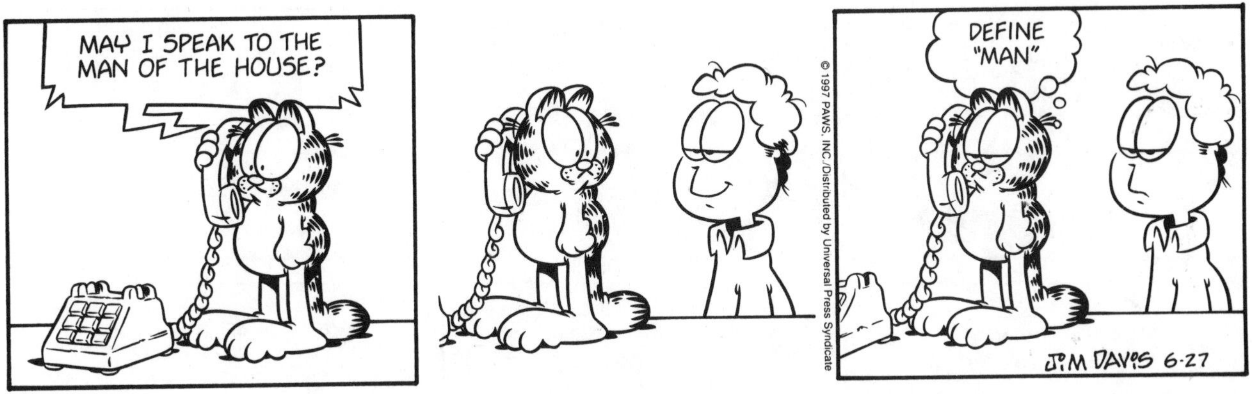
MAY I SPEAK TO THE MAN OF THE HOUSE?
DEFINE "MAN"
© 1997 PAWS, INC./Distributed by Universal Press Syndicate
JIM DAVIS 6-27

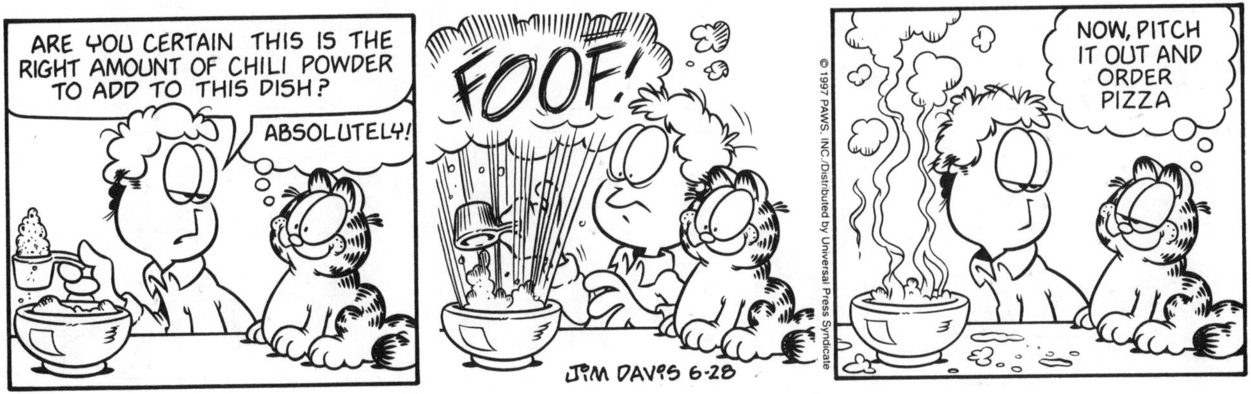
ARE YOU CERTAIN THIS IS THE RIGHT AMOUNT OF CHILI POWDER TO ADD TO THIS DISH?
ABSOLUTELY!
FOOF!
NOW, PITCH IT OUT AND ORDER PIZZA
© 1997 PAWS, INC./Distributed by Universal Press Syndicate
JIM DAVIS 6-28

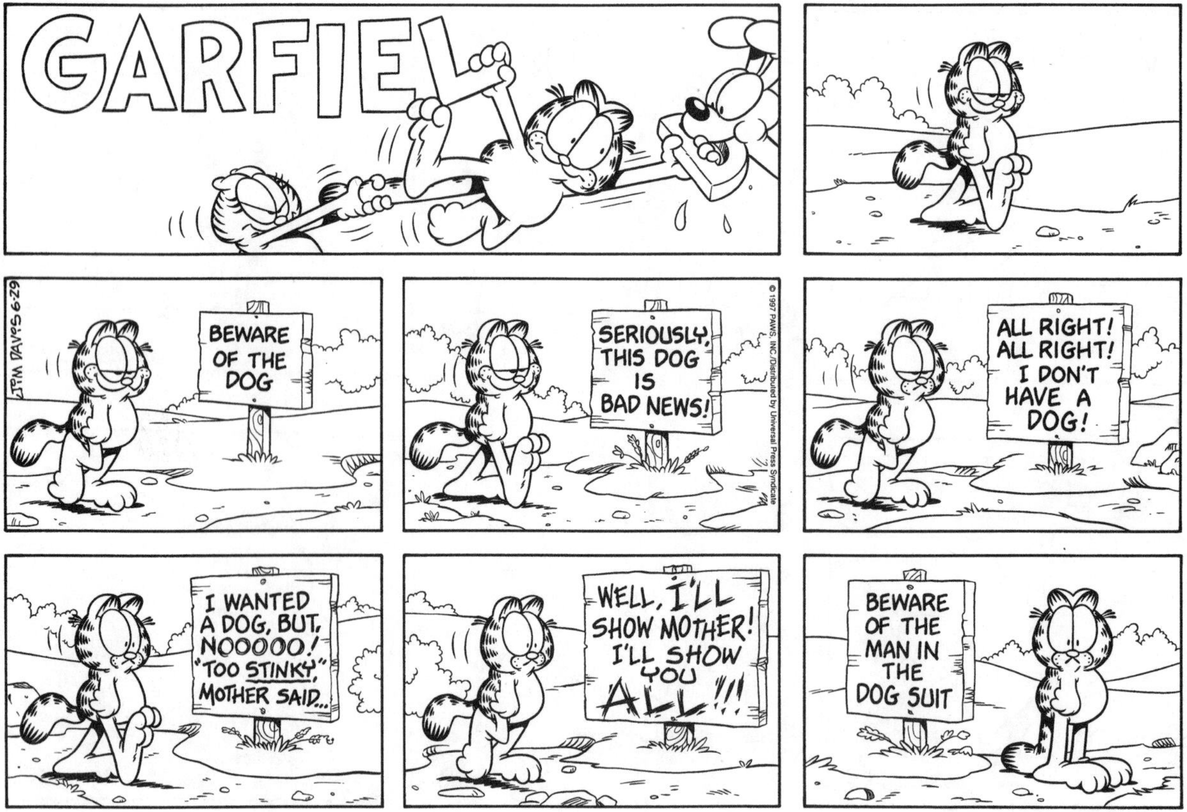
GARFIEL
JIM DAVIS 6-29
BEWARE OF THE DOG
© 1997 PAWS, INC./Distributed by Universal Press Syndicate
SERIOUSLY, THIS DOG IS BAD NEWS!
ALL RIGHT! ALL RIGHT! I DON'T HAVE A DOG!
I WANTED A DOG, BUT, NOOOOO! "TOO STINKY," MOTHER SAID...
WELL, I'LL SHOW MOTHER! I'LL SHOW YOU ALL!!!
BEWARE OF THE MAN IN THE DOG SUIT

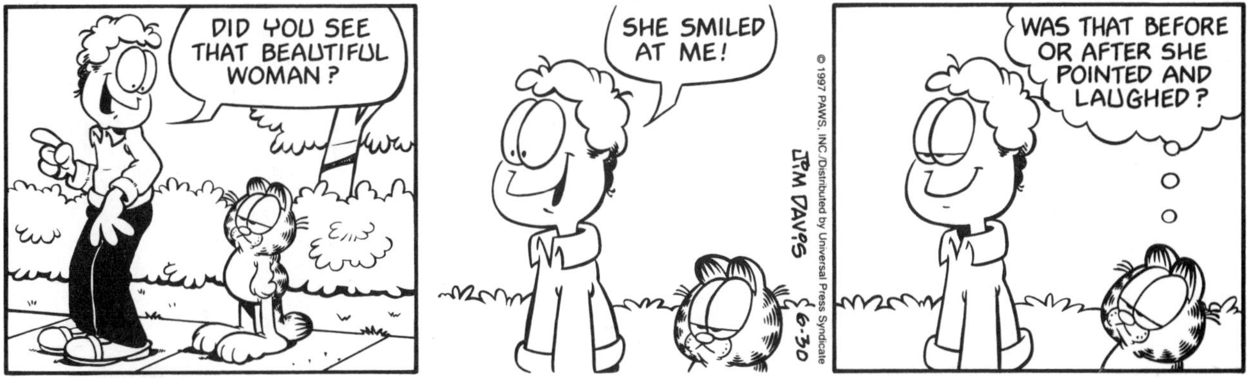
DID YOU SEE THAT BEAUTIFUL WOMAN?
SHE SMILED AT ME!
WAS THAT BEFORE OR AFTER SHE POINTED AND LAUGHED?
JIM DAVIS 6-30
© 1997 PAWS, INC./Distributed by Universal Press Syndicate

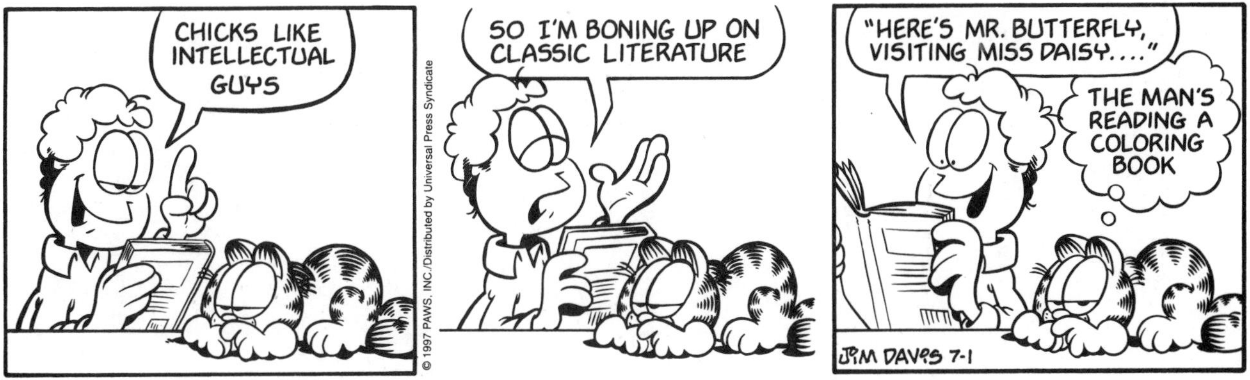
CHICKS LIKE INTELLECTUAL GUYS
SO I'M BONING UP ON CLASSIC LITERATURE
"HERE'S MR. BUTTERFLY, VISITING MISS DAISY...."
THE MAN'S READING A COLORING BOOK
JIM DAVIS 7-1
© 1997 PAWS, INC./Distributed by Universal Press Syndicate

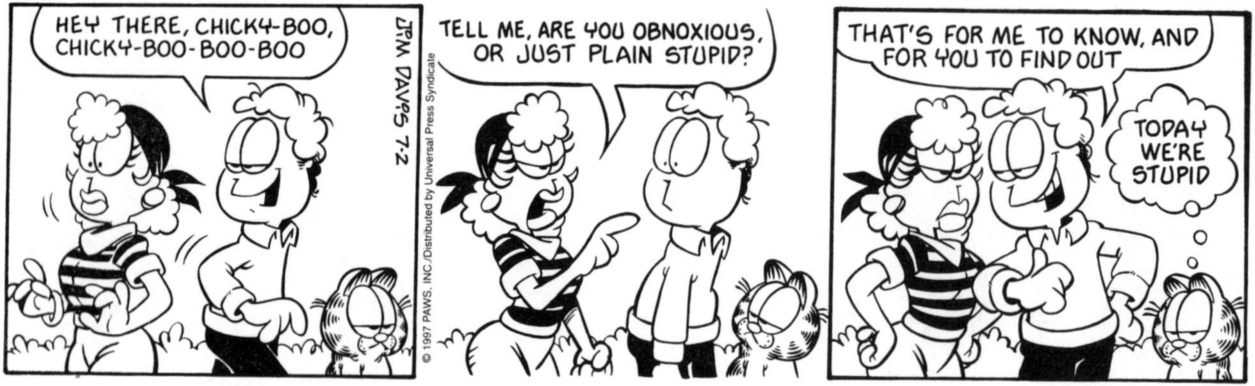
HEY THERE, CHICKY-BOO, CHICKY-BOO-BOO-BOO
JIM DAVIS 7-2
© 1997 PAWS, INC./Distributed by Universal Press Syndicate
TELL ME, ARE YOU OBNOXIOUS, OR JUST PLAIN STUPID?
THAT'S FOR ME TO KNOW, AND FOR YOU TO FIND OUT
TODAY WE'RE STUPID

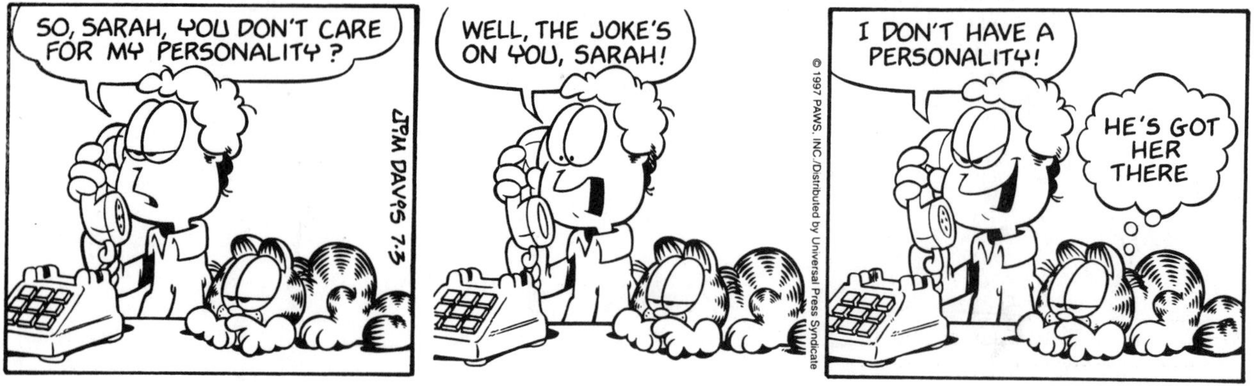
SO, SARAH, YOU DON'T CARE FOR MY PERSONALITY?
JIM DAVIS 7-3
WELL, THE JOKE'S ON YOU, SARAH!
© 1997 PAWS, INC./Distributed by Universal Press Syndicate
I DON'T HAVE A PERSONALITY!
HE'S GOT HER THERE

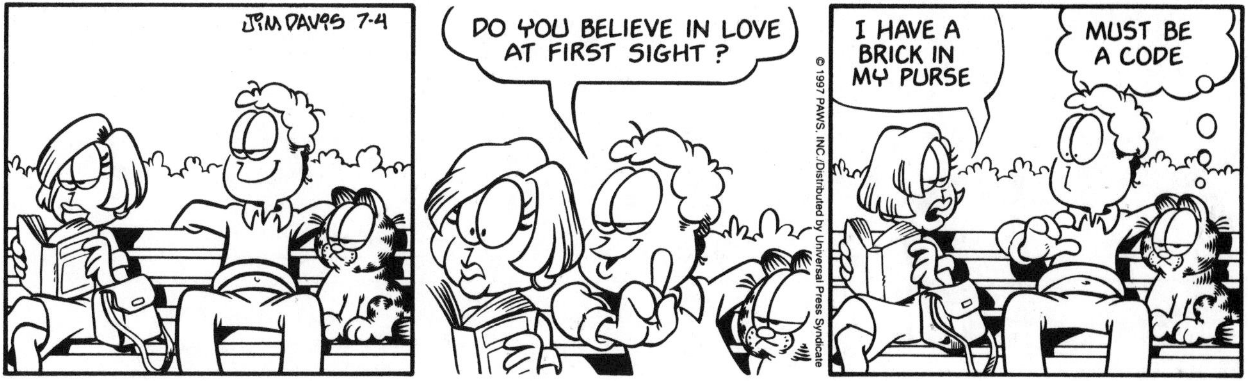
JIM DAVIS 7-4
DO YOU BELIEVE IN LOVE AT FIRST SIGHT ?
© 1997 PAWS, INC./Distributed by Universal Press Syndicate
I HAVE A BRICK IN MY PURSE
MUST BE A CODE

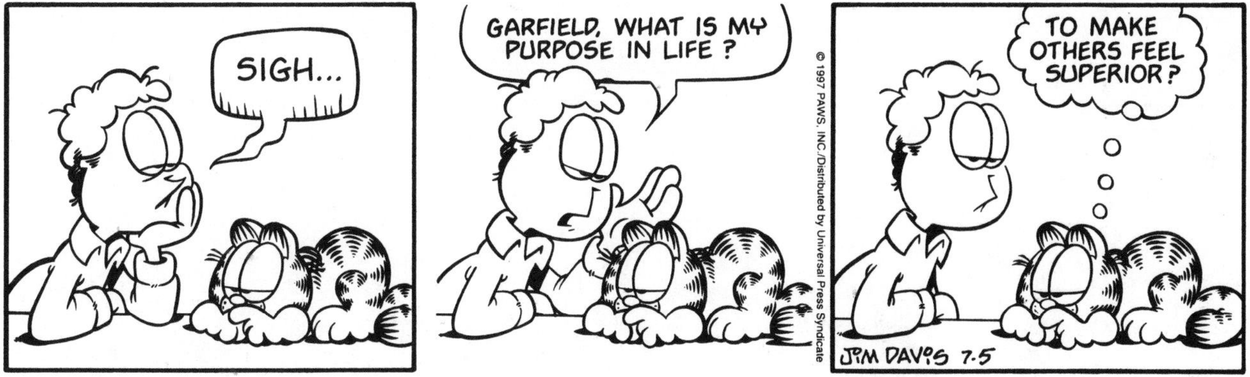
SIGH...
GARFIELD, WHAT IS MY PURPOSE IN LIFE ?
© 1997 PAWS, INC./Distributed by Universal Press Syndicate
TO MAKE OTHERS FEEL SUPERIOR ?
JIM DAVIS 7-5

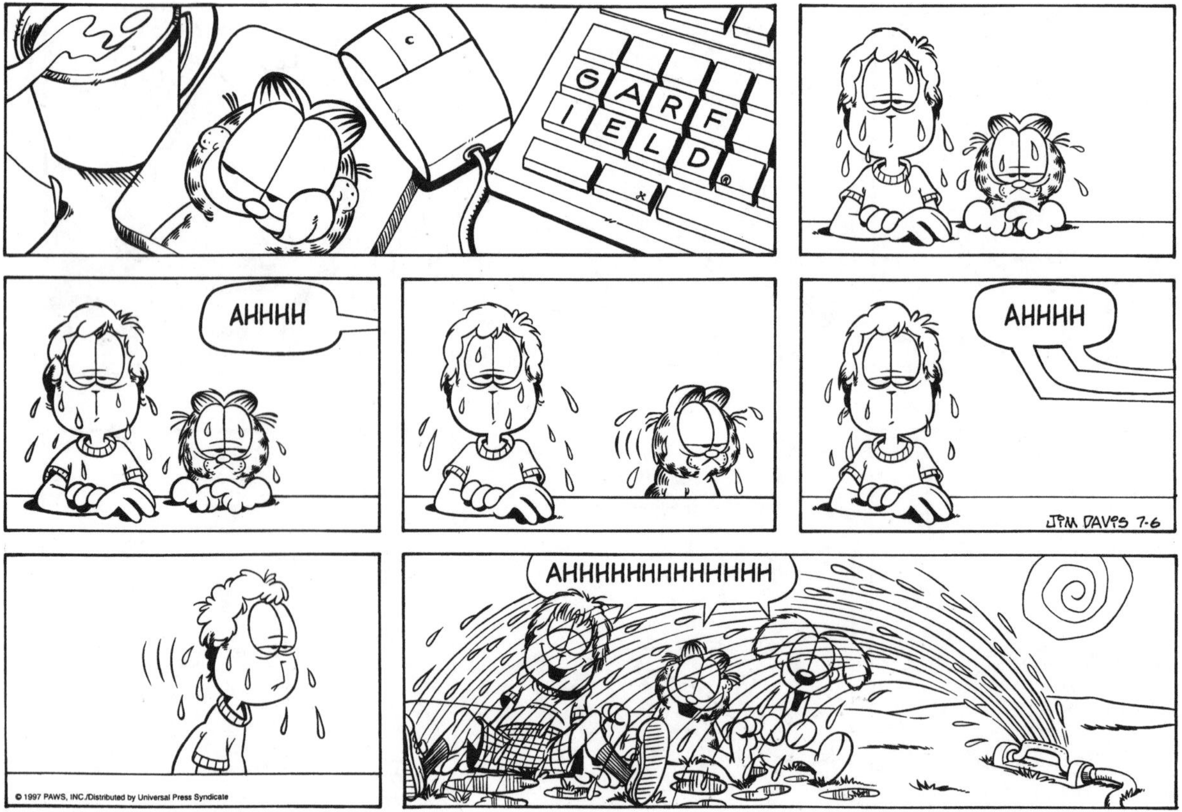
GARFIELD®
AHHHH
AHHHH
JIM DAVIS 7-6
AHHHHHHHHHHHHH
© 1997 PAWS, INC./Distributed by Universal Press Syndicate

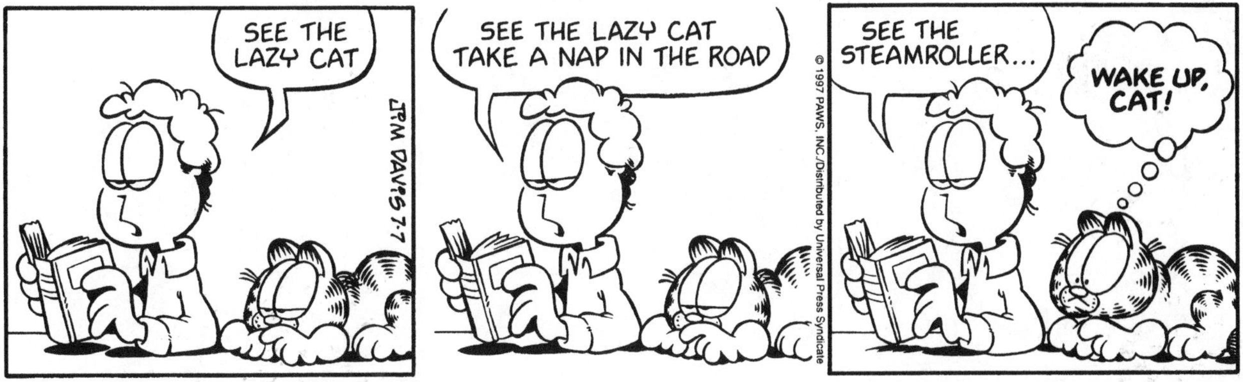
SEE THE LAZY CAT
JIM DAVIS 7-7
SEE THE LAZY CAT TAKE A NAP IN THE ROAD
© 1997 PAWS, INC./Distributed by Universal Press Syndicate
SEE THE STEAMROLLER...
WAKE UP, CAT!

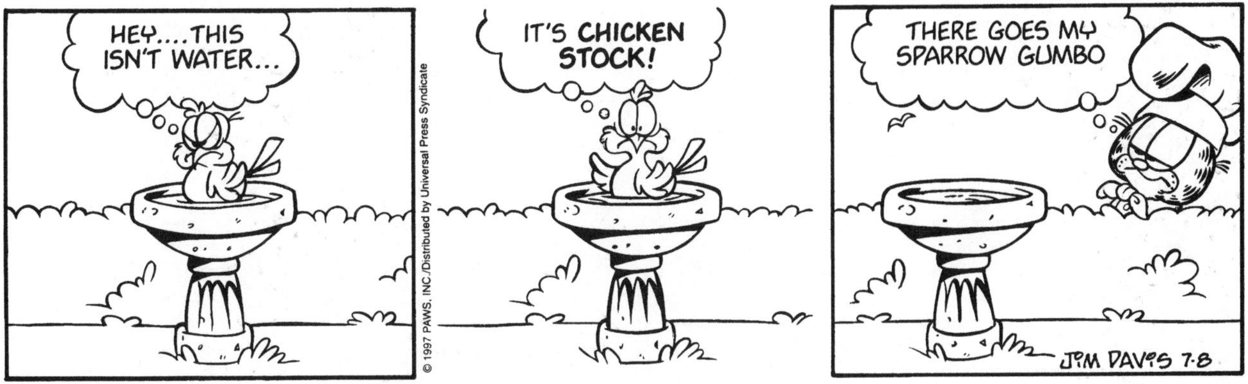
HEY....THIS ISN'T WATER...
© 1997 PAWS, INC./Distributed by Universal Press Syndicate
IT'S CHICKEN STOCK!
THERE GOES MY SPARROW GUMBO
JIM DAVIS 7-8

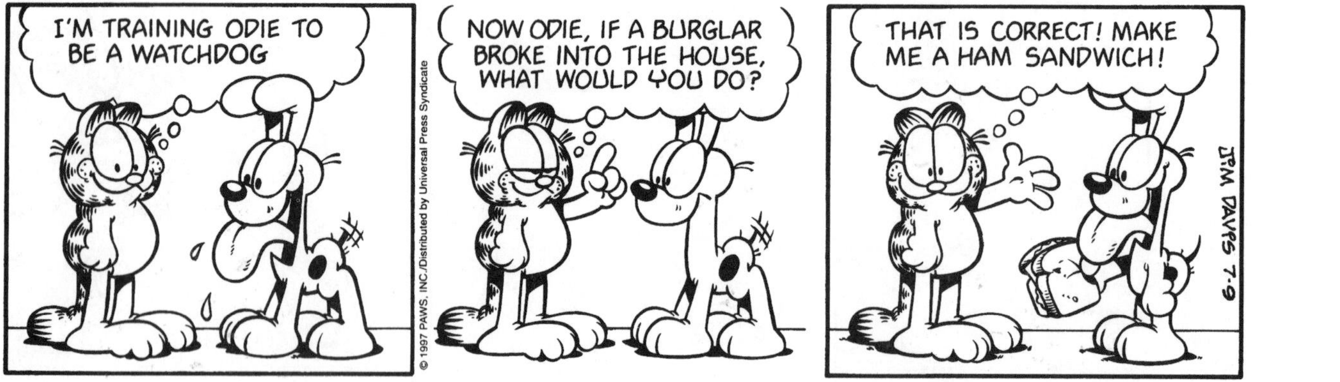
I'M TRAINING ODIE TO BE A WATCHDOG
NOW ODIE, IF A BURGLAR BROKE INTO THE HOUSE, WHAT WOULD YOU DO?
THAT IS CORRECT! MAKE ME A HAM SANDWICH!
JIM DAVIS 7-9
© 1997 PAWS, INC./Distributed by Universal Press Syndicate

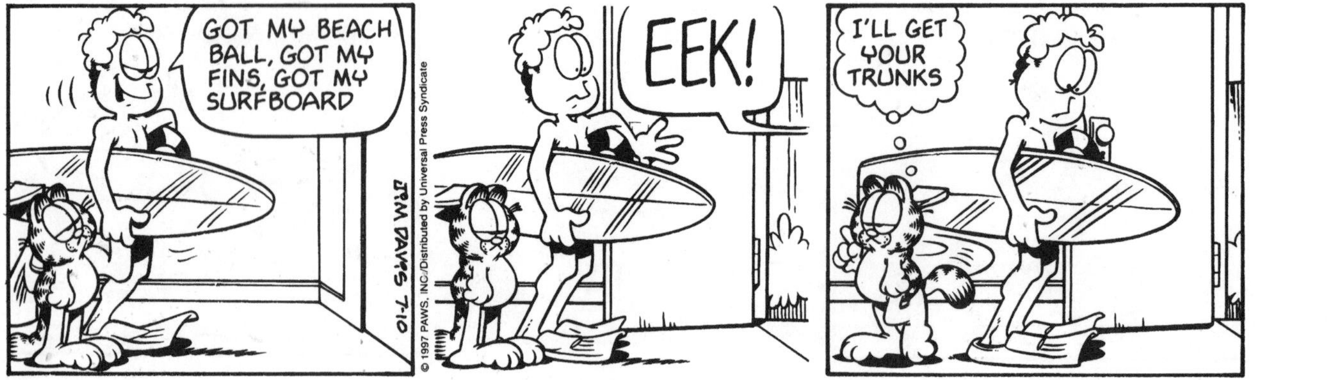
GOT MY BEACH BALL, GOT MY FINS, GOT MY SURFBOARD
EEK!
I'LL GET YOUR TRUNKS
JIM DAVIS 7-10
© 1997 PAWS, INC./Distributed by Universal Press Syndicate

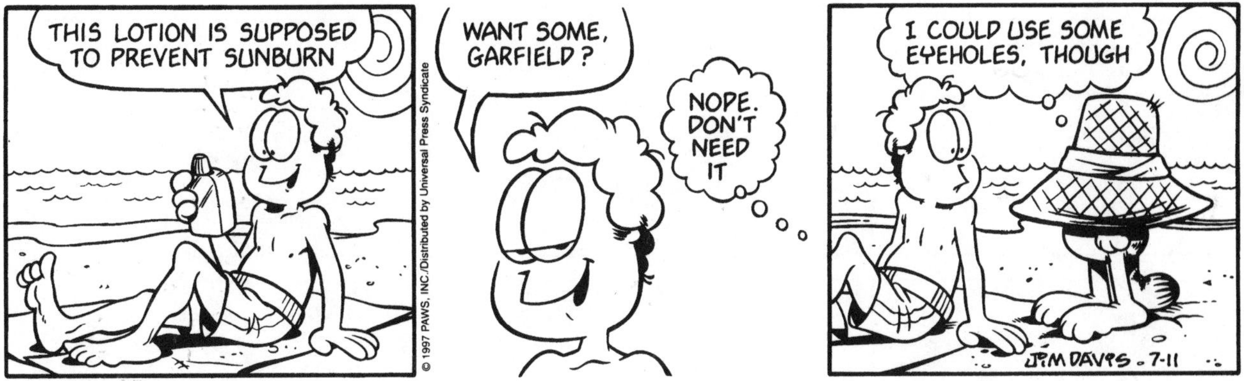
THIS LOTION IS SUPPOSED TO PREVENT SUNBURN
© 1997 PAWS, INC./Distributed by Universal Press Syndicate
WANT SOME, GARFIELD?
NOPE. DON'T NEED IT
I COULD USE SOME EYEHOLES, THOUGH
JIM DAVIS 7-11

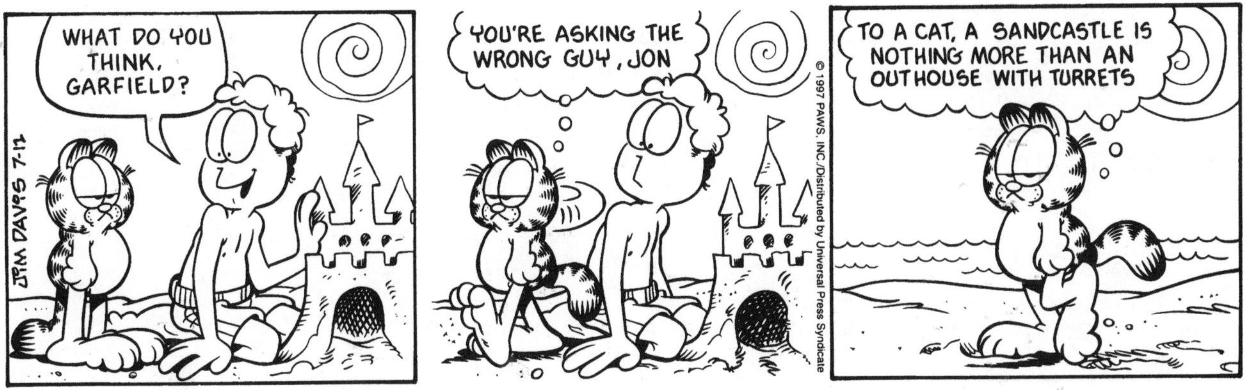
JIM DAVIS 7-12
WHAT DO YOU THINK, GARFIELD?
YOU'RE ASKING THE WRONG GUY, JON
© 1997 PAWS, INC./Distributed by Universal Press Syndicate
TO A CAT, A SANDCASTLE IS NOTHING MORE THAN AN OUTHOUSE WITH TURRETS

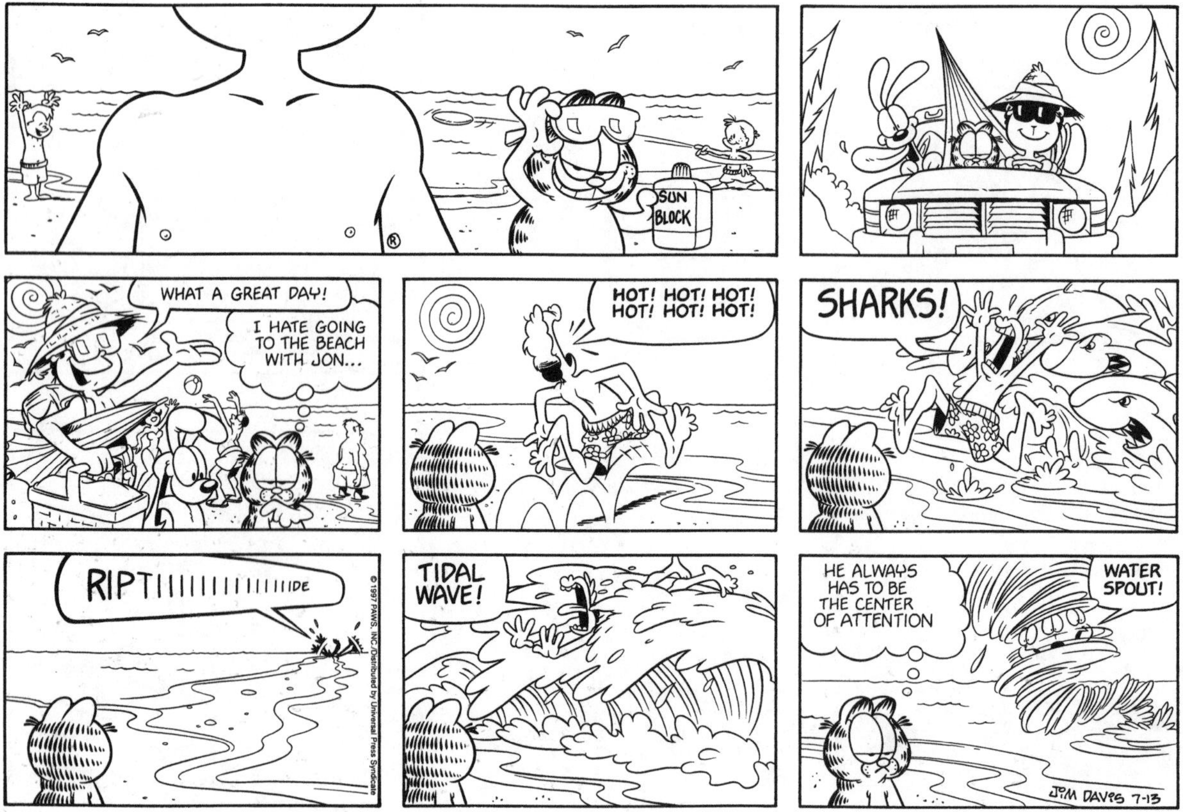
WHAT A GREAT DAY!
I HATE GOING TO THE BEACH WITH JON...
HOT! HOT! HOT! HOT! HOT! HOT!
SHARKS!
RIPTIIIIIIIIIIIIIIIIIDE
© 1997 PAWS, INC./Distributed by Universal Press Syndicate
TIDAL WAVE!
HE ALWAYS HAS TO BE THE CENTER OF ATTENTION
WATER SPOUT!
JIM DAVIS 7-13

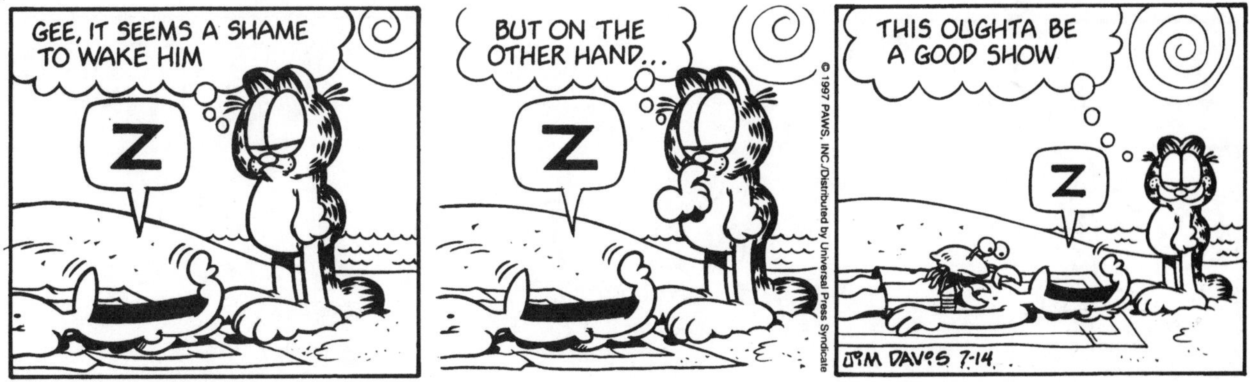
GEE, IT SEEMS A SHAME TO WAKE HIM
Z
BUT ON THE OTHER HAND...
Z
THIS OUGHTA BE A GOOD SHOW
Z
JIM DAVIS 7-14

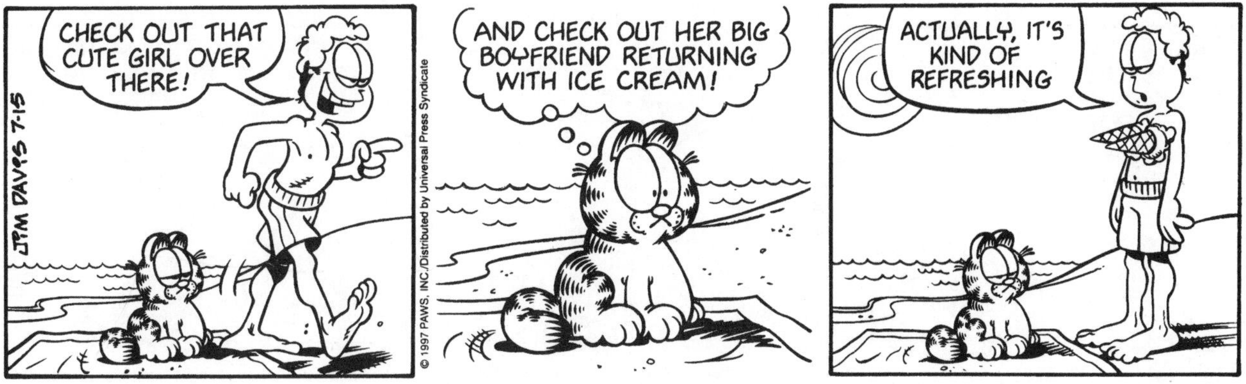
CHECK OUT THAT CUTE GIRL OVER THERE!
JIM DAVIS 7-15
AND CHECK OUT HER BIG BOYFRIEND RETURNING WITH ICE CREAM!
ACTUALLY, IT'S KIND OF REFRESHING

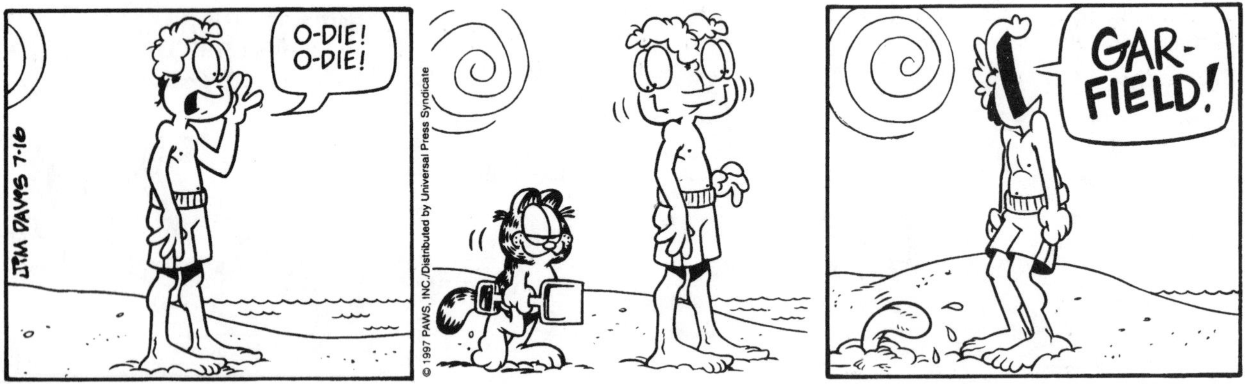

JIM DAVIS 7-16
O-DIE! O-DIE!
© 1997 PAWS, INC./Distributed by Universal Press Syndicate
GAR-FIELD!

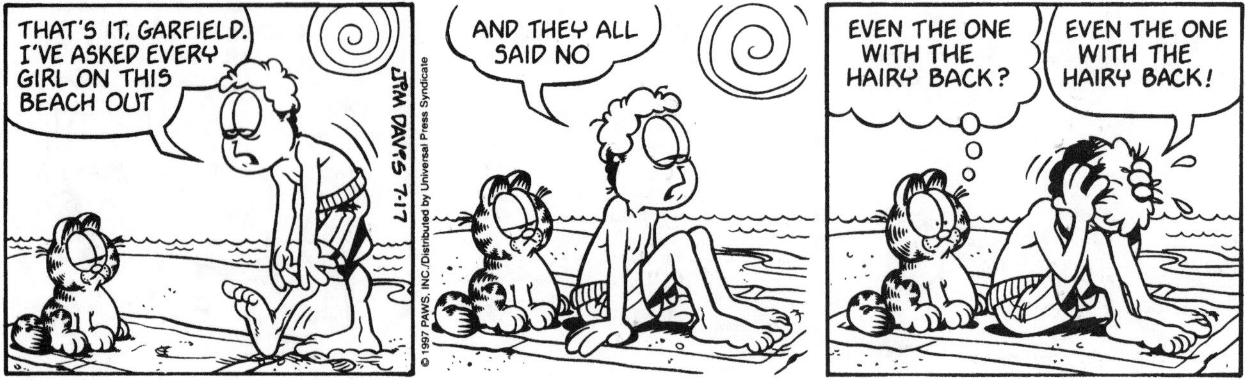

THAT'S IT, GARFIELD. I'VE ASKED EVERY GIRL ON THIS BEACH OUT
JIM DAVIS 7-17
© 1997 PAWS, INC./Distributed by Universal Press Syndicate
AND THEY ALL SAID NO
EVEN THE ONE WITH THE HAIRY BACK?
EVEN THE ONE WITH THE HAIRY BACK!

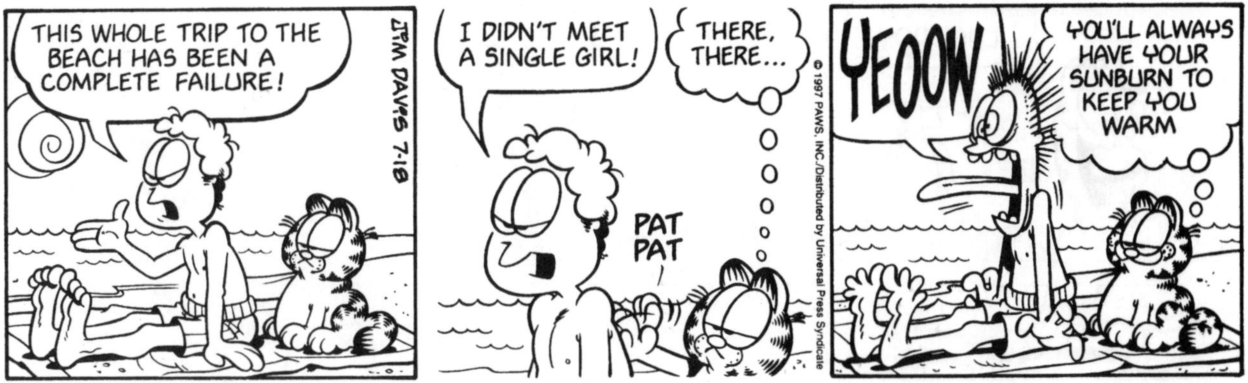
THIS WHOLE TRIP TO THE BEACH HAS BEEN A COMPLETE FAILURE!
JIM DAVIS 7-18
I DIDN'T MEET A SINGLE GIRL!
PAT PAT
THERE, THERE...
© 1997 PAWS, INC./Distributed by Universal Press Syndicate
YEOOW
YOU'LL ALWAYS HAVE YOUR SUNBURN TO KEEP YOU WARM

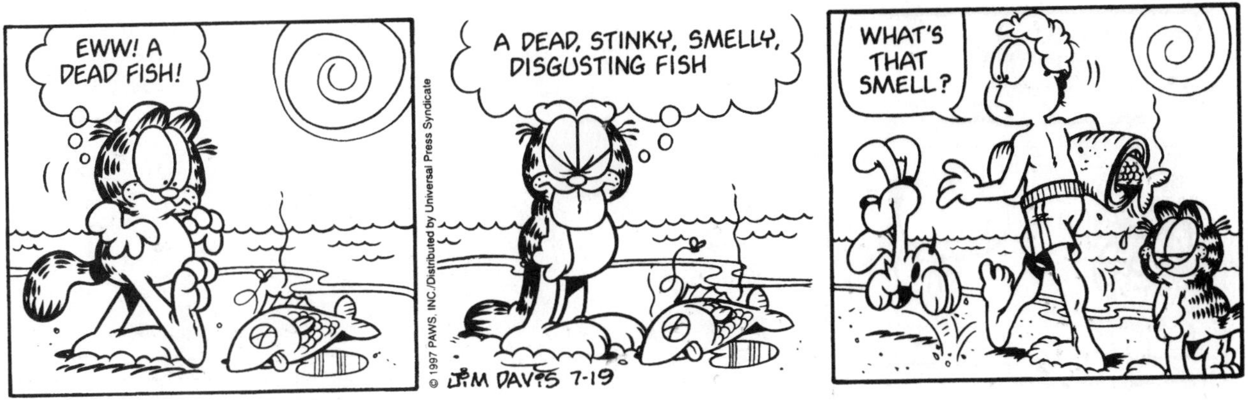
EWW! A DEAD FISH!
© 1997 PAWS, INC./Distributed by Universal Press Syndicate
A DEAD, STINKY, SMELLY, DISGUSTING FISH
JIM DAVIS 7-19
WHAT'S THAT SMELL?

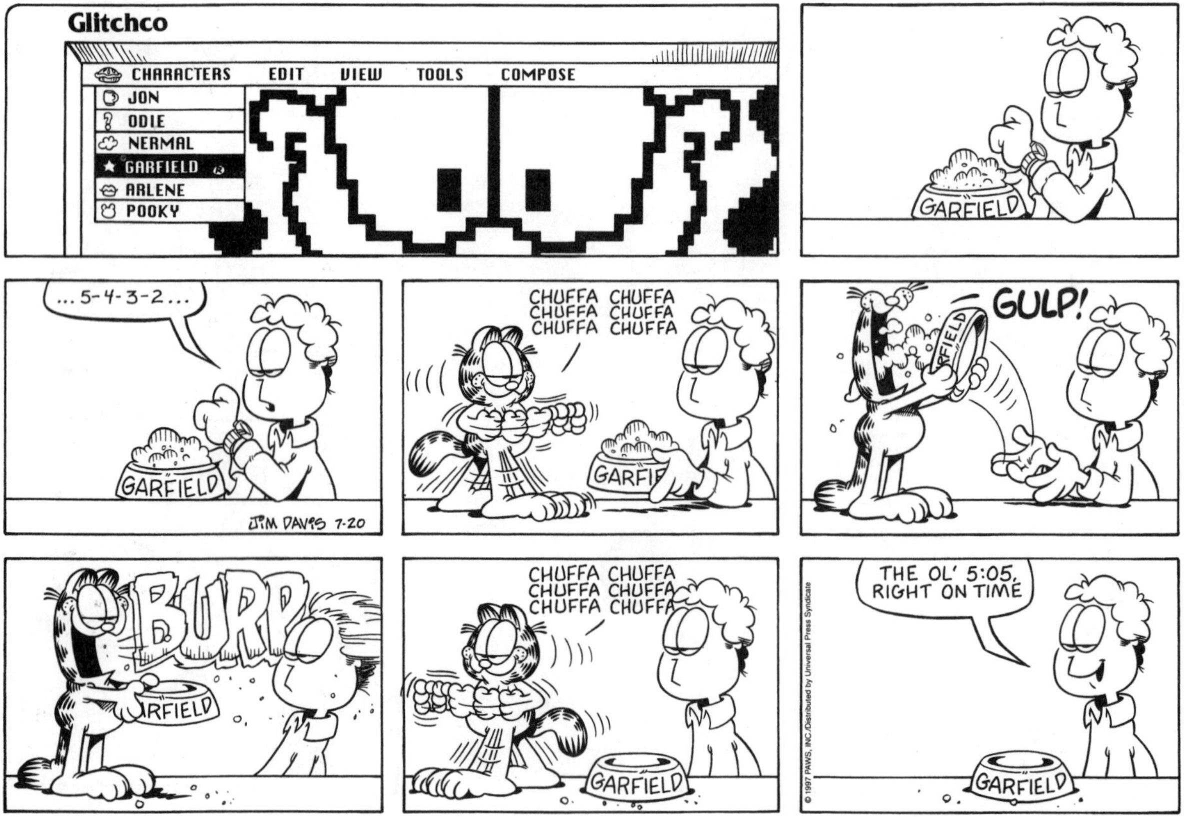
Glitchco
CHARACTERS EDIT VIEW TOOLS COMPOSE
JON
ODIE
NERMAL
GARFIELD ®
ARLENE
POOKY
GARFIELD
...5-4-3-2...
GARFIELD
JIM DAVIS 7-20
CHUFFA CHUFFA
CHUFFA CHUFFA
CHUFFA CHUFFA
GARFIELD
GULP!
GARFIELD
BURP
RFIELD
CHUFFA CHUFFA
CHUFFA CHUFFA
CHUFFA CHUFFA
GARFIELD
© 1997 PAWS, INC./Distributed by Universal Press Syndicate
THE OL' 5:05,
RIGHT ON TIME
GARFIELD

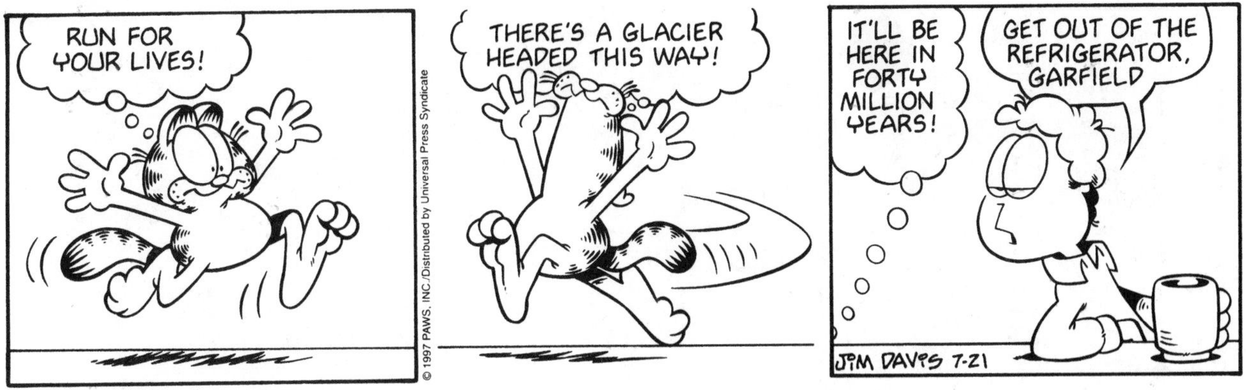
RUN FOR YOUR LIVES!
THERE'S A GLACIER HEADED THIS WAY!
IT'LL BE HERE IN FORTY MILLION YEARS!
GET OUT OF THE REFRIGERATOR, GARFIELD
JIM DAVIS 7-21

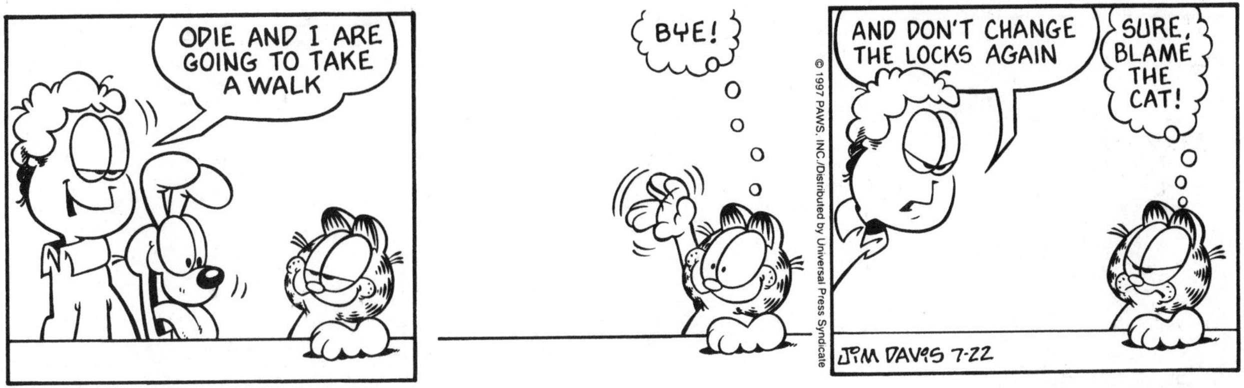
ODIE AND I ARE GOING TO TAKE A WALK
BYE!
AND DON'T CHANGE THE LOCKS AGAIN
SURE, BLAME THE CAT!
JIM DAVIS 7-22

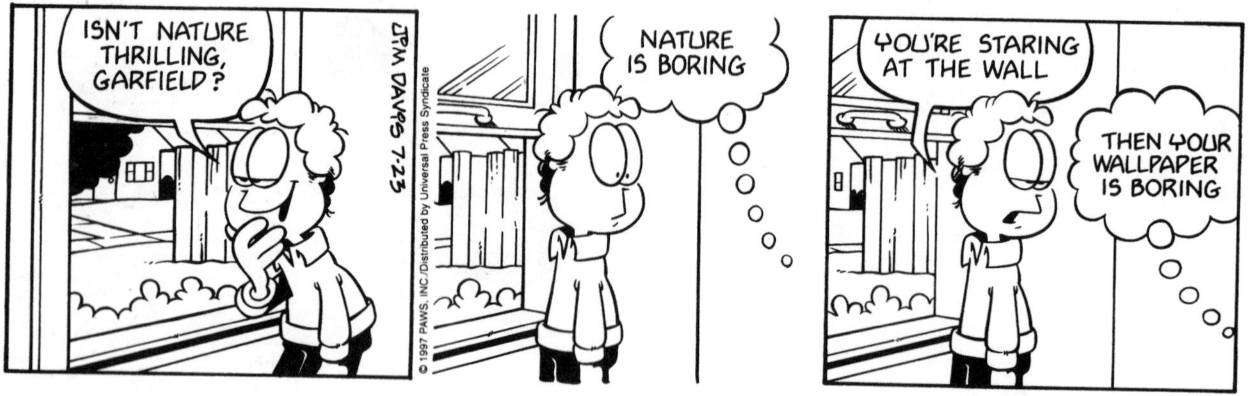
ISN'T NATURE THRILLING, GARFIELD?
JIM DAVIS 7-23
© 1997 PAWS, INC./Distributed by Universal Press Syndicate
NATURE IS BORING
YOU'RE STARING AT THE WALL
THEN YOUR WALLPAPER IS BORING

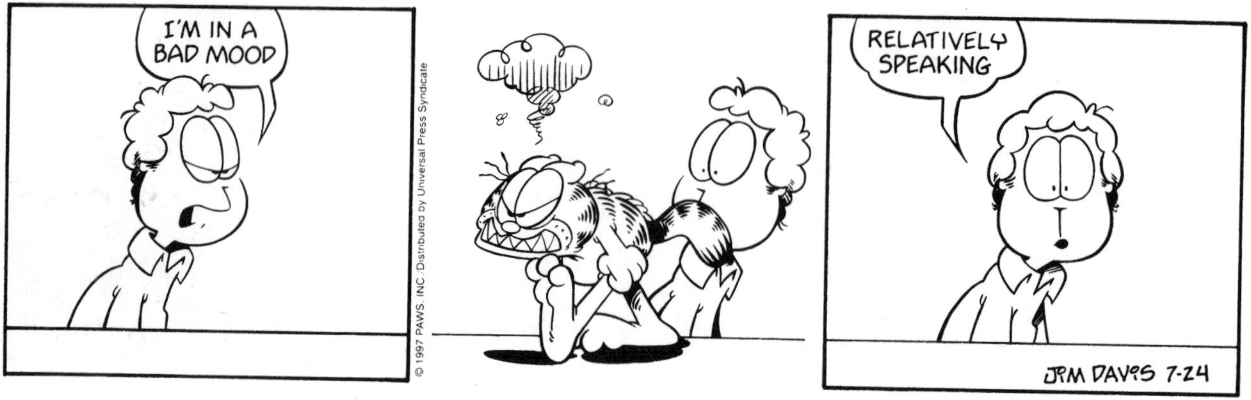
I'M IN A BAD MOOD
© 1997 PAWS, INC./Distributed by Universal Press Syndicate
RELATIVELY SPEAKING
JIM DAVIS 7-24

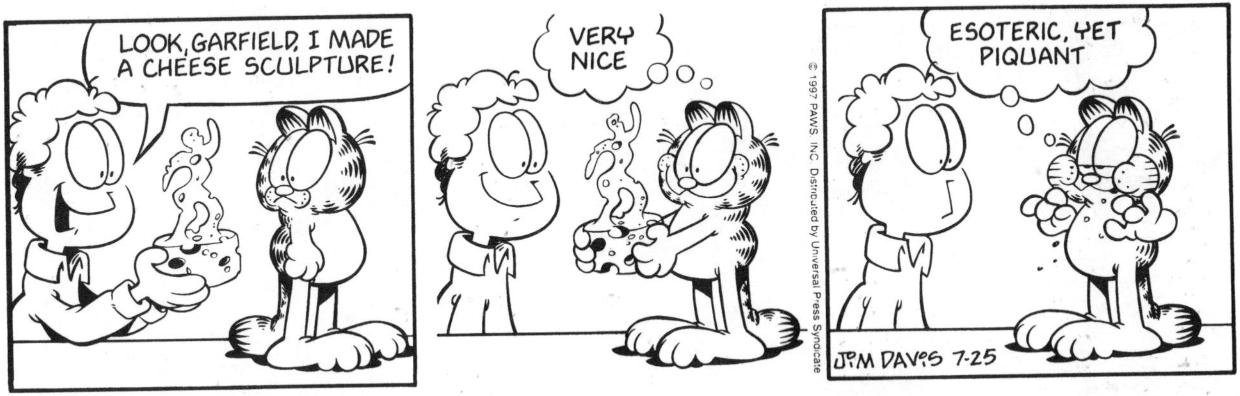
LOOK, GARFIELD, I MADE A CHEESE SCULPTURE!
VERY NICE
ESOTERIC, YET PIQUANT
JIM DAVIS 7-25
© 1997 PAWS, INC. Distributed by Universal Press Syndicate

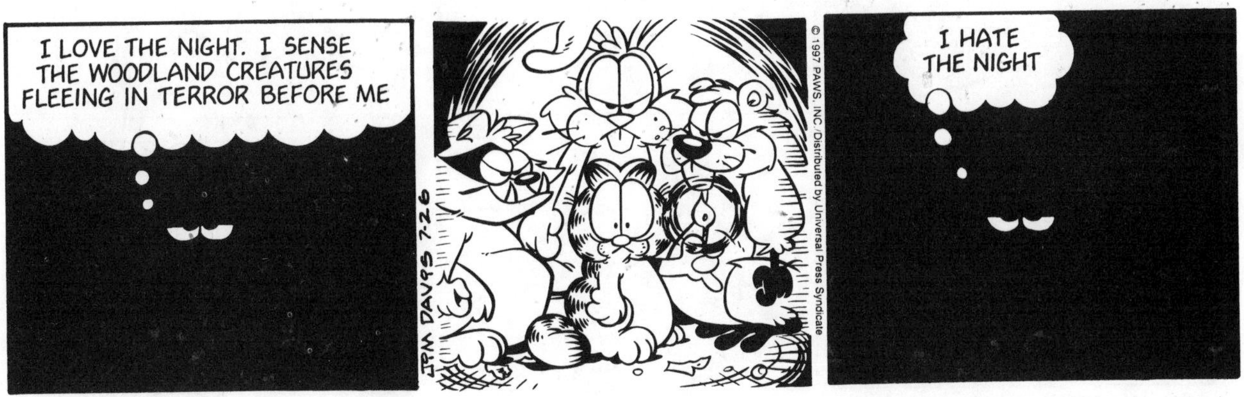
I LOVE THE NIGHT. I SENSE THE WOODLAND CREATURES FLEEING IN TERROR BEFORE ME
JIM DAVIS 7-26
© 1997 PAWS, INC./Distributed by Universal Press Syndicate
I HATE THE NIGHT

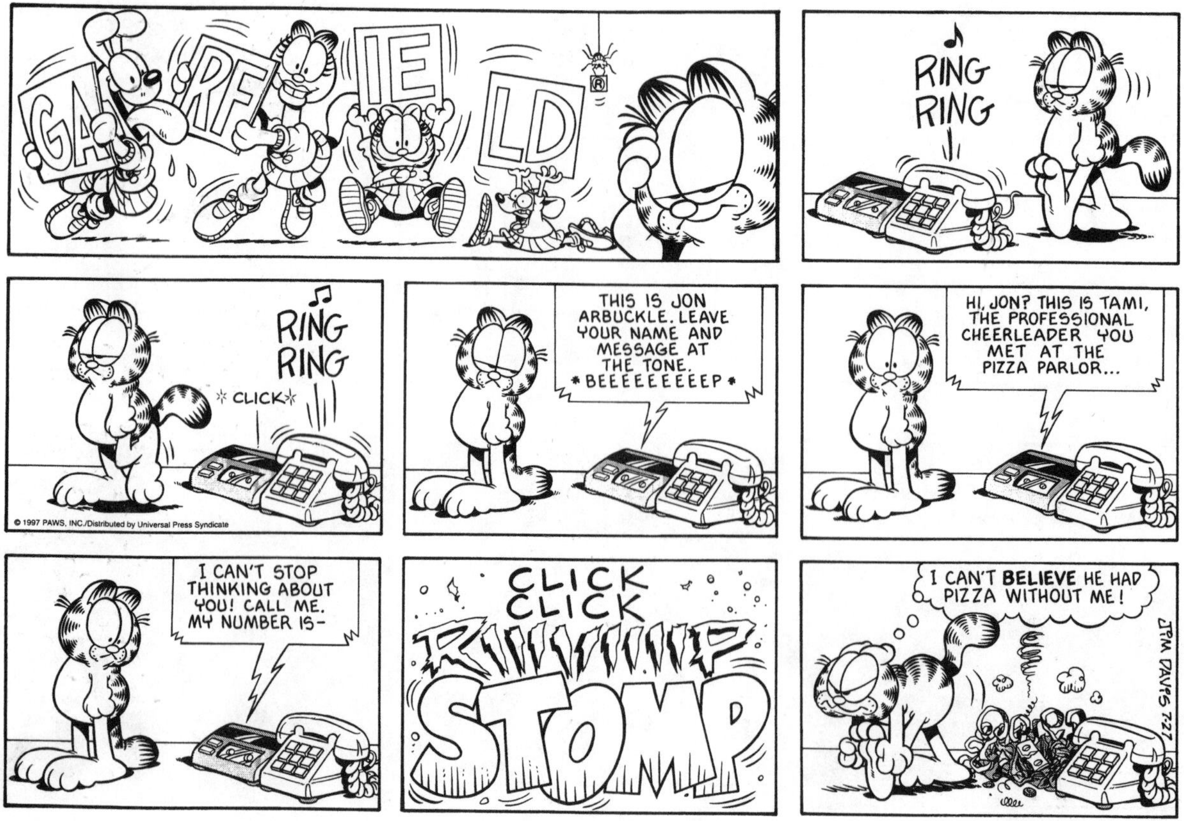
GARFIELD ®
RING RING
RING RING
CLICK
© 1997 PAWS, INC./Distributed by Universal Press Syndicate
THIS IS JON ARBUCKLE. LEAVE YOUR NAME AND MESSAGE AT THE TONE. *BEEEEEEEEEP*
HI, JON? THIS IS TAMI, THE PROFESSIONAL CHEERLEADER YOU MET AT THE PIZZA PARLOR...
I CAN'T STOP THINKING ABOUT YOU! CALL ME. MY NUMBER IS-
CLICK CLICK
RMMMMP
STOMP
I CAN'T **BELIEVE** HE HAD PIZZA WITHOUT ME!
JPM DAVIS 7-27

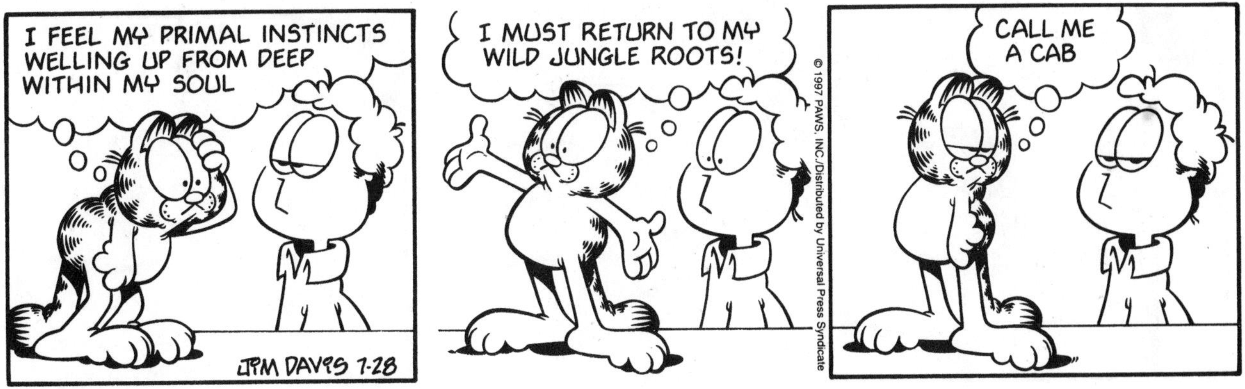
I FEEL MY PRIMAL INSTINCTS WELLING UP FROM DEEP WITHIN MY SOUL
JIM DAVIS 7-28
I MUST RETURN TO MY WILD JUNGLE ROOTS!
© 1997 PAWS, INC./Distributed by Universal Press Syndicate
CALL ME A CAB

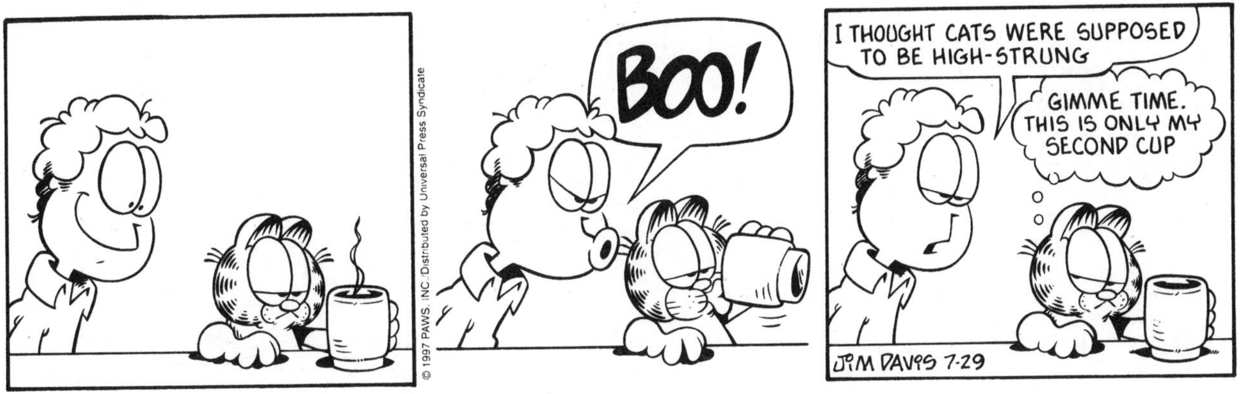
© 1997 PAWS, INC./Distributed by Universal Press Syndicate
BOO!
I THOUGHT CATS WERE SUPPOSED TO BE HIGH-STRUNG
GIMME TIME. THIS IS ONLY MY SECOND CUP
JIM DAVIS 7-29

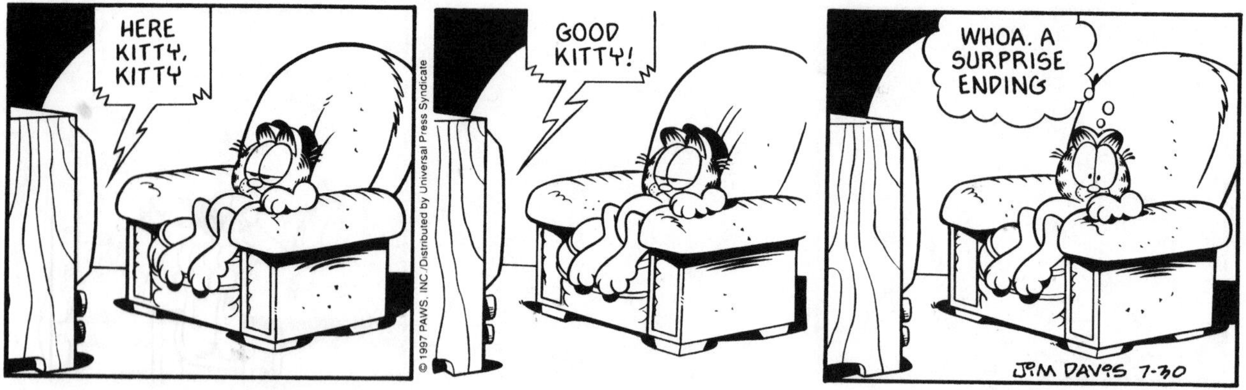
HERE KITTY, KITTY
GOOD KITTY!
WHOA. A SURPRISE ENDING
JIM DAVIS 7-30

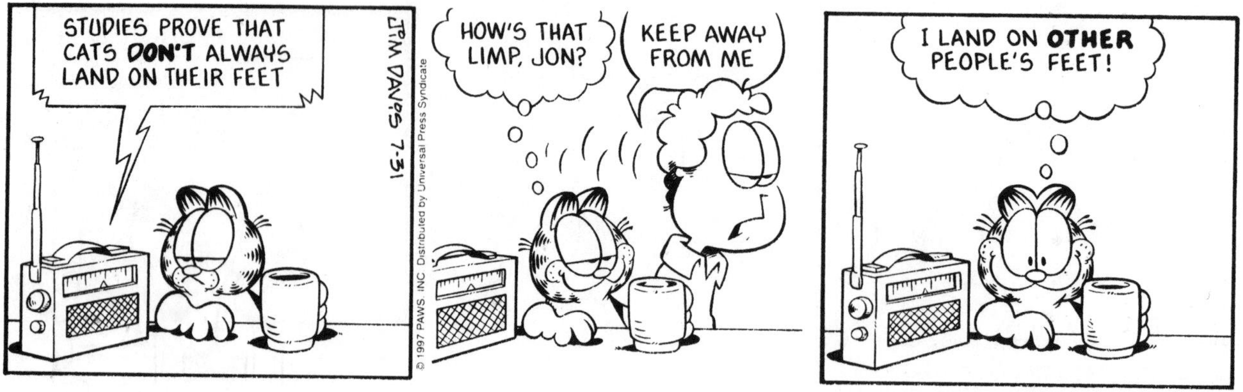
STUDIES PROVE THAT CATS **DON'T** ALWAYS LAND ON THEIR FEET
JIM DAVIS 7-31
HOW'S THAT LIMP, JON?
KEEP AWAY FROM ME
I LAND ON **OTHER** PEOPLE'S FEET!

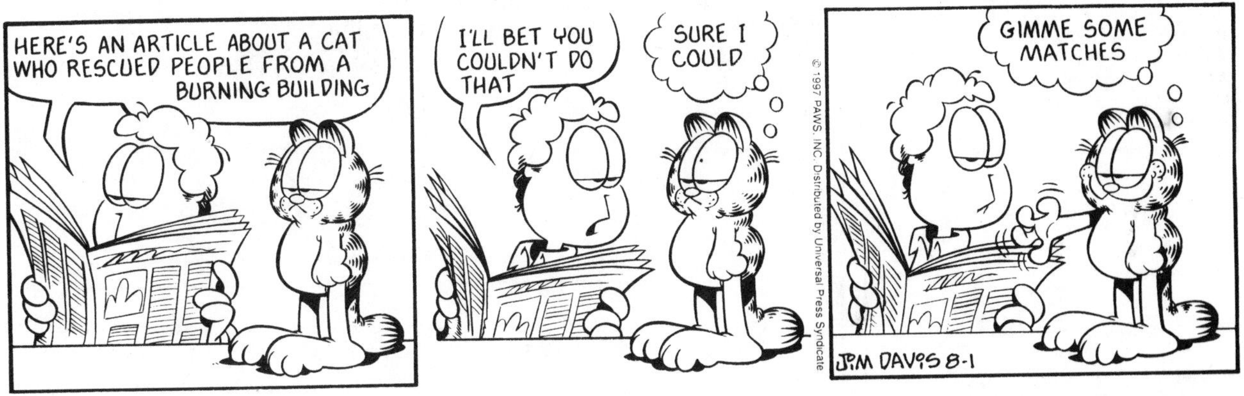
HERE'S AN ARTICLE ABOUT A CAT WHO RESCUED PEOPLE FROM A BURNING BUILDING
I'LL BET YOU COULDN'T DO THAT
SURE I COULD
© 1997 PAWS, INC. Distributed by Universal Press Syndicate
GIMME SOME MATCHES
JIM DAVIS 8-1

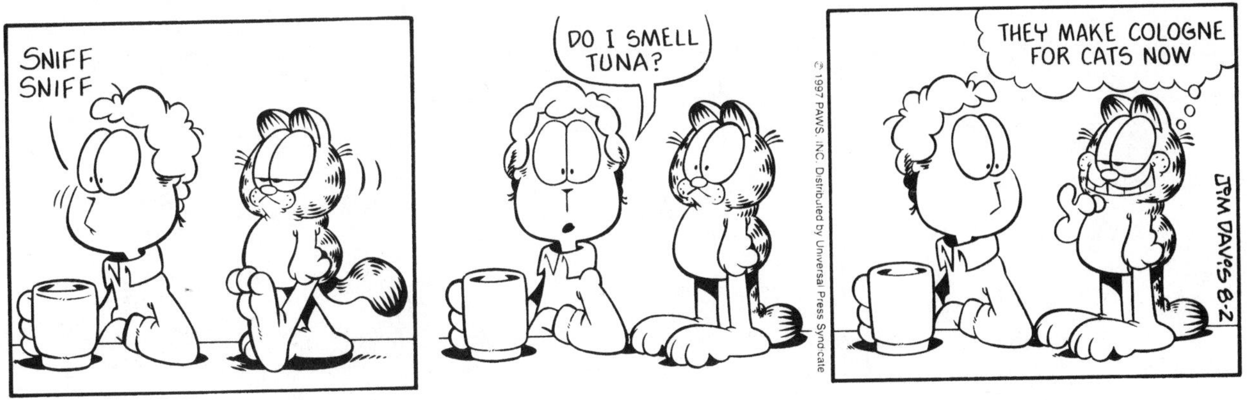
SNIFF SNIFF
DO I SMELL TUNA?
© 1997 PAWS, INC. Distributed by Universal Press Syndicate
THEY MAKE COLOGNE FOR CATS NOW
JIM DAVIS 8-2

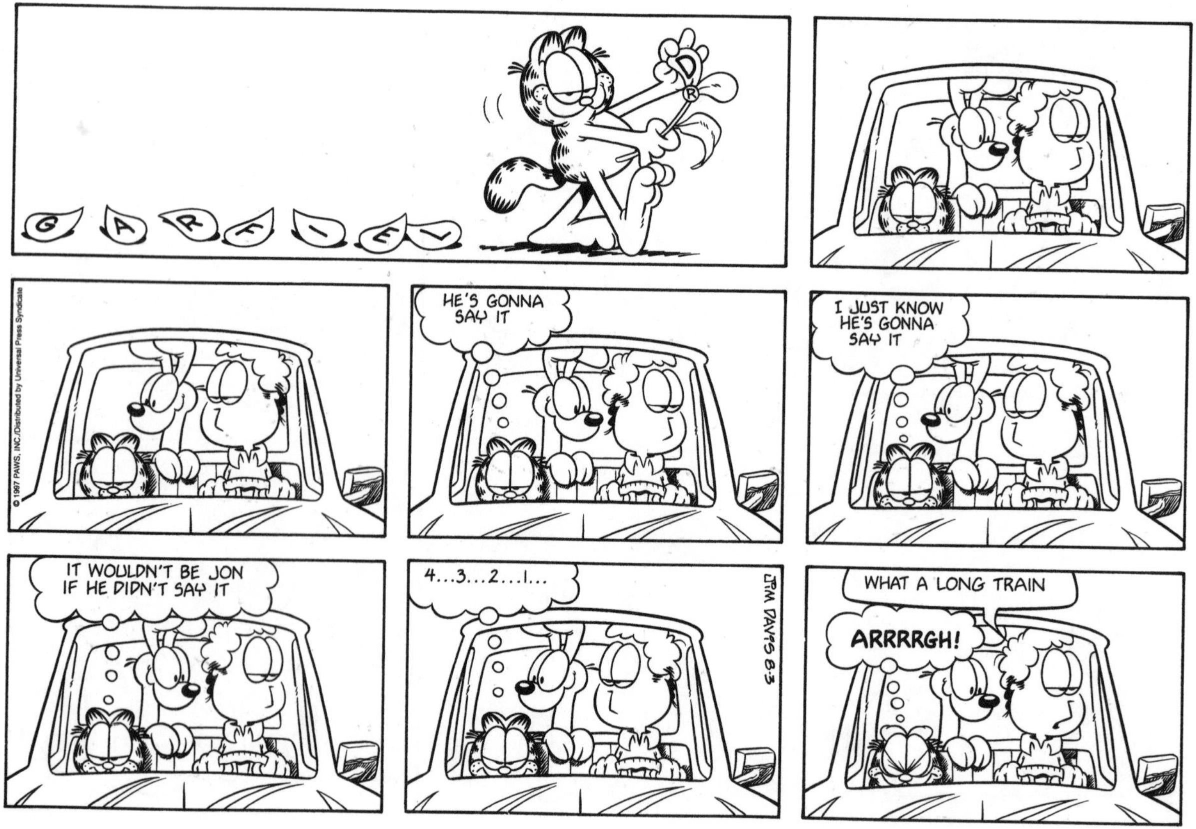
G A R F I E L D
© 1997 PAWS, INC./Distributed by Universal Press Syndicate
HE'S GONNA SAY IT
I JUST KNOW HE'S GONNA SAY IT
IT WOULDN'T BE JON IF HE DIDN'T SAY IT
4...3...2...1...
JIM DAVIS 8-3
WHAT A LONG TRAIN
ARRRRGH!

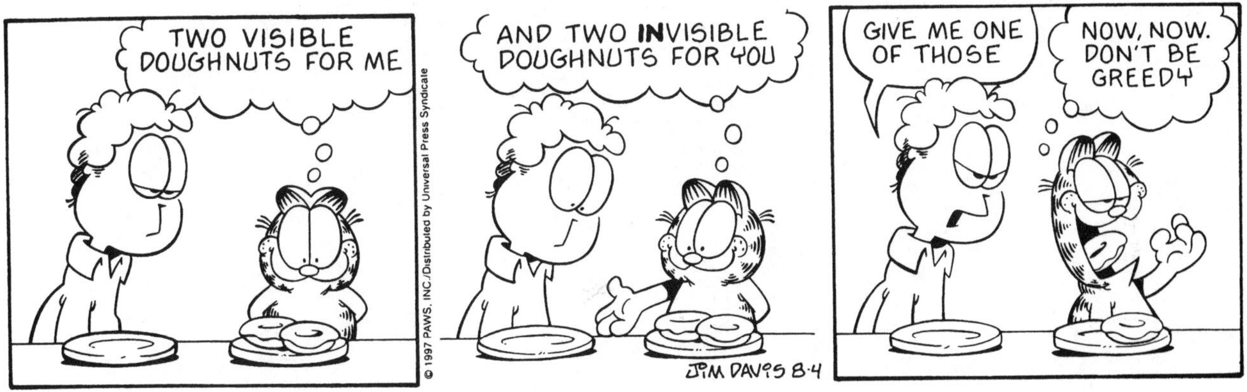
TWO VISIBLE DOUGHNUTS FOR ME
© 1997 PAWS. INC./Distributed by Universal Press Syndicate
AND TWO INVISIBLE DOUGHNUTS FOR YOU
JIM DAVIS 8·4
GIVE ME ONE OF THOSE
NOW, NOW. DON'T BE GREEDY

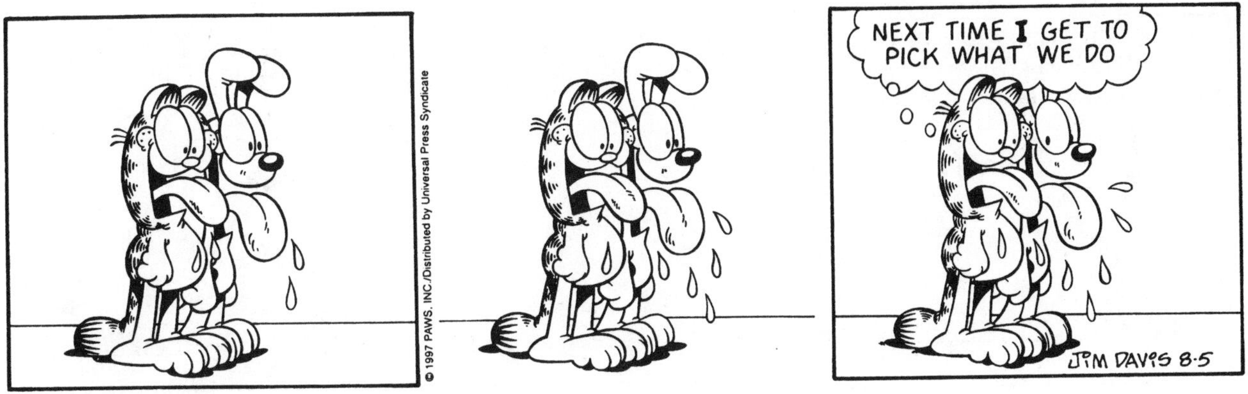
© 1997 PAWS. INC./Distributed by Universal Press Syndicate
NEXT TIME I GET TO PICK WHAT WE DO
JIM DAVIS 8·5

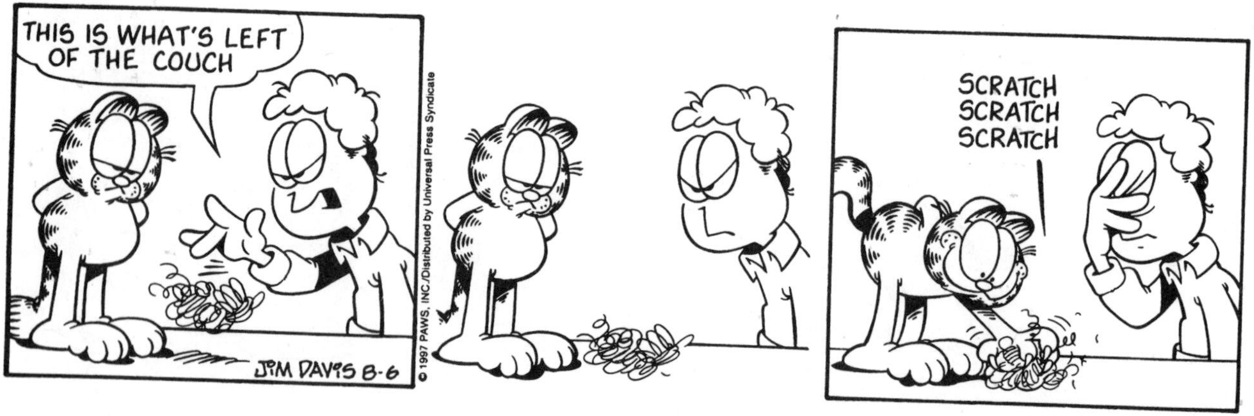
THIS IS WHAT'S LEFT OF THE COUCH
SCRATCH SCRATCH SCRATCH
JIM DAVIS 8-6
© 1997 PAWS, INC./Distributed by Universal Press Syndicate

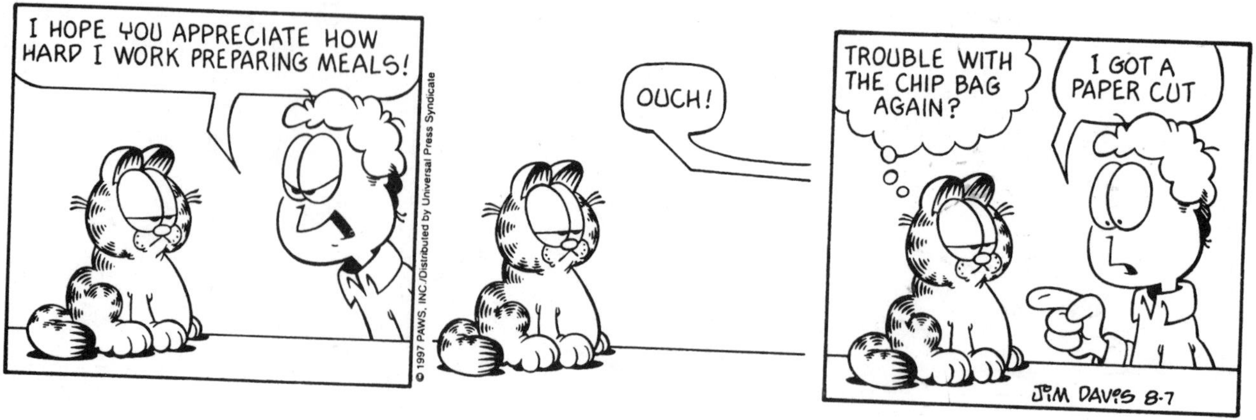
I HOPE YOU APPRECIATE HOW HARD I WORK PREPARING MEALS!
OUCH!
TROUBLE WITH THE CHIP BAG AGAIN?
I GOT A PAPER CUT
JIM DAVIS 8-7
© 1997 PAWS, INC./Distributed by Universal Press Syndicate

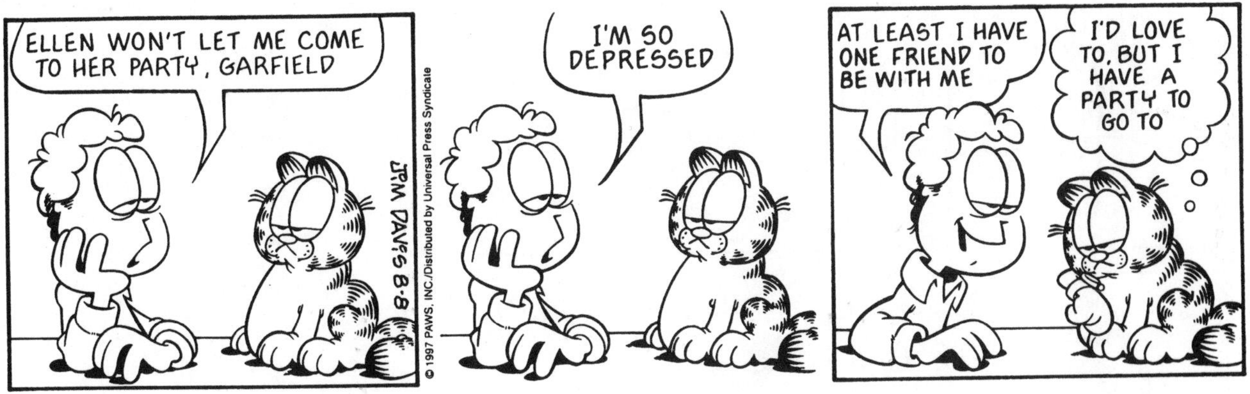

ELLEN WON'T LET ME COME TO HER PARTY, GARFIELD
JIM DAVIS 8-8
© 1997 PAWS, INC./Distributed by Universal Press Syndicate
I'M SO DEPRESSED
AT LEAST I HAVE ONE FRIEND TO BE WITH ME
I'D LOVE TO, BUT I HAVE A PARTY TO GO TO

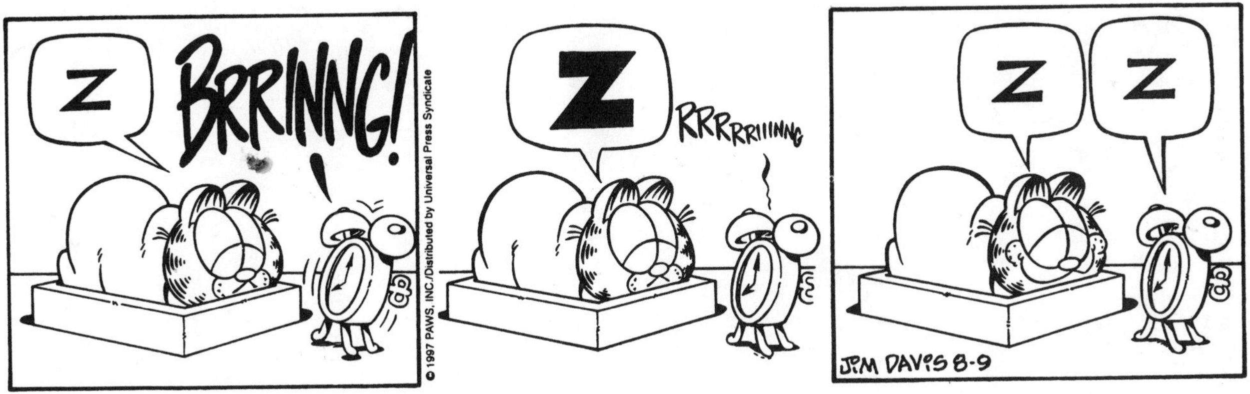

Z
BRRINNG!
© 1997 PAWS, INC./Distributed by Universal Press Syndicate
Z
RRRRRIIINNG
Z
Z
JIM DAVIS 8-9

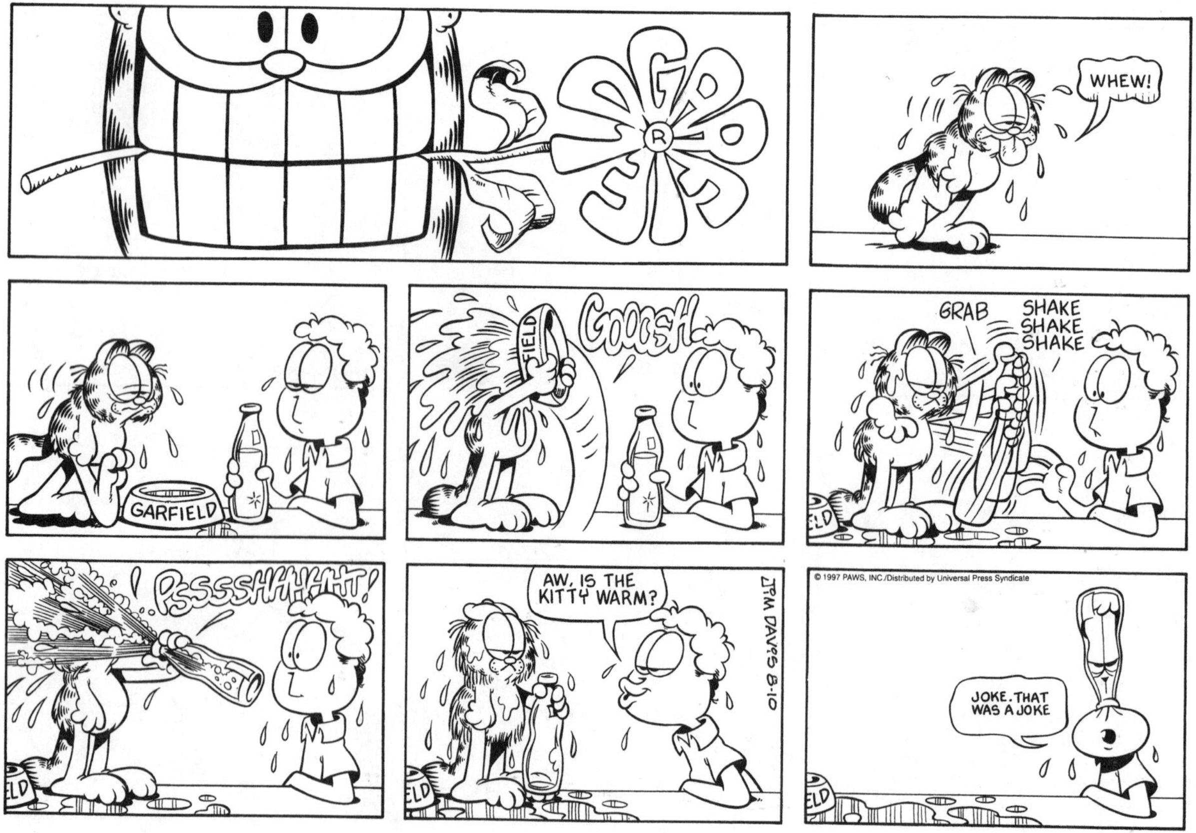
WHEW!
GARFIELD
FIELD
GOOOSH
GRAB
SHAKE
SHAKE
SHAKE
PSSSSHHHHHT!
AW, IS THE KITTY WARM?
JIM DAVIS 8-10
© 1997 PAWS, INC./Distributed by Universal Press Syndicate
JOKE. THAT WAS A JOKE

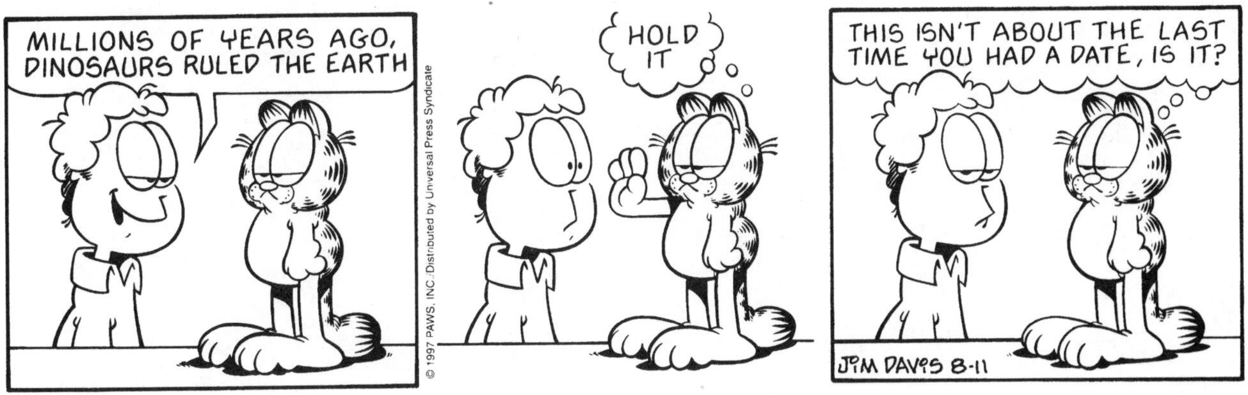
MILLIONS OF YEARS AGO, DINOSAURS RULED THE EARTH
HOLD IT
THIS ISN'T ABOUT THE LAST TIME YOU HAD A DATE, IS IT?
JIM DAVIS 8-11
© 1997 PAWS, INC./Distributed by Universal Press Syndicate

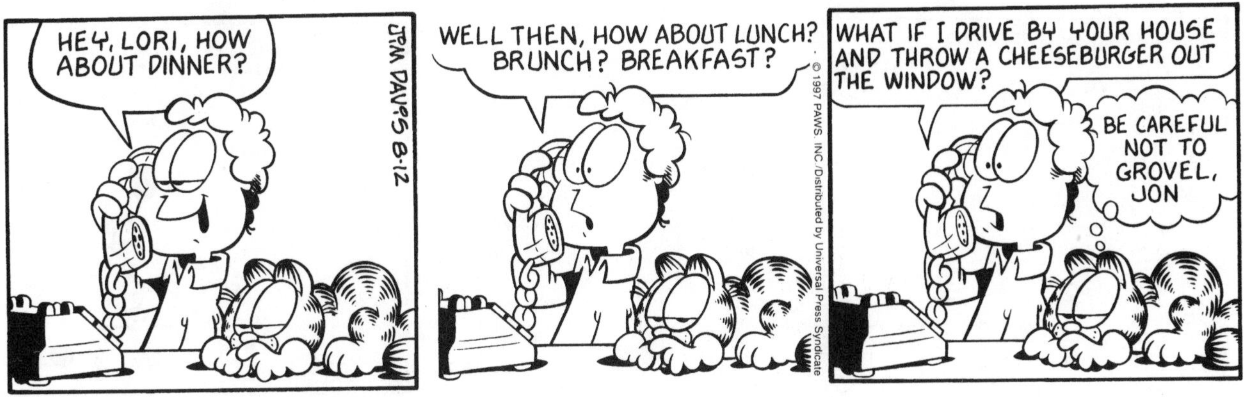
HEY, LORI, HOW ABOUT DINNER?
JIM DAVIS 8-12
WELL THEN, HOW ABOUT LUNCH? BRUNCH? BREAKFAST?
WHAT IF I DRIVE BY YOUR HOUSE AND THROW A CHEESEBURGER OUT THE WINDOW?
BE CAREFUL NOT TO GROVEL, JON
© 1997 PAWS, INC./Distributed by Universal Press Syndicate

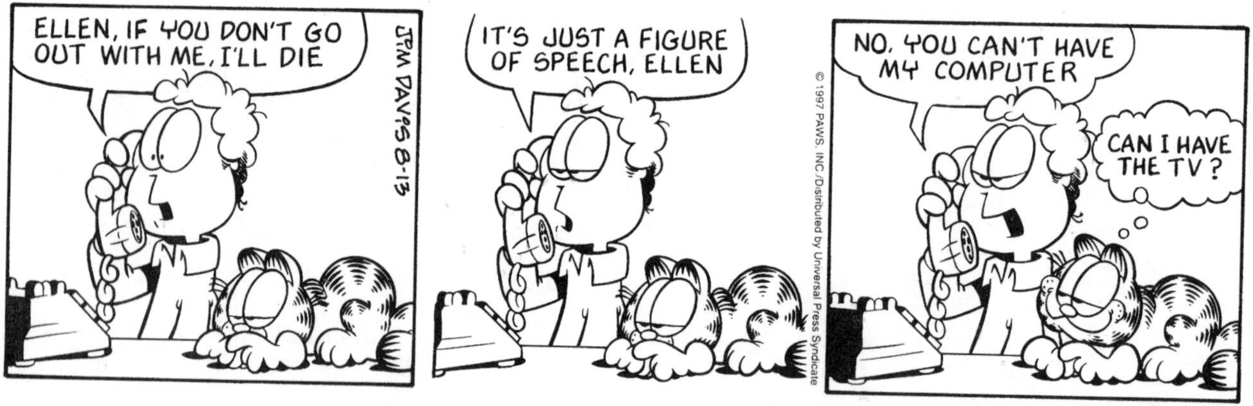
ELLEN, IF YOU DON'T GO OUT WITH ME, I'LL DIE
JIM DAVIS 8-13
IT'S JUST A FIGURE OF SPEECH, ELLEN
NO, YOU CAN'T HAVE MY COMPUTER
CAN I HAVE THE TV?

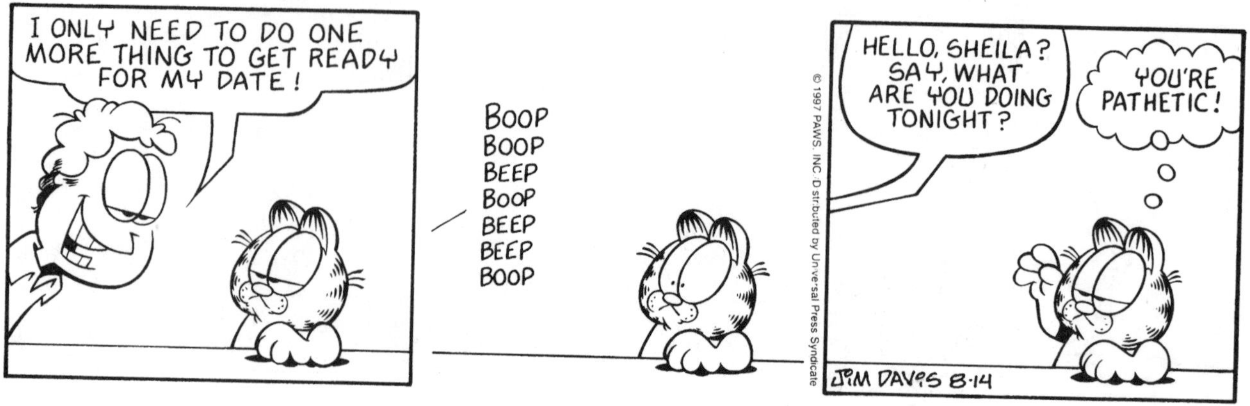
I ONLY NEED TO DO ONE MORE THING TO GET READY FOR MY DATE!
BOOP BOOP BEEP BOOP BEEP BEEP BOOP
HELLO, SHEILA? SAY, WHAT ARE YOU DOING TONIGHT?
YOU'RE PATHETIC!
JIM DAVIS 8-14

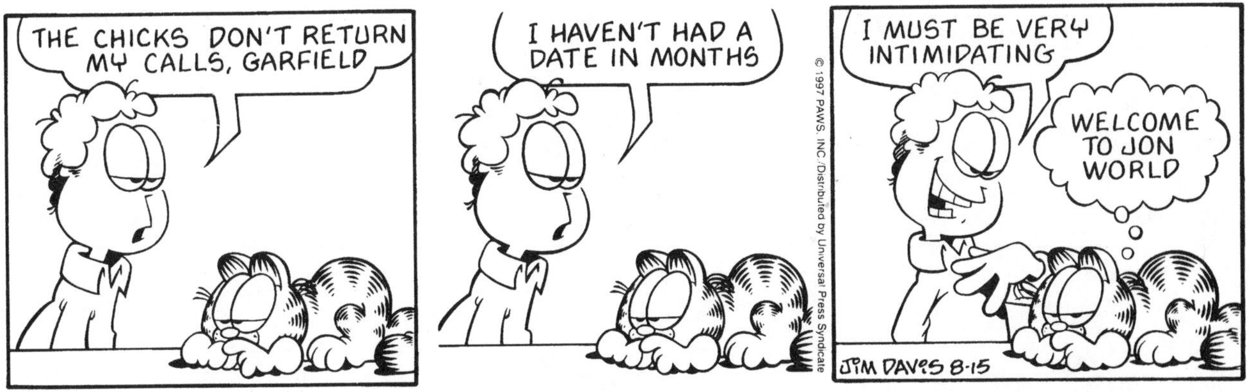
THE CHICKS DON'T RETURN MY CALLS, GARFIELD
I HAVEN'T HAD A DATE IN MONTHS
© 1997 PAWS, INC./Distributed by Universal Press Syndicate
I MUST BE VERY INTIMIDATING
WELCOME TO JON WORLD
JIM DAVIS 8-15

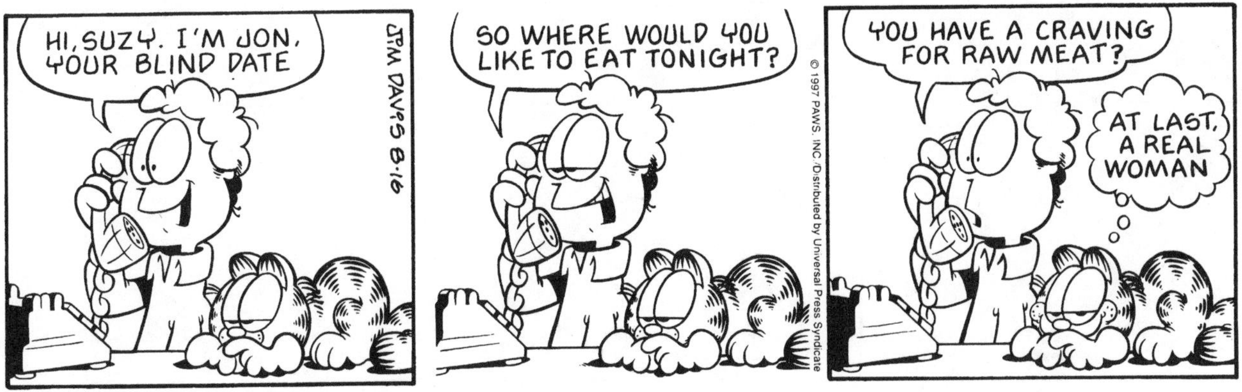
HI, SUZY. I'M JON, YOUR BLIND DATE
JIM DAVIS 8-16
SO WHERE WOULD YOU LIKE TO EAT TONIGHT?
© 1997 PAWS, INC./Distributed by Universal Press Syndicate
YOU HAVE A CRAVING FOR RAW MEAT?
AT LAST, A REAL WOMAN

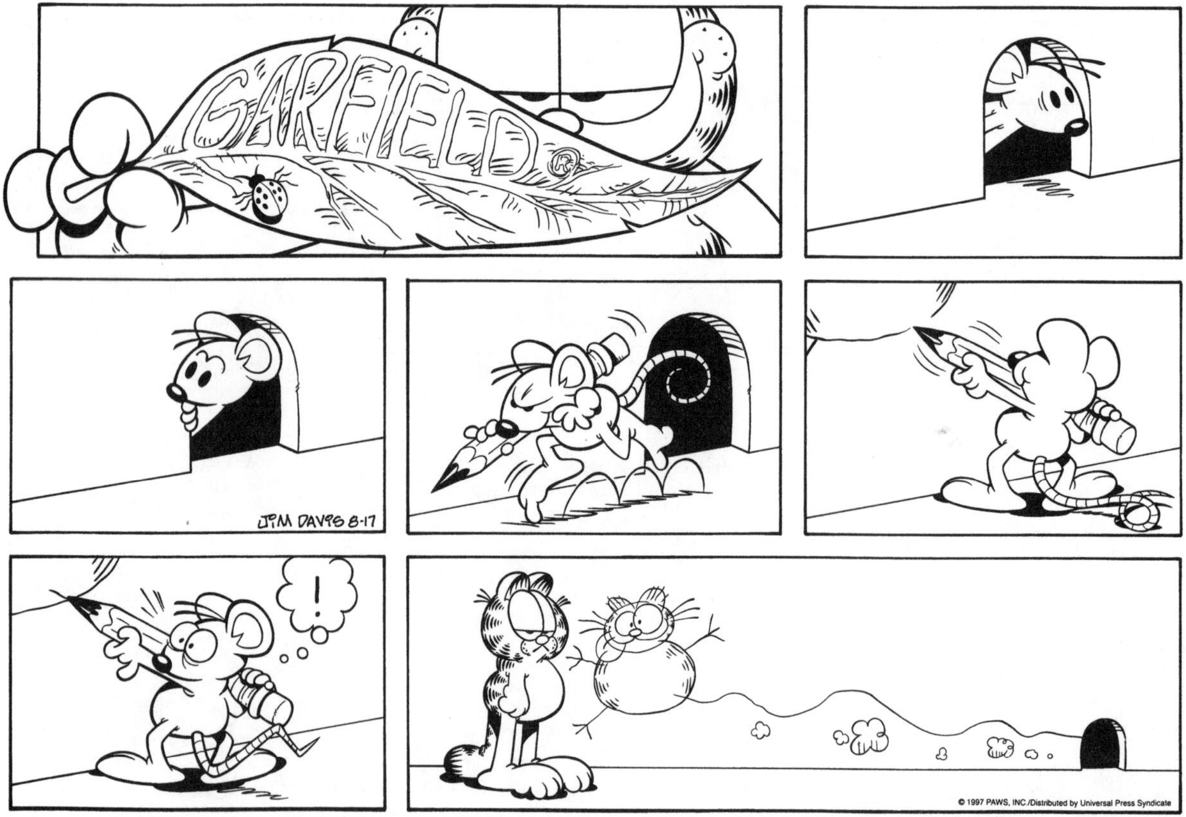
GARFIELD®
JIM DAVIS 8-17
!
© 1997 PAWS, INC./Distributed by Universal Press Syndicate

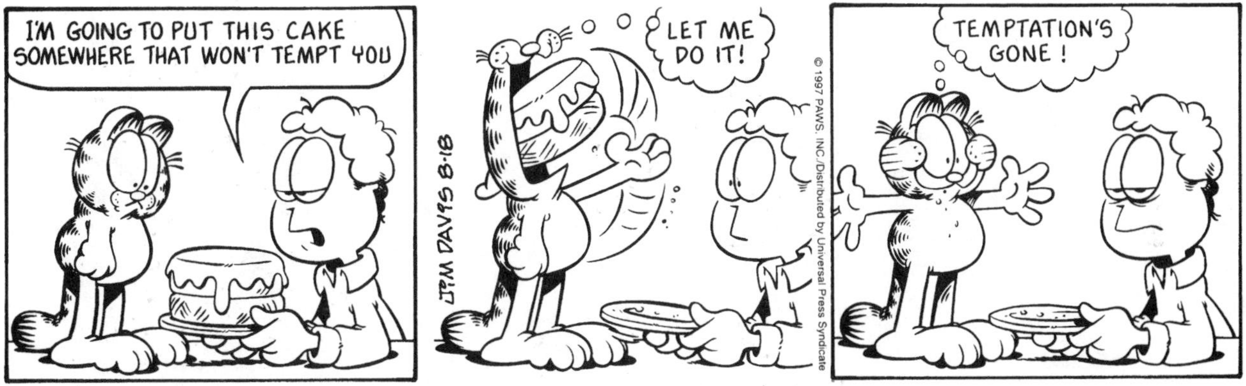
I'M GOING TO PUT THIS CAKE SOMEWHERE THAT WON'T TEMPT YOU
LET ME DO IT!
JIM DAVIS 8-18
TEMPTATION'S GONE!
© 1997 PAWS, INC./Distributed by Universal Press Syndicate

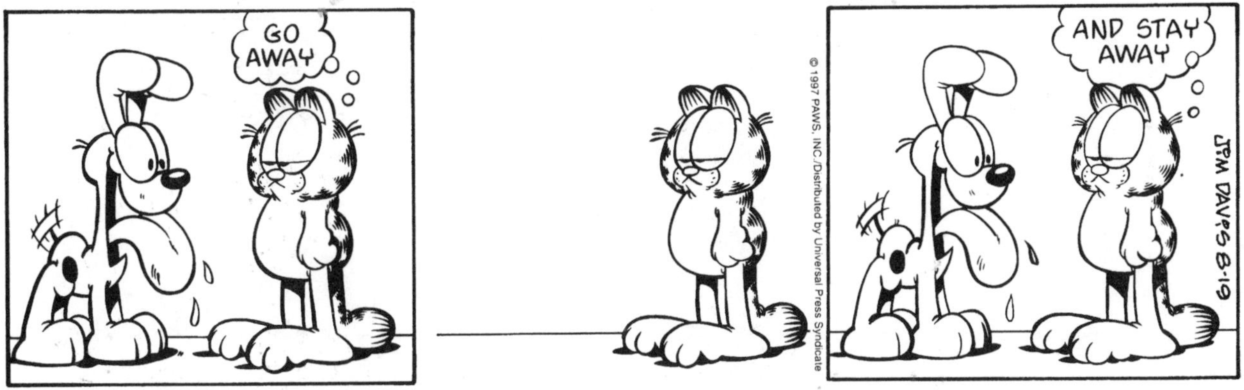
GO AWAY
AND STAY AWAY
JIM DAVIS 8-19
© 1997 PAWS, INC./Distributed by Universal Press Syndicate

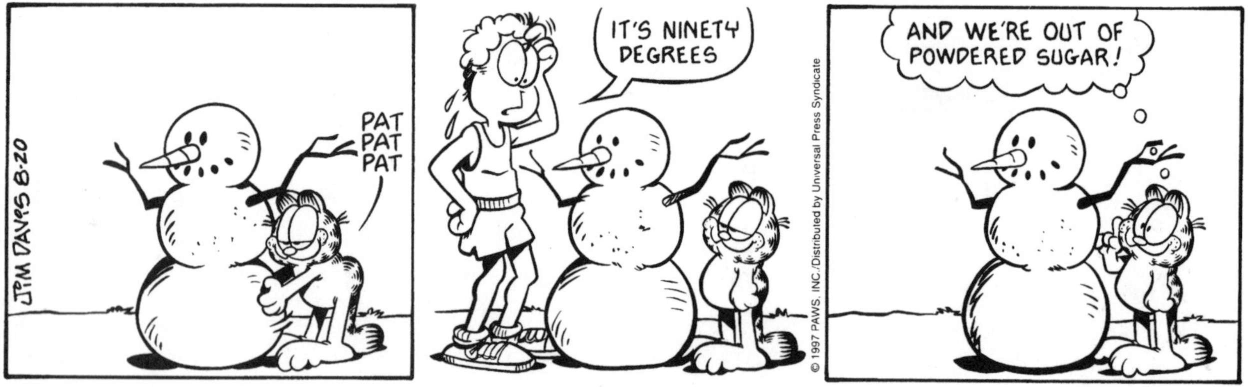
JIM DAVIS 8-20
PAT PAT PAT
IT'S NINETY DEGREES
AND WE'RE OUT OF POWDERED SUGAR!
© 1997 PAWS, INC./Distributed by Universal Press Syndicate

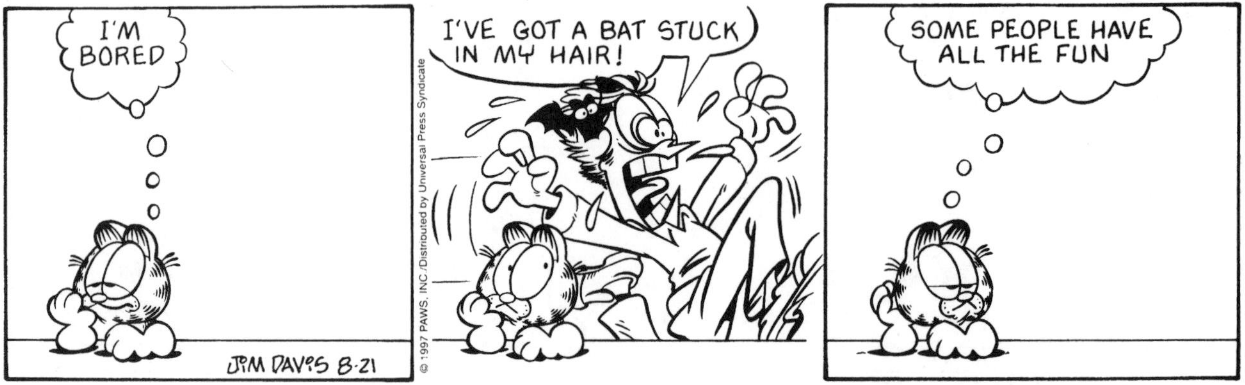
I'M BORED
JIM DAVIS 8-21
© 1997 PAWS, INC./Distributed by Universal Press Syndicate
I'VE GOT A BAT STUCK IN MY HAIR!
SOME PEOPLE HAVE ALL THE FUN

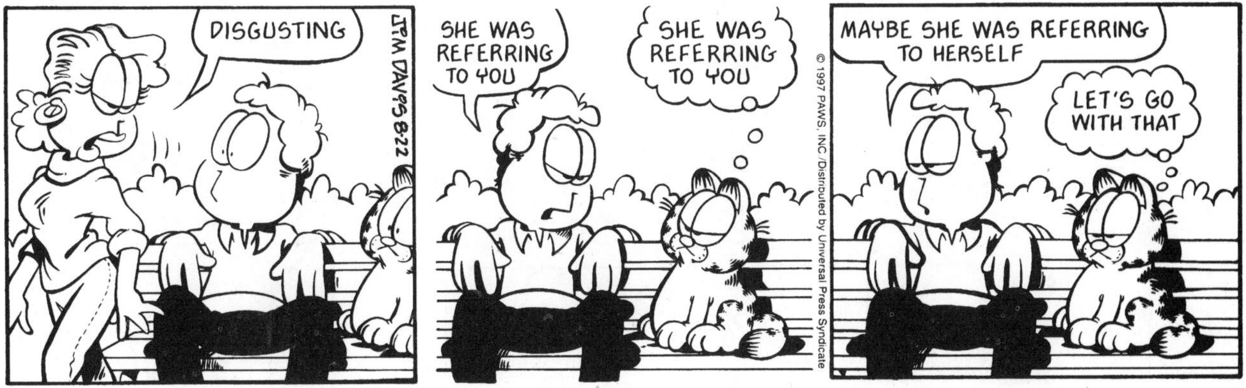
DISGUSTING
JIM DAVIS 8-22
SHE WAS REFERRING TO YOU
SHE WAS REFERRING TO YOU
© 1997 PAWS, INC./Distributed by Universal Press Syndicate
MAYBE SHE WAS REFERRING TO HERSELF
LET'S GO WITH THAT

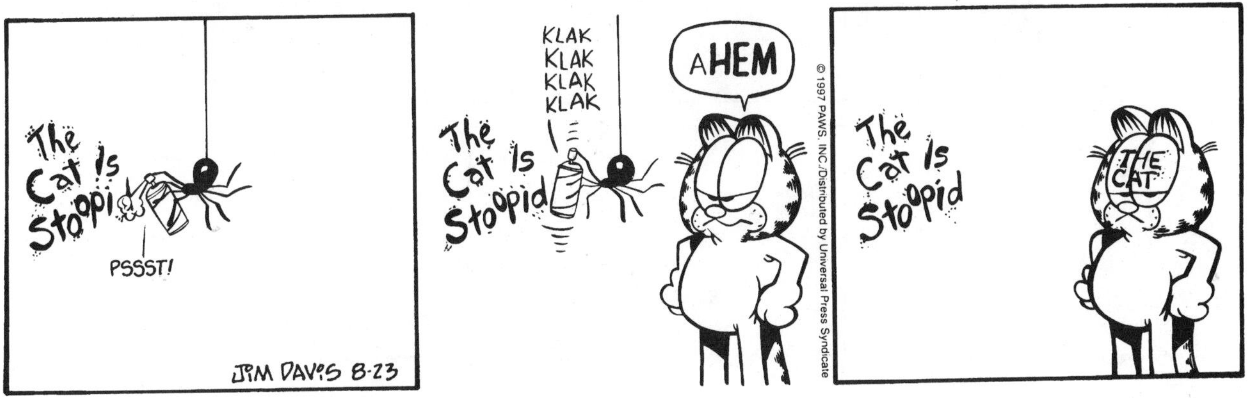
The Cat Is Stoopi
PSSST!
JIM DAVIS 8-23
The Cat Is Stoopid
KLAK KLAK KLAK KLAK
AHEM
© 1997 PAWS, INC./Distributed by Universal Press Syndicate
The Cat Is Stoopid
THE CAT

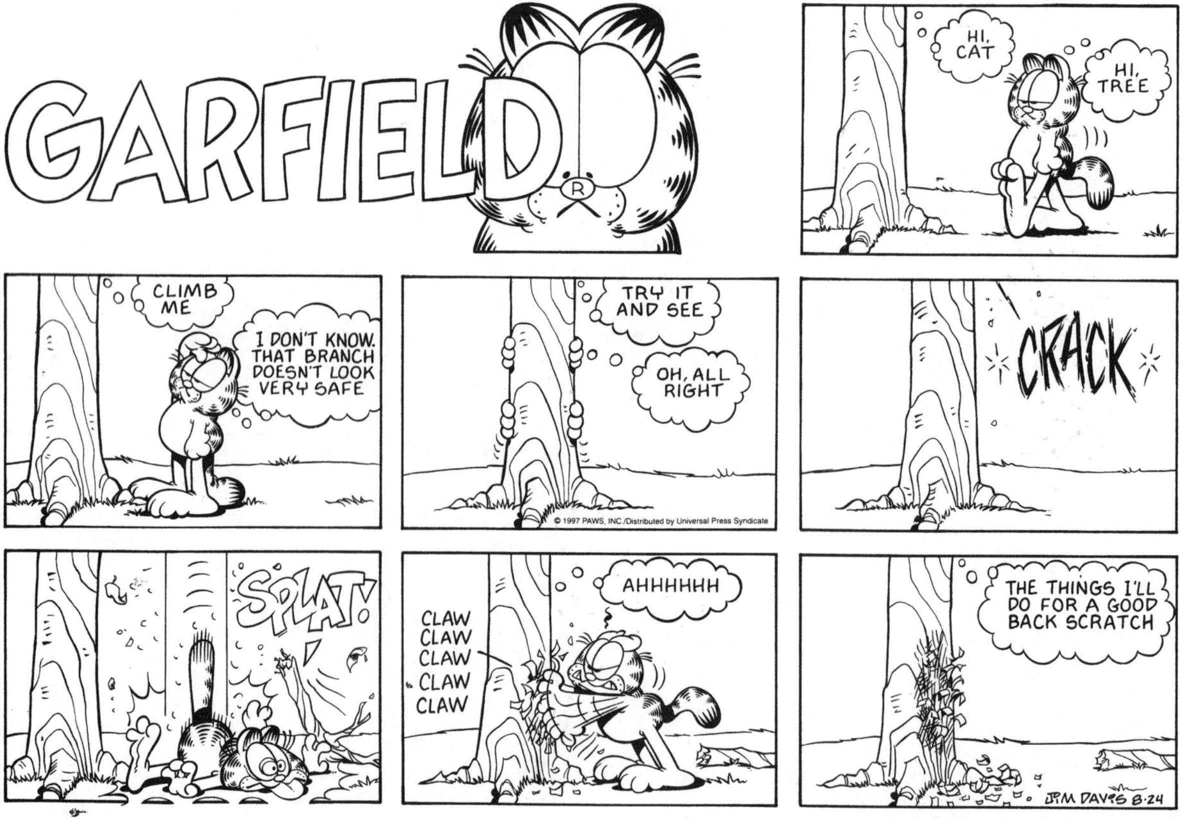
GARFIELD
HI, CAT
HI, TREE
CLIMB ME
I DON'T KNOW. THAT BRANCH DOESN'T LOOK VERY SAFE
TRY IT AND SEE
OH, ALL RIGHT
© 1997 PAWS, INC./Distributed by Universal Press Syndicate
CRACK
SPLAT
CLAW CLAW CLAW CLAW CLAW CLAW
AHHHHHH
THE THINGS I'LL DO FOR A GOOD BACK SCRATCH
JIM DAVIS 8-24

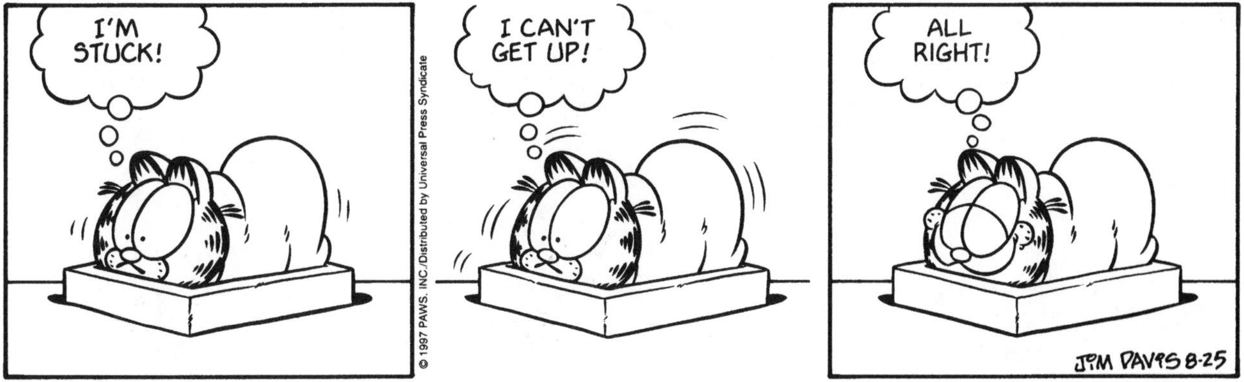
I'M STUCK!
© 1997 PAWS. INC./Distributed by Universal Press Syndicate
I CAN'T GET UP!
ALL RIGHT!
JIM DAVIS 8-25

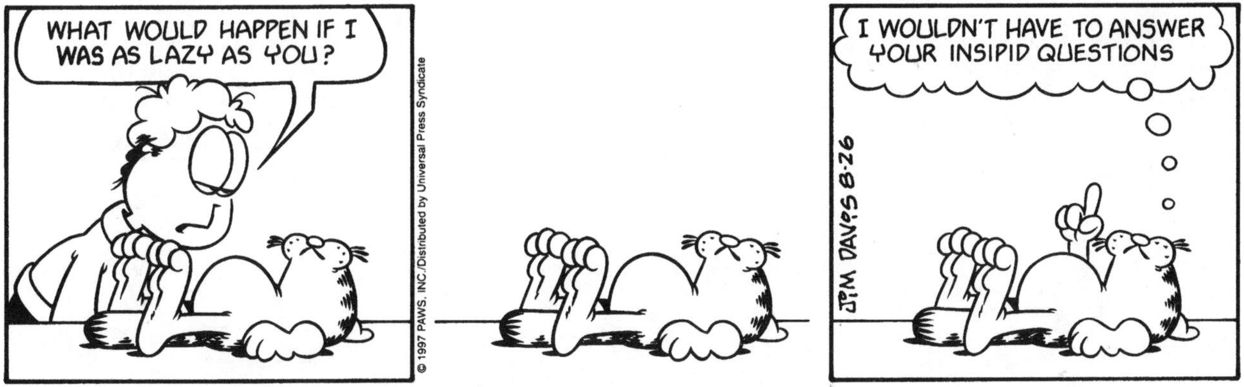
WHAT WOULD HAPPEN IF I WAS AS LAZY AS YOU?
© 1997 PAWS. INC./Distributed by Universal Press Syndicate
JIM DAVIS 8-26
I WOULDN'T HAVE TO ANSWER YOUR INSIPID QUESTIONS

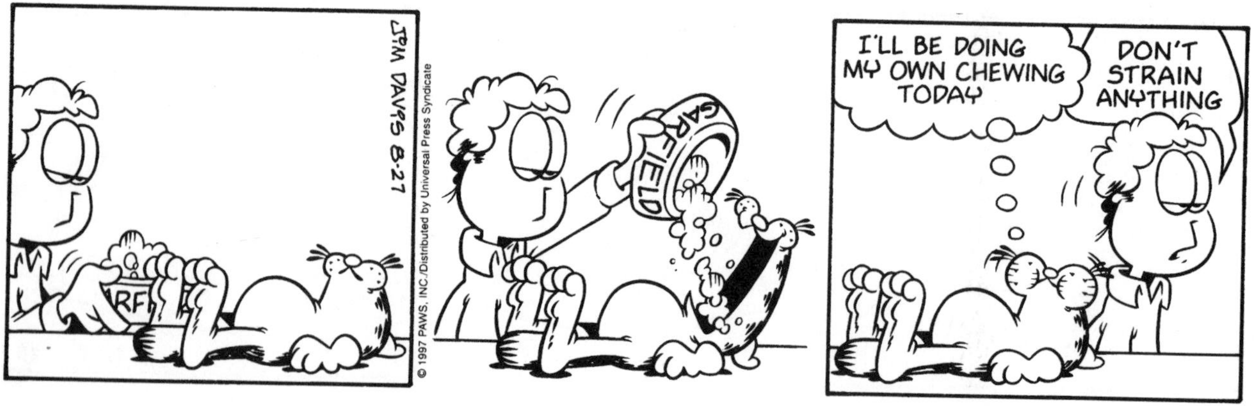
JIM DAVIS 8-27
© 1997 PAWS, INC./Distributed by Universal Press Syndicate
GARFIELD
I'LL BE DOING MY OWN CHEWING TODAY
DON'T STRAIN ANYTHING

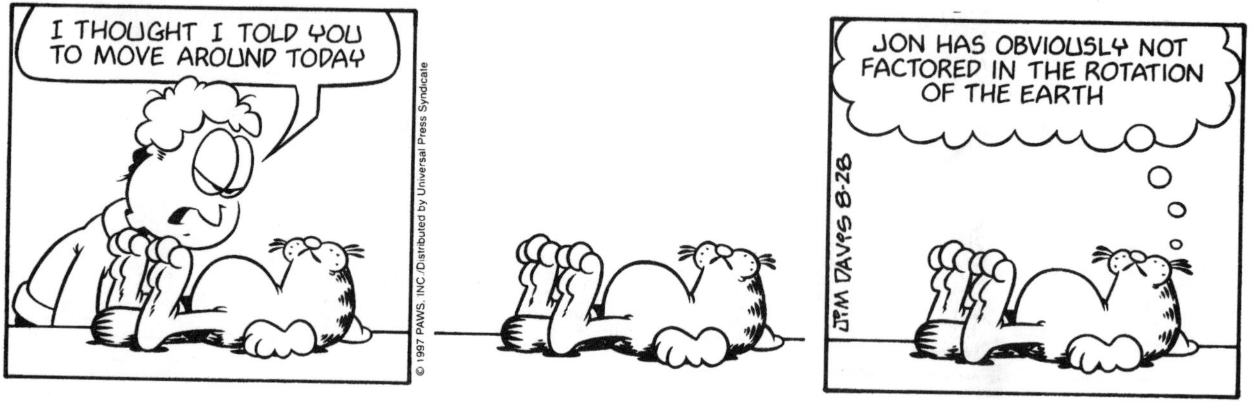
I THOUGHT I TOLD YOU TO MOVE AROUND TODAY
© 1997 PAWS, INC./Distributed by Universal Press Syndicate
JON HAS OBVIOUSLY NOT FACTORED IN THE ROTATION OF THE EARTH
JIM DAVIS 8-28

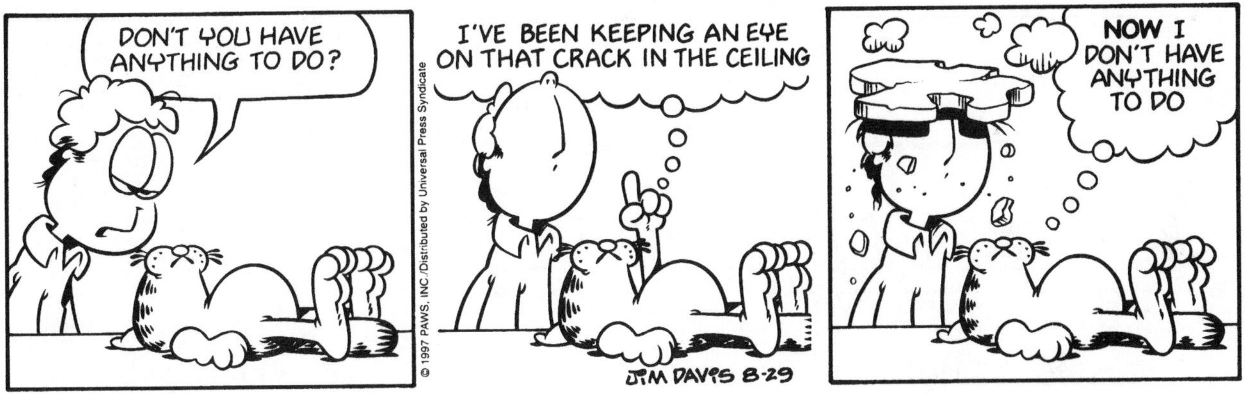
DON'T YOU HAVE ANYTHING TO DO?
© 1997 PAWS, INC./Distributed by Universal Press Syndicate
I'VE BEEN KEEPING AN EYE ON THAT CRACK IN THE CEILING
JIM DAVIS 8-29
NOW I DON'T HAVE ANYTHING TO DO

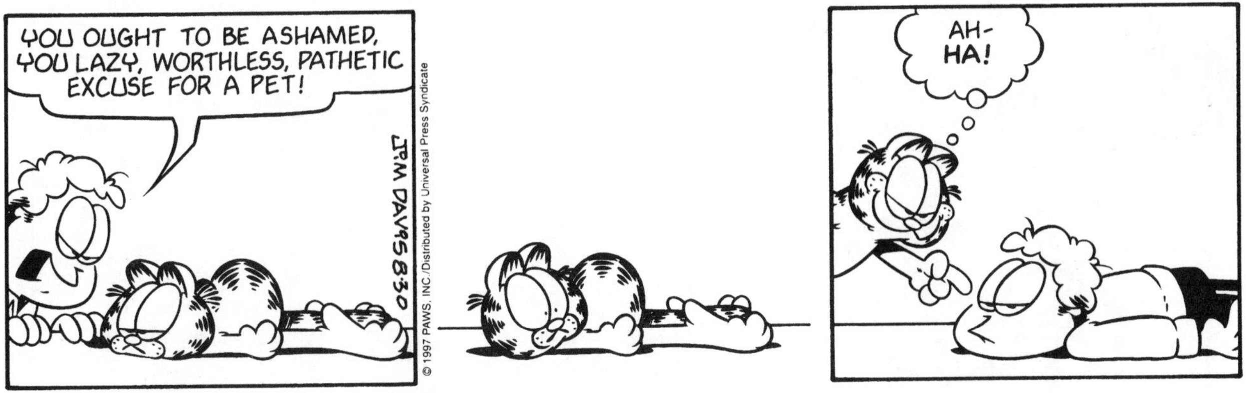
YOU OUGHT TO BE ASHAMED, YOU LAZY, WORTHLESS, PATHETIC EXCUSE FOR A PET!
JIM DAVIS 8-30
© 1997 PAWS, INC./Distributed by Universal Press Syndicate
AH-HA!

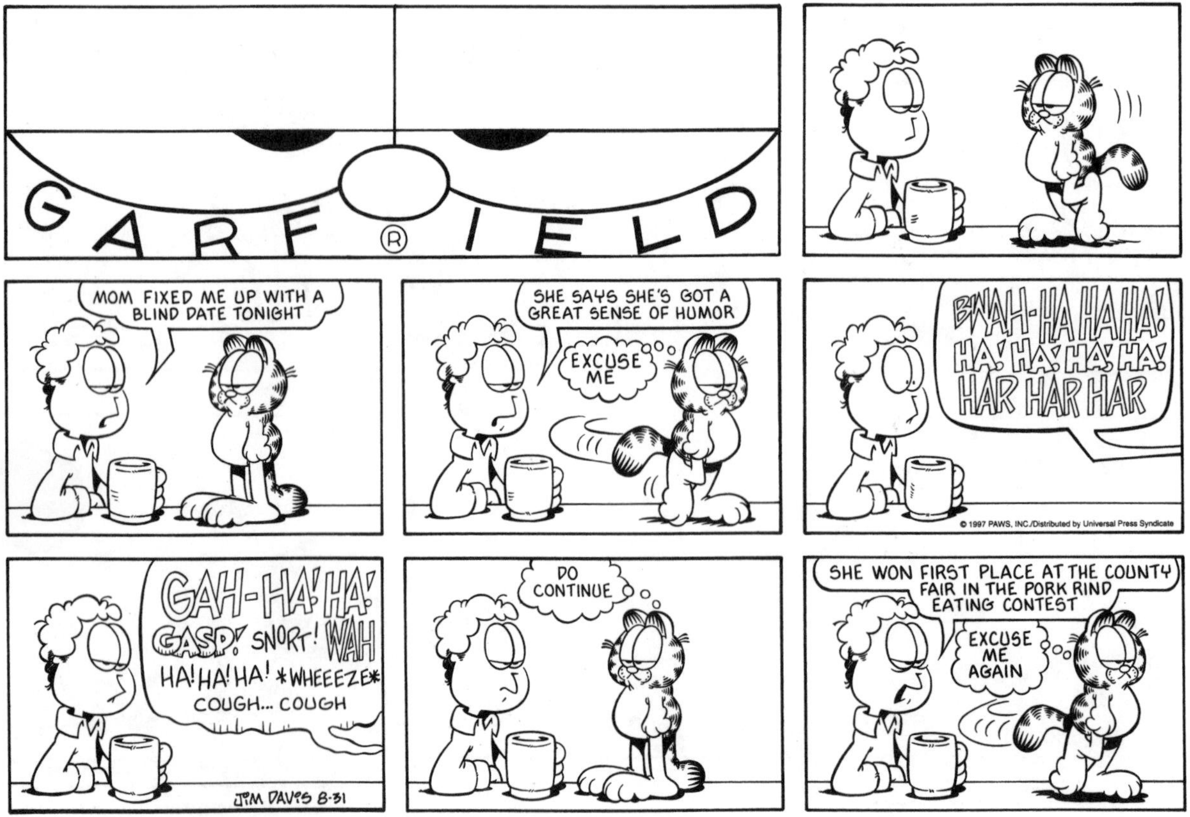
GARFIELD®
MOM FIXED ME UP WITH A BLIND DATE TONIGHT
SHE SAYS SHE'S GOT A GREAT SENSE OF HUMOR
EXCUSE ME
BWAH-HA HAHA! HA! HA! HA! HA! HAR HAR HAR
© 1997 PAWS, INC./Distributed by Universal Press Syndicate
GAH-HA! HA! GASP! SNORT! WAH HA! HA! HA! *WHEEEZE* COUGH... COUGH
JIM DAVIS 8-31
DO CONTINUE
SHE WON FIRST PLACE AT THE COUNTY FAIR IN THE PORK RIND EATING CONTEST
EXCUSE ME AGAIN

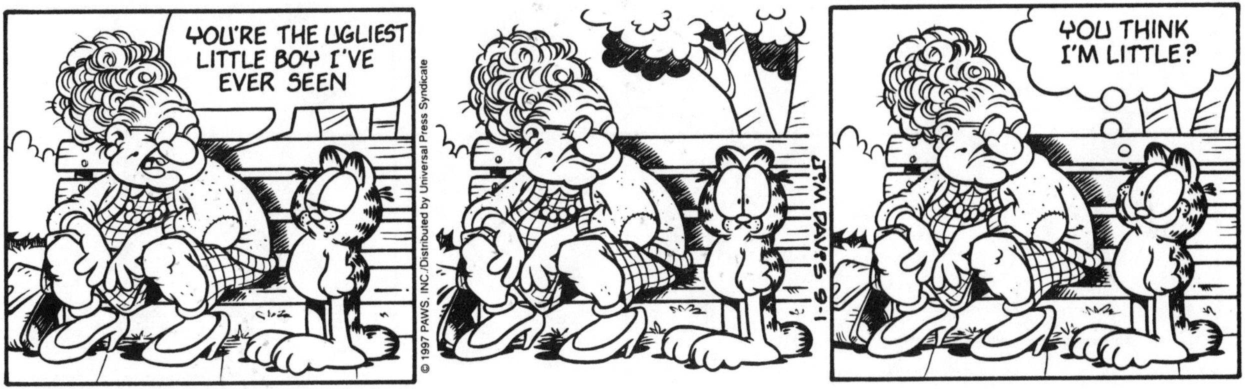
YOU'RE THE UGLIEST LITTLE BOY I'VE EVER SEEN
© 1997 PAWS, INC./Distributed by Universal Press Syndicate
JIM DAVIS 9-1
YOU THINK I'M LITTLE?

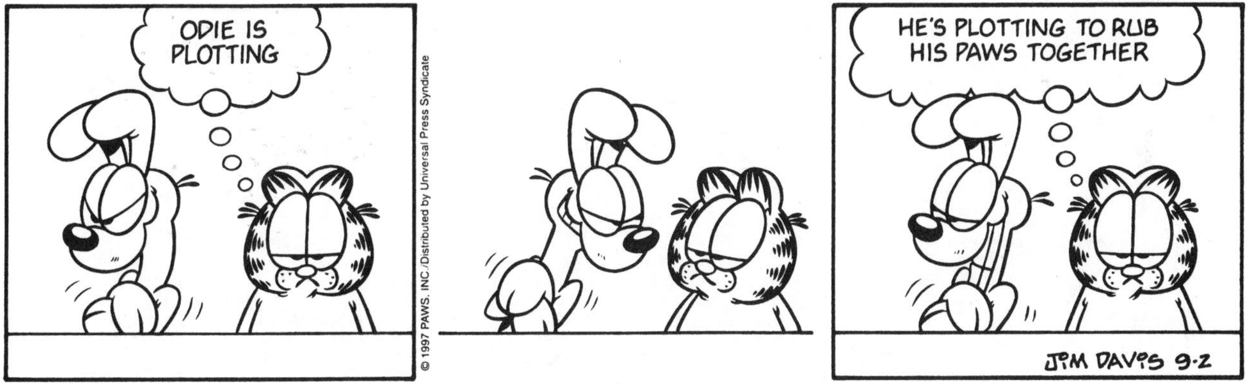
ODIE IS PLOTTING
© 1997 PAWS, INC./Distributed by Universal Press Syndicate
HE'S PLOTTING TO RUB HIS PAWS TOGETHER
JIM DAVIS 9-2

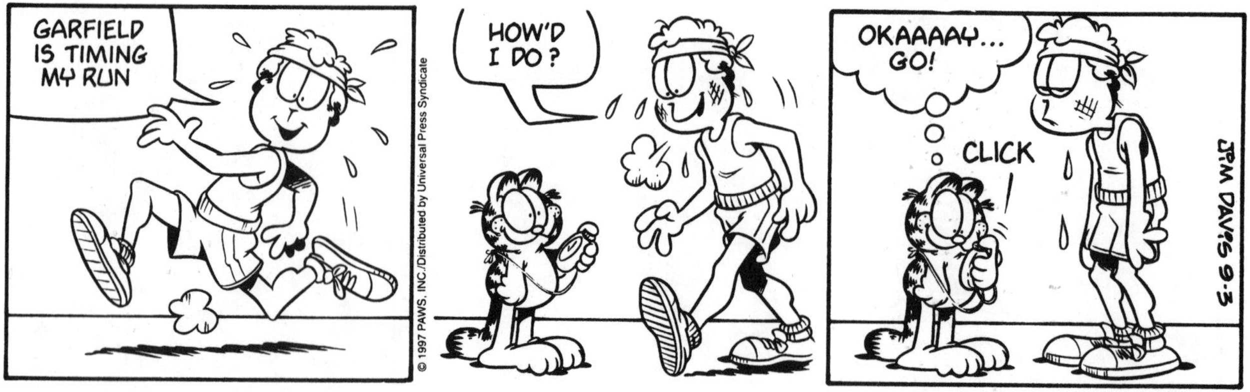
GARFIELD IS TIMING MY RUN
HOW'D I DO?
OKAAAAY... GO!
CLICK
JIM DAVIS 9-3

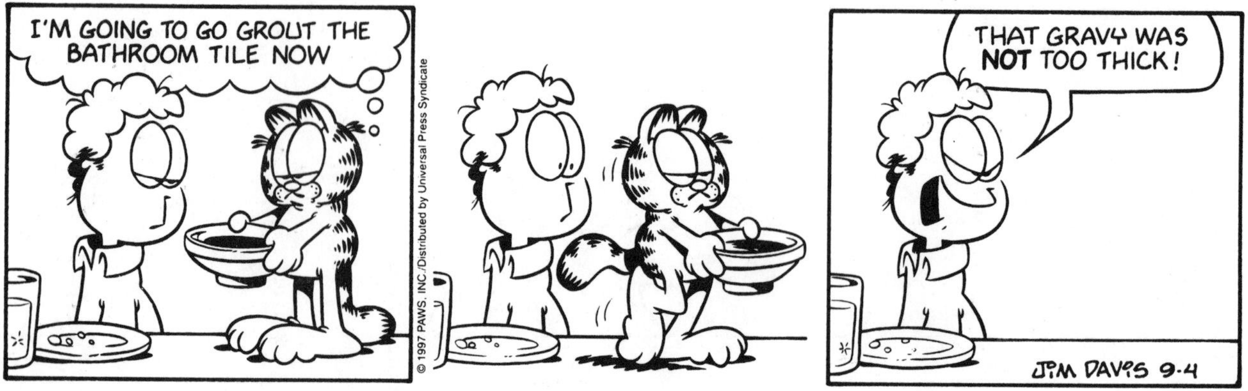
I'M GOING TO GO GROUT THE BATHROOM TILE NOW
THAT GRAVY WAS **NOT** TOO THICK!
JIM DAVIS 9-4

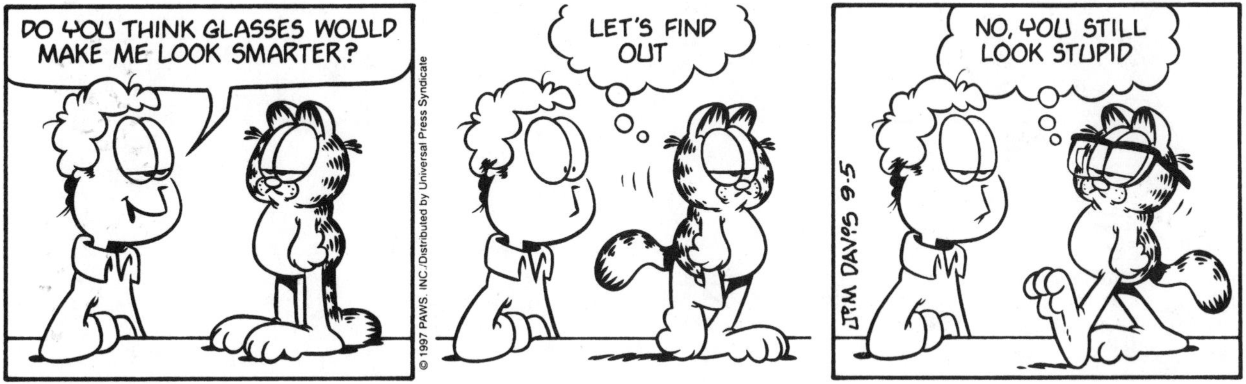
DO YOU THINK GLASSES WOULD MAKE ME LOOK SMARTER?
LET'S FIND OUT
NO, YOU STILL LOOK STUPID
© 1997 PAWS. INC./Distributed by Universal Press Syndicate
JIM DAVIS 9-5

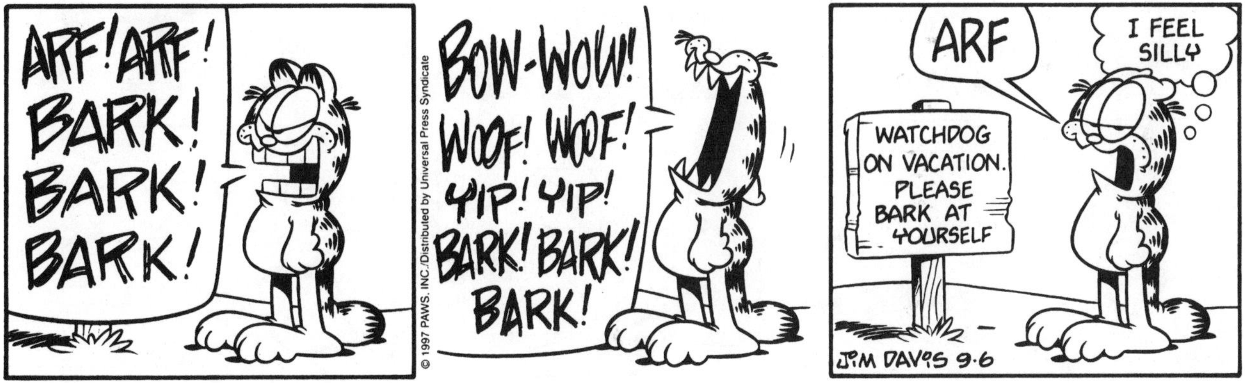
ARF! ARF! BARK! BARK! BARK!
BOW-WOW! WOOF! WOOF! YIP! YIP! BARK! BARK! BARK!
WATCHDOG ON VACATION. PLEASE BARK AT YOURSELF
ARF
I FEEL SILLY
© 1997 PAWS. INC./Distributed by Universal Press Syndicate
JIM DAVIS 9-6

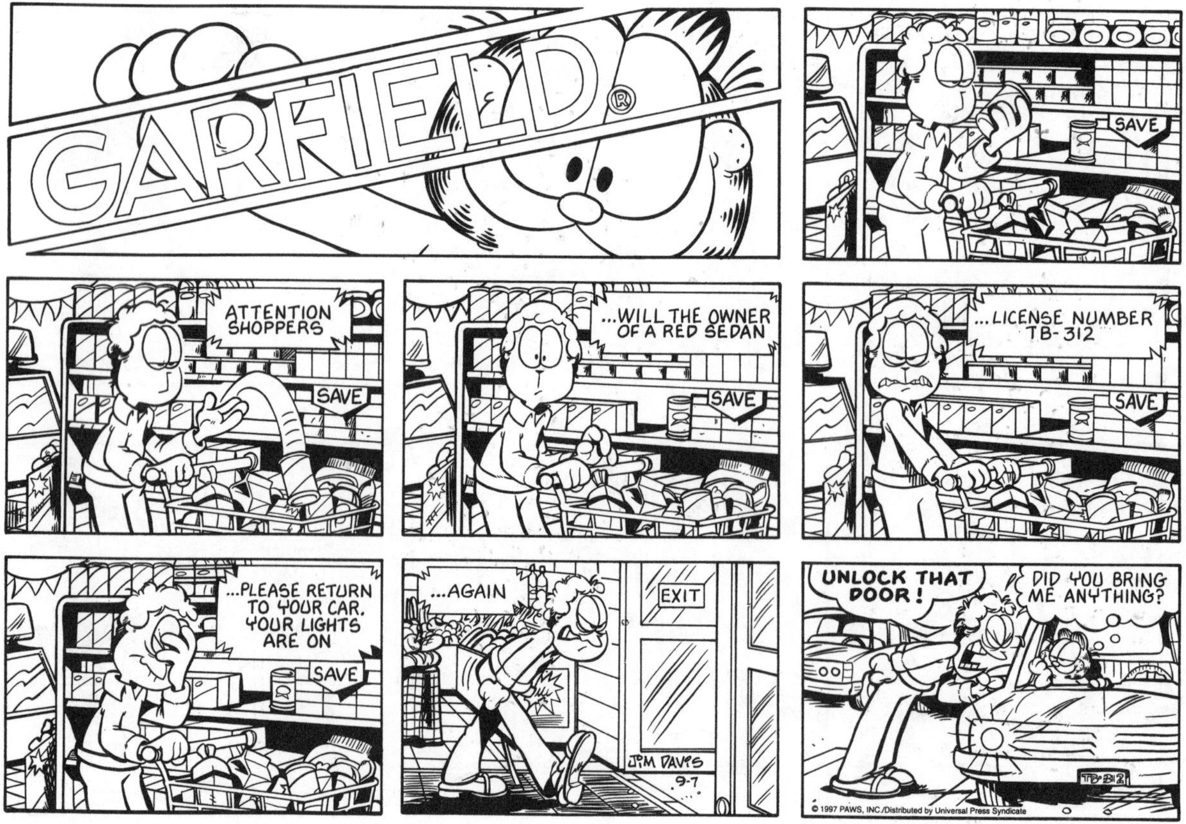
GARFIELD®
SAVE
ATTENTION SHOPPERS
SAVE
...WILL THE OWNER OF A RED SEDAN
SAVE
...LICENSE NUMBER TB-312
SAVE
...PLEASE RETURN TO YOUR CAR. YOUR LIGHTS ARE ON
SAVE
...AGAIN
EXIT
JIM DAVIS 9-7
UNLOCK THAT DOOR!
DID YOU BRING ME ANYTHING?
TB-312
© 1997 PAWS, INC./Distributed by Universal Press Syndicate

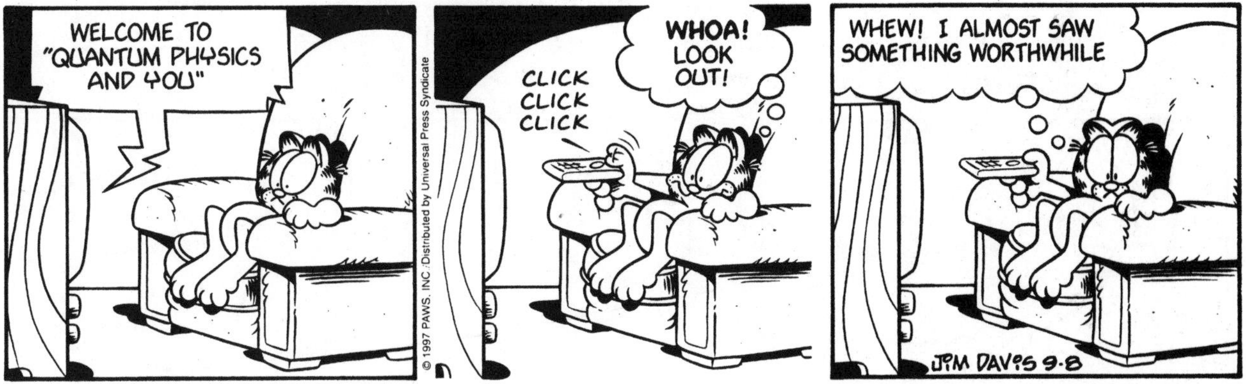
WELCOME TO "QUANTUM PHYSICS AND YOU"
CLICK CLICK CLICK
WHOA! LOOK OUT!
WHEW! I ALMOST SAW SOMETHING WORTHWHILE
JIM DAVIS 9-8
© 1997 PAWS, INC./Distributed by Universal Press Syndicate

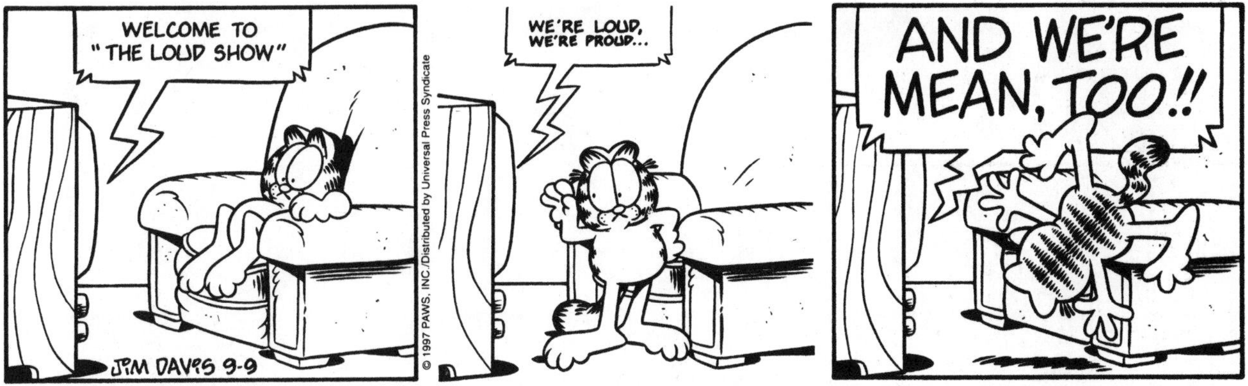
WELCOME TO "THE LOUD SHOW"
JIM DAVIS 9-9
WE'RE LOUD, WE'RE PROUD...
AND WE'RE MEAN, TOO!!
© 1997 PAWS, INC./Distributed by Universal Press Syndicate

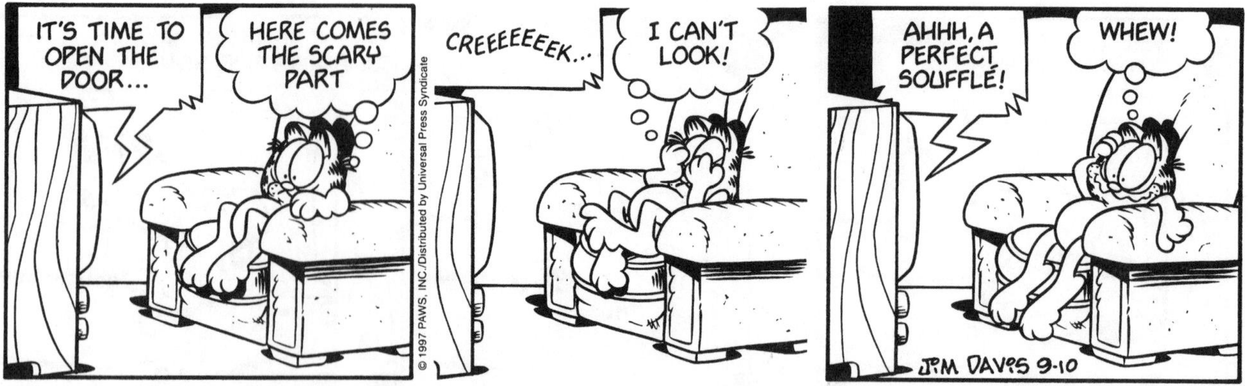
IT'S TIME TO OPEN THE DOOR...
HERE COMES THE SCARY PART
© 1997 PAWS, INC./Distributed by Universal Press Syndicate
CREEEEEEEK...
I CAN'T LOOK!
AHHH, A PERFECT SOUFFLÉ!
WHEW!
JIM DAVIS 9-10

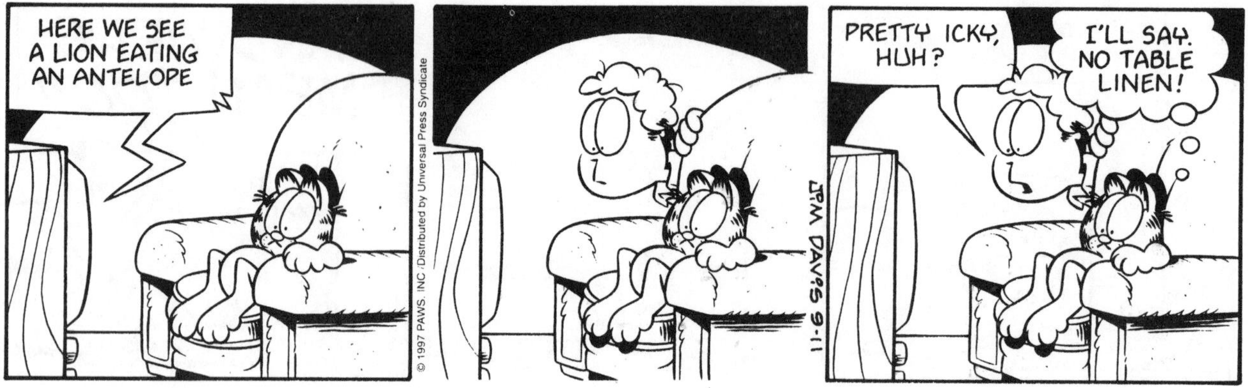
HERE WE SEE A LION EATING AN ANTELOPE
© 1997 PAWS, INC./Distributed by Universal Press Syndicate
JIM DAVIS 9-11
PRETTY ICKY, HUH?
I'LL SAY. NO TABLE LINEN!

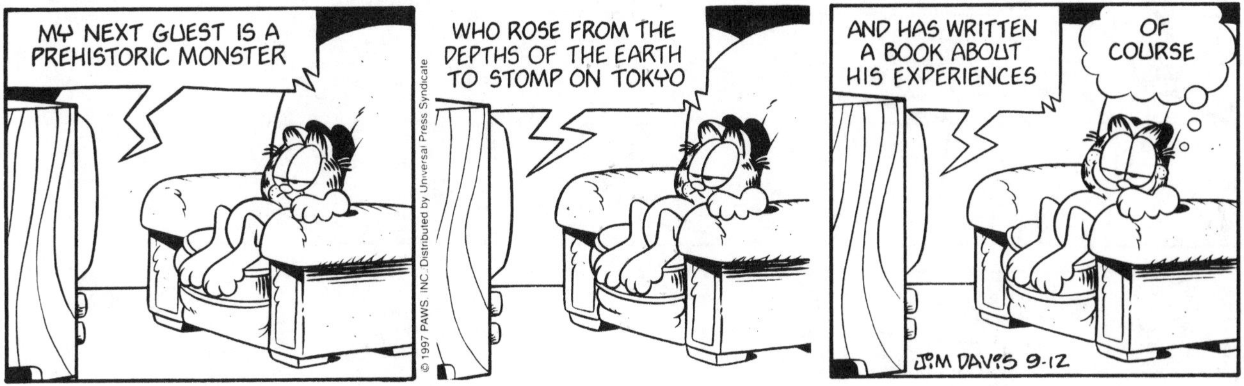
MY NEXT GUEST IS A PREHISTORIC MONSTER
© 1997 PAWS, INC./Distributed by Universal Press Syndicate
WHO ROSE FROM THE DEPTHS OF THE EARTH TO STOMP ON TOKYO
AND HAS WRITTEN A BOOK ABOUT HIS EXPERIENCES
OF COURSE
JIM DAVIS 9-12

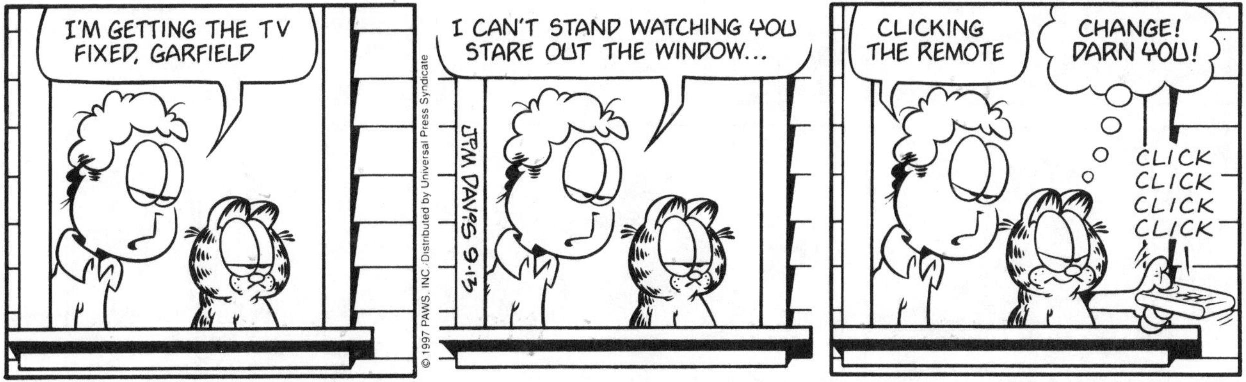
I'M GETTING THE TV FIXED, GARFIELD
© 1997 PAWS, INC./Distributed by Universal Press Syndicate
JIM DAVIS 9-13
I CAN'T STAND WATCHING YOU STARE OUT THE WINDOW...
CLICKING THE REMOTE
CHANGE! DARN YOU!
CLICK
CLICK
CLICK
CLICK

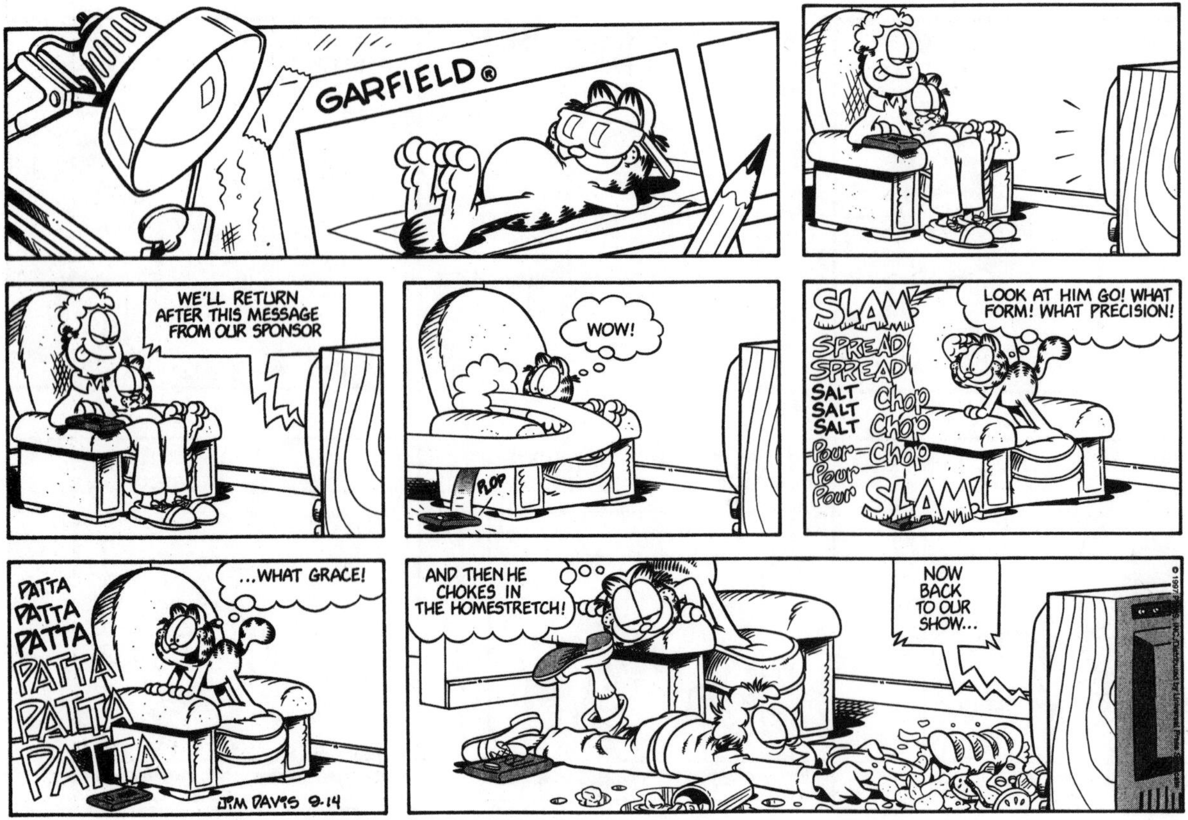
GARFIELD®
WE'LL RETURN AFTER THIS MESSAGE FROM OUR SPONSOR
WOW!
PLOP
SLAM!
LOOK AT HIM GO! WHAT FORM! WHAT PRECISION!
SPREAD SPREAD
SALT SALT SALT
Chop Chop Chop Chop
Pour Pour Pour
SLAM!
PATTA PATTA PATTA PATTA PATTA PATTA PATTA
...WHAT GRACE!
JIM DAVIS 9-14
AND THEN HE CHOKES IN THE HOMESTRETCH!
NOW BACK TO OUR SHOW...
© 1997

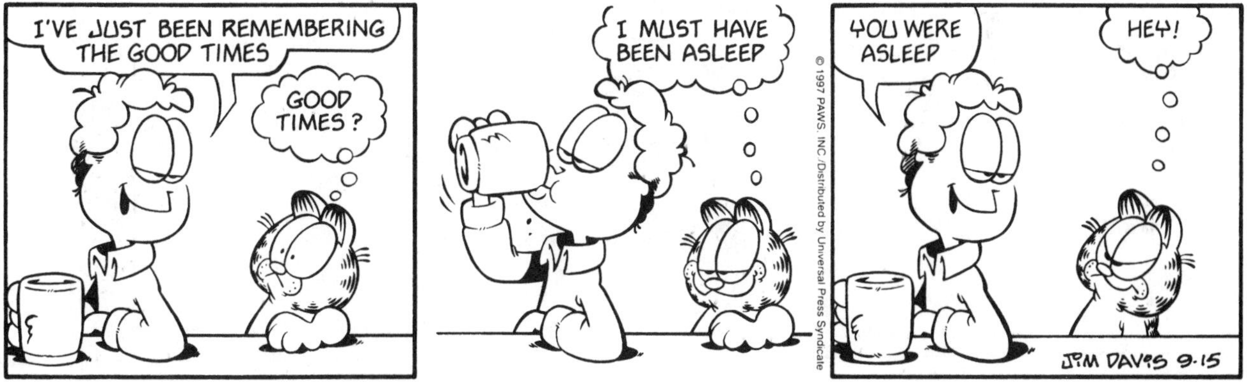
I'VE JUST BEEN REMEMBERING THE GOOD TIMES
GOOD TIMES?
I MUST HAVE BEEN ASLEEP
© 1997 PAWS, INC./Distributed by Universal Press Syndicate
YOU WERE ASLEEP
HEY!
JIM DAVIS 9-15

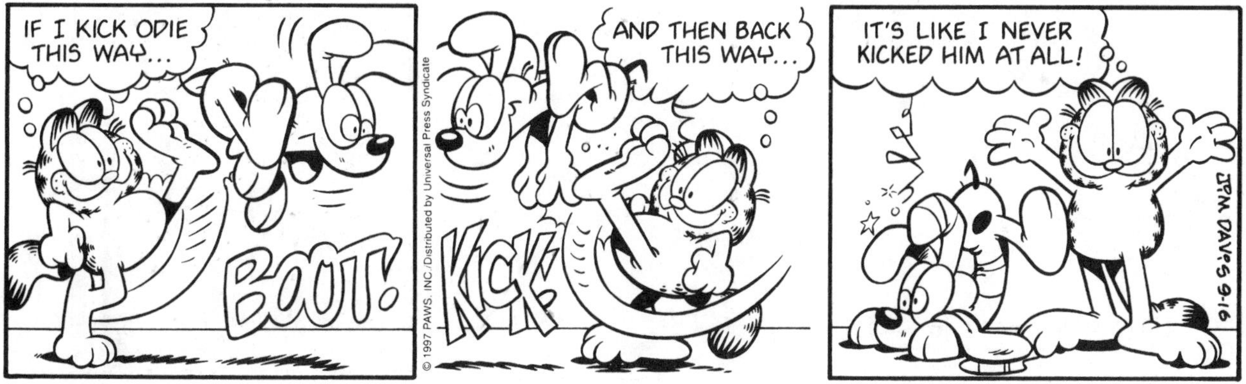
IF I KICK ODIE THIS WAY...
BOOT!
© 1997 PAWS, INC./Distributed by Universal Press Syndicate
KICK!
AND THEN BACK THIS WAY...
IT'S LIKE I NEVER KICKED HIM AT ALL!
JIM DAVIS 9-16

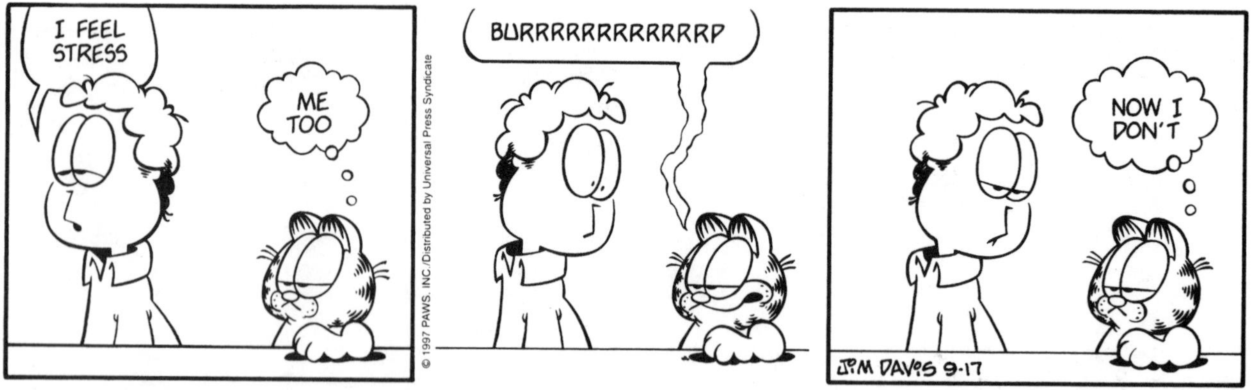
I FEEL STRESS
ME TOO
BURRRRRRRRRRRRP
NOW I DON'T
JIM DAVIS 9-17
© 1997 PAWS. INC./Distributed by Universal Press Syndicate

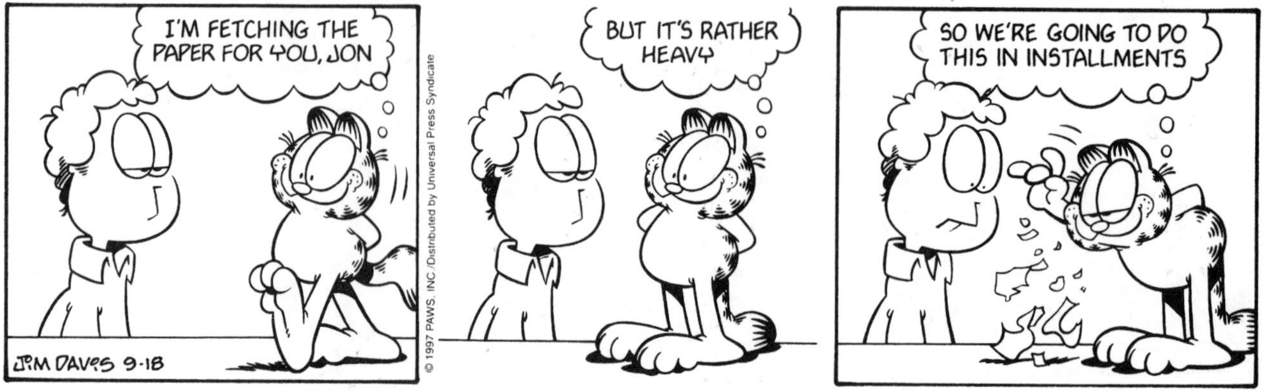
I'M FETCHING THE PAPER FOR YOU, JON
BUT IT'S RATHER HEAVY
SO WE'RE GOING TO DO THIS IN INSTALLMENTS
JIM DAVIS 9-18
© 1997 PAWS. INC./Distributed by Universal Press Syndicate

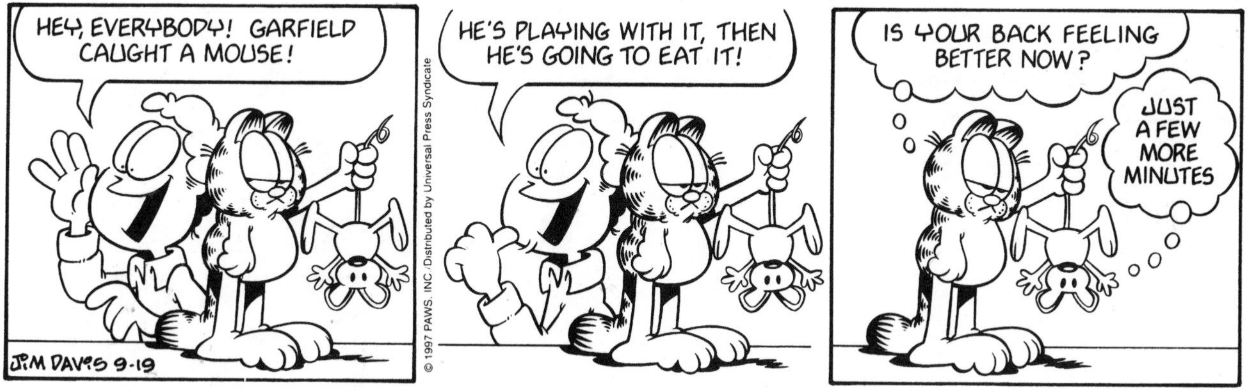
HEY, EVERYBODY! GARFIELD CAUGHT A MOUSE!
JIM DAVIS 9-19
HE'S PLAYING WITH IT, THEN HE'S GOING TO EAT IT!
IS YOUR BACK FEELING BETTER NOW?
JUST A FEW MORE MINUTES

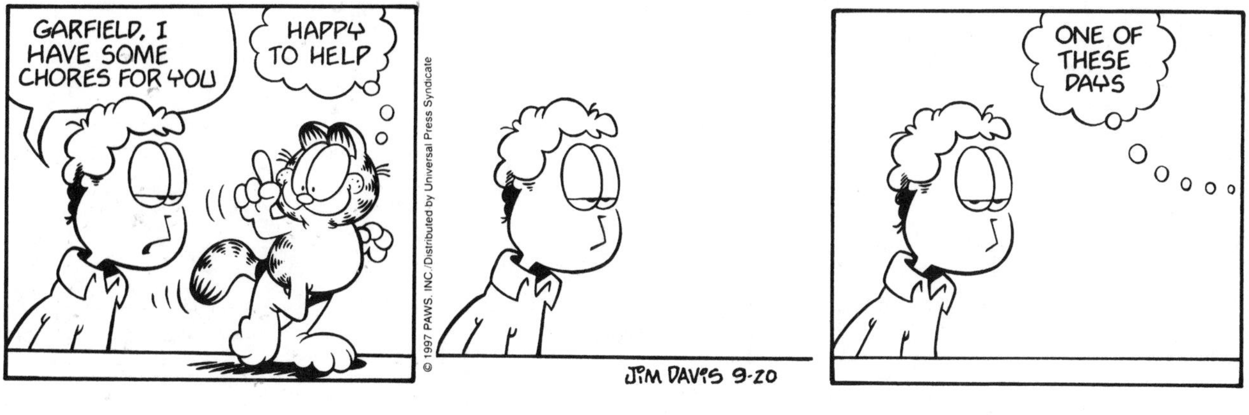
GARFIELD, I HAVE SOME CHORES FOR YOU
HAPPY TO HELP
JIM DAVIS 9-20
ONE OF THESE DAYS

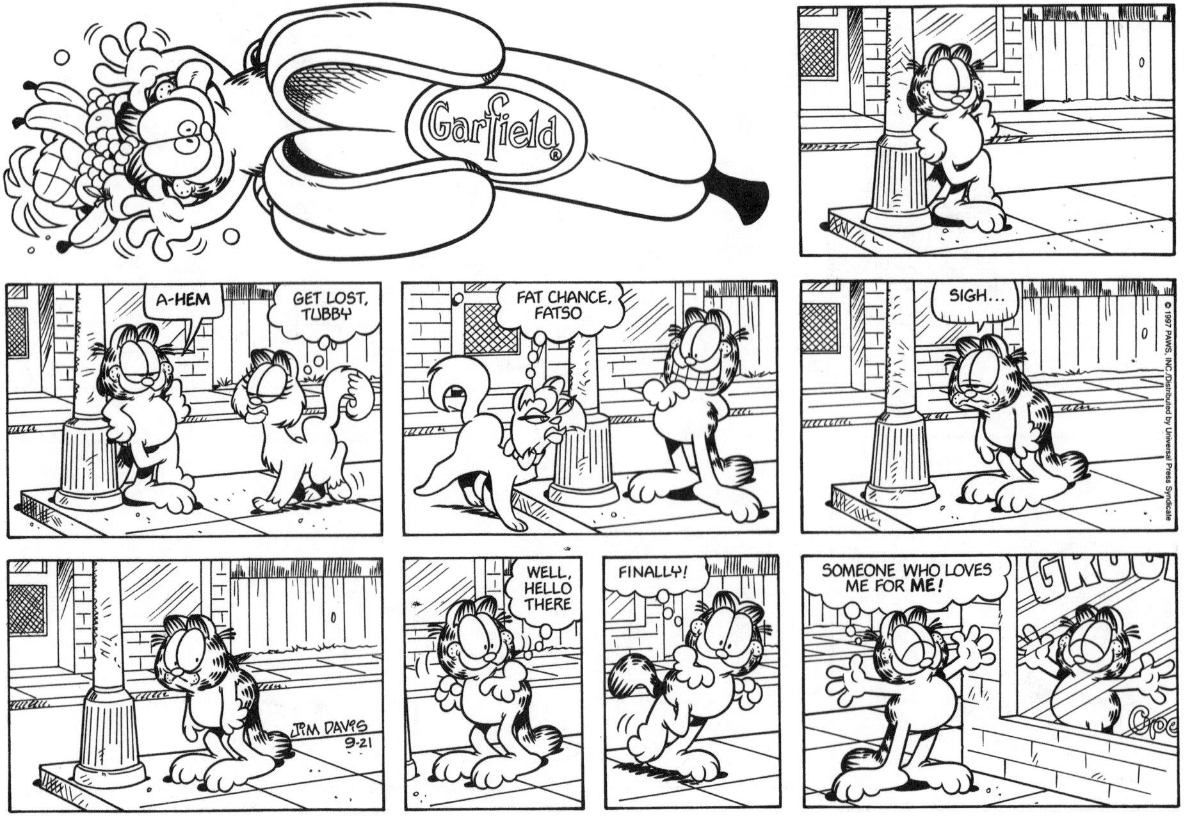

Garfield®
A-HEM
GET LOST, TUBBY
FAT CHANCE, FATSO
SIGH...
© 1997 PAWS, INC./Distributed by Universal Press Syndicate
JIM DAVIS 9-21
WELL, HELLO THERE
FINALLY!
SOMEONE WHO LOVES ME FOR ME!

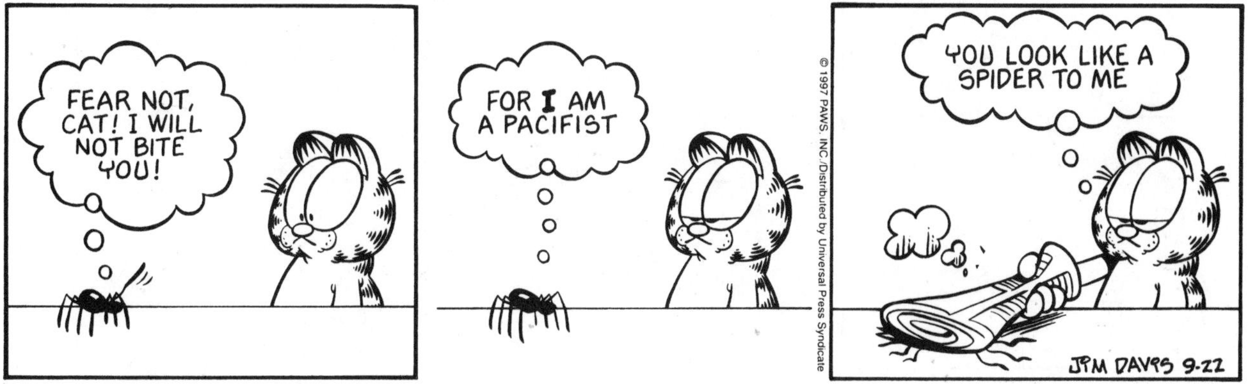
FEAR NOT, CAT! I WILL NOT BITE YOU!
FOR I AM A PACIFIST
© 1997 PAWS. INC./Distributed by Universal Press Syndicate
YOU LOOK LIKE A SPIDER TO ME
JIM DAVIS 9-22

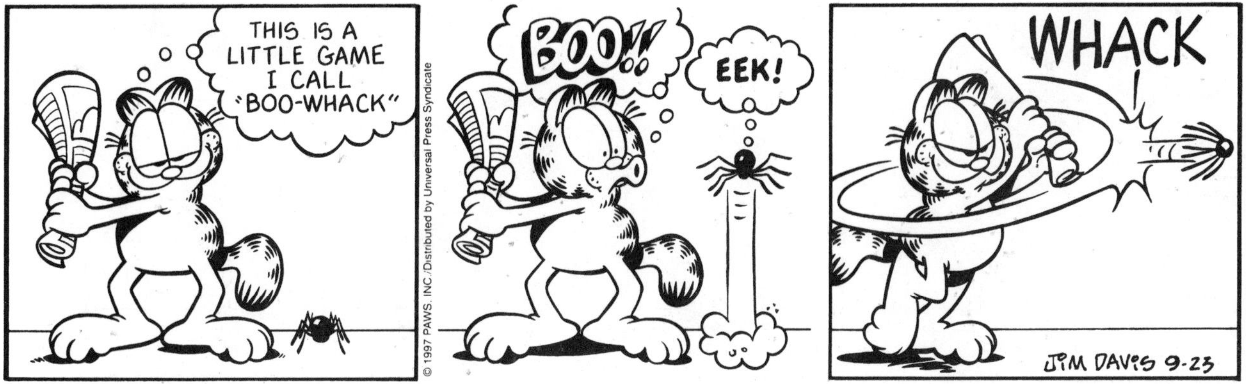
THIS IS A LITTLE GAME I CALL "BOO-WHACK"
© 1997 PAWS. INC./Distributed by Universal Press Syndicate
BOO!!
EEK!
WHACK
JIM DAVIS 9-23

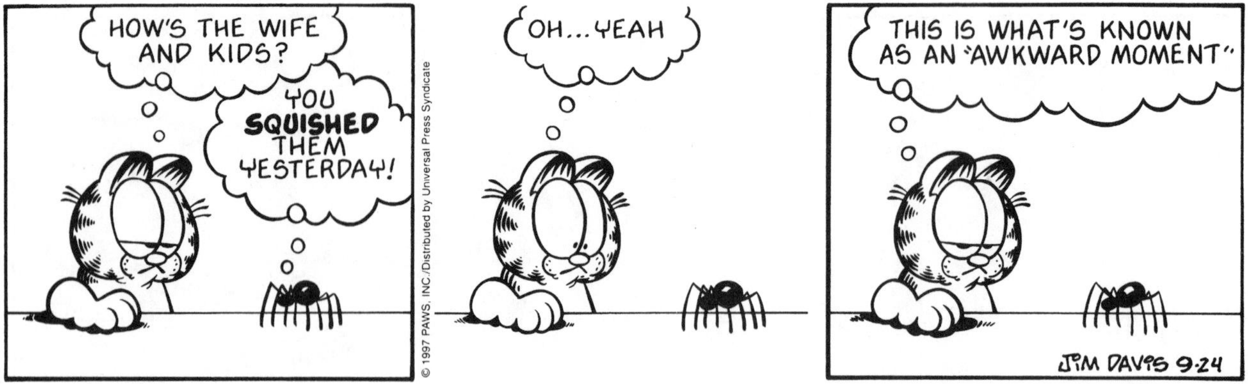
HOW'S THE WIFE AND KIDS?
YOU SQUISHED THEM YESTERDAY!
OH... YEAH
THIS IS WHAT'S KNOWN AS AN "AWKWARD MOMENT"
JIM DAVIS 9-24

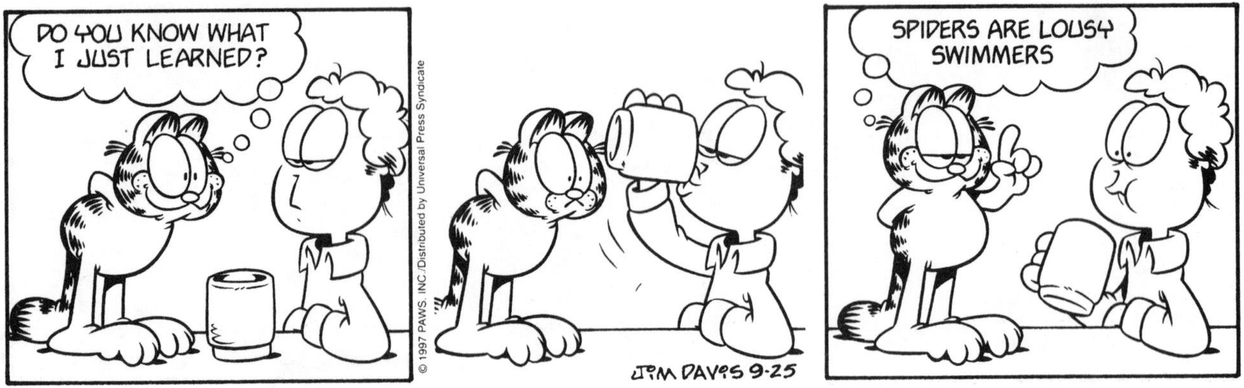
DO YOU KNOW WHAT I JUST LEARNED?
SPIDERS ARE LOUSY SWIMMERS
JIM DAVIS 9-25

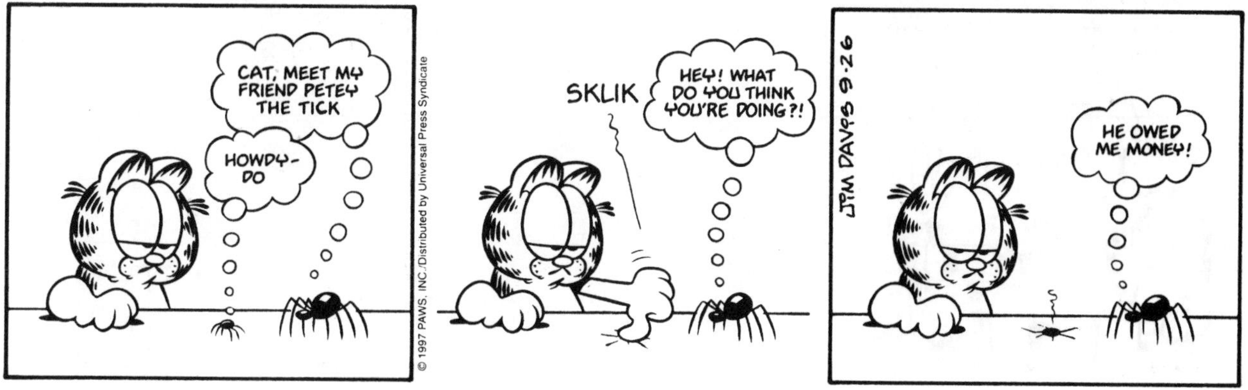
CAT, MEET MY FRIEND PETEY THE TICK
HOWDY-DO
© 1997 PAWS. INC./Distributed by Universal Press Syndicate
SKLIK
HEY! WHAT DO YOU THINK YOU'RE DOING?!
JIM DAVIS 9-26
HE OWED ME MONEY!

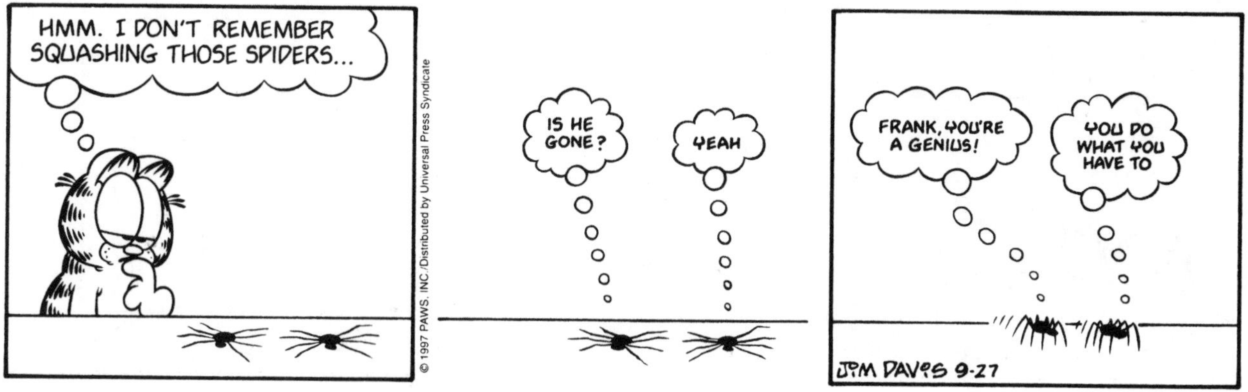
HMM. I DON'T REMEMBER SQUASHING THOSE SPIDERS...
© 1997 PAWS. INC./Distributed by Universal Press Syndicate
IS HE GONE?
YEAH
FRANK, YOU'RE A GENIUS!
YOU DO WHAT YOU HAVE TO
JIM DAVIS 9-27

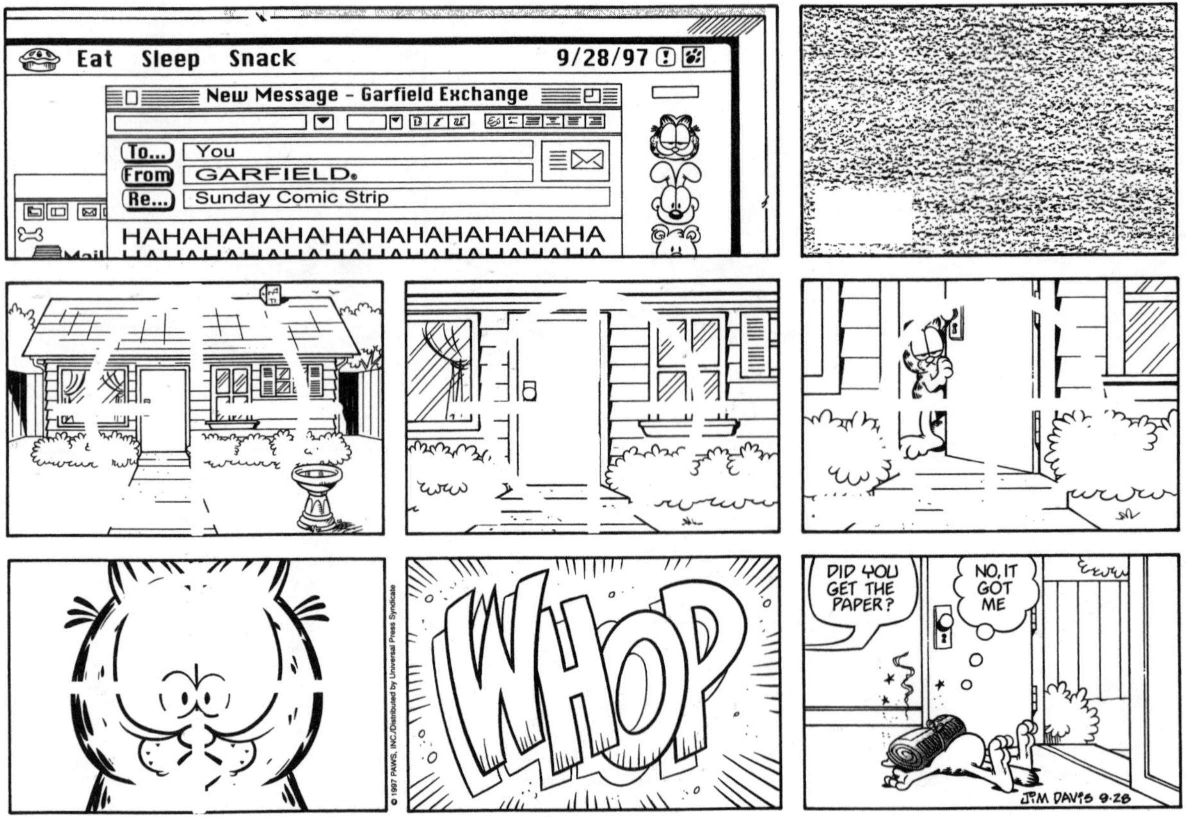
Eat Sleep Snack
9/28/97
New Message - Garfield Exchange
To... You
From GARFIELD®
Re... Sunday Comic Strip
HAHAHAHAHAHAHAHAHAHAHAHAHA
WHOP
DID YOU GET THE PAPER?
NO, IT GOT ME
JIM DAVIS 9-28

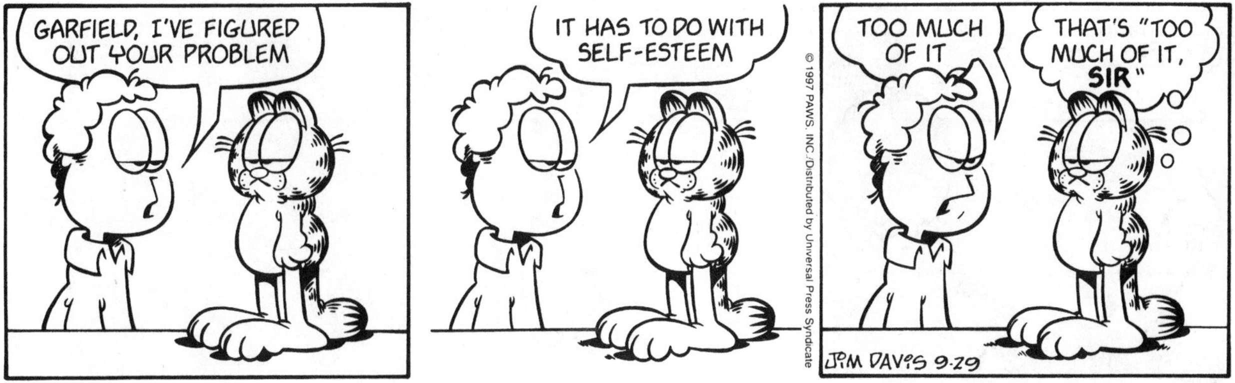
GARFIELD, I'VE FIGURED OUT YOUR PROBLEM
IT HAS TO DO WITH SELF-ESTEEM
TOO MUCH OF IT
THAT'S "TOO MUCH OF IT, SIR"
© 1997 PAWS, INC./Distributed by Universal Press Syndicate
JIM DAVIS 9-29

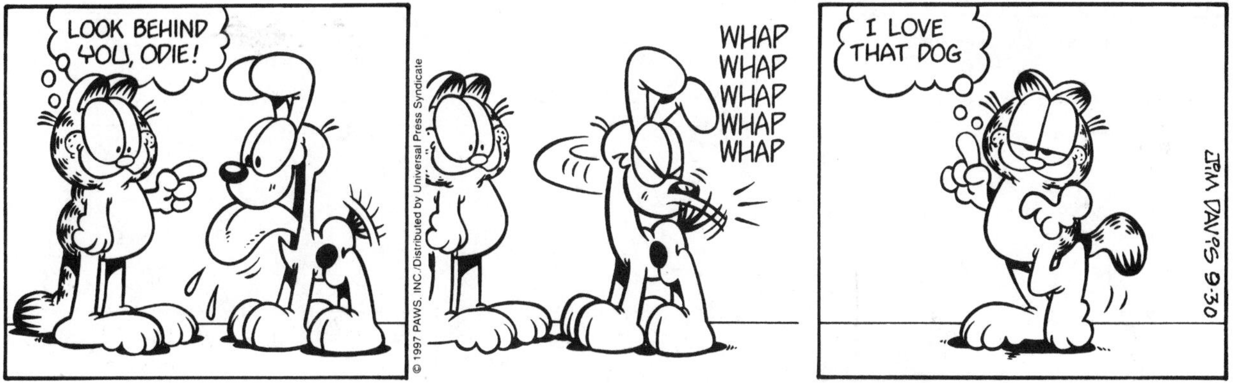
LOOK BEHIND YOU, ODIE!
© 1997 PAWS, INC./Distributed by Universal Press Syndicate
WHAP WHAP WHAP WHAP WHAP
I LOVE THAT DOG
JIM DAVIS 9-30

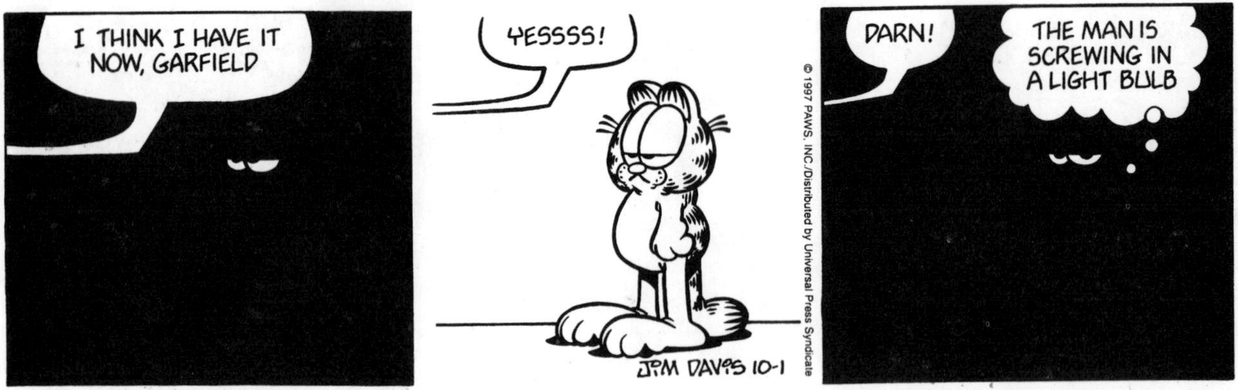
I THINK I HAVE IT NOW, GARFIELD
YESSSS!
JIM DAVIS 10-1
© 1997 PAWS, INC./Distributed by Universal Press Syndicate
DARN!
THE MAN IS SCREWING IN A LIGHT BULB

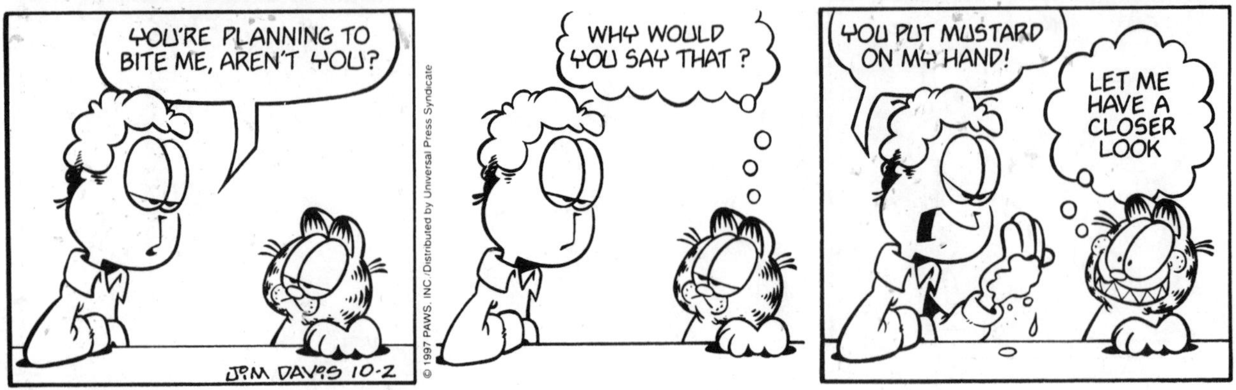
YOU'RE PLANNING TO BITE ME, AREN'T YOU?
JIM DAVIS 10-2
© 1997 PAWS, INC./Distributed by Universal Press Syndicate
WHY WOULD YOU SAY THAT ?
YOU PUT MUSTARD ON MY HAND!
LET ME HAVE A CLOSER LOOK

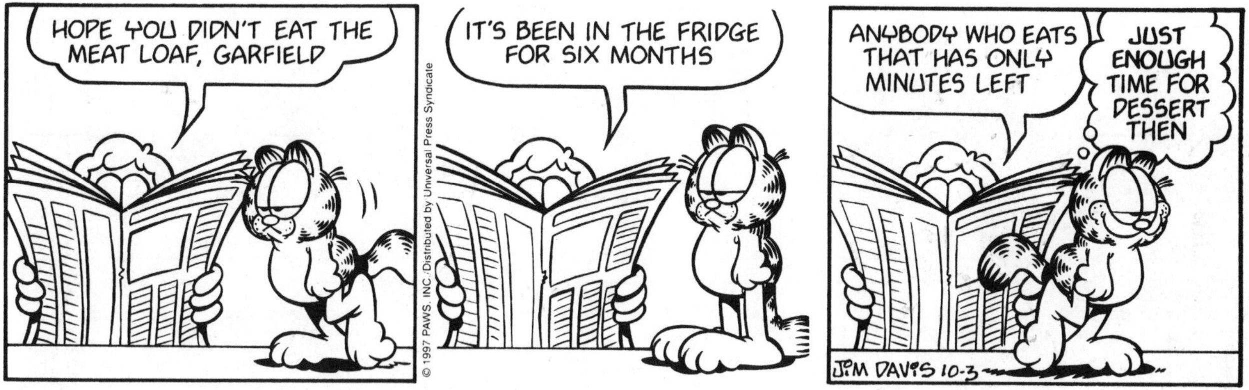
HOPE YOU DIDN'T EAT THE MEAT LOAF, GARFIELD
IT'S BEEN IN THE FRIDGE FOR SIX MONTHS
ANYBODY WHO EATS THAT HAS ONLY MINUTES LEFT
JUST ENOUGH TIME FOR DESSERT THEN
JIM DAVIS 10-3

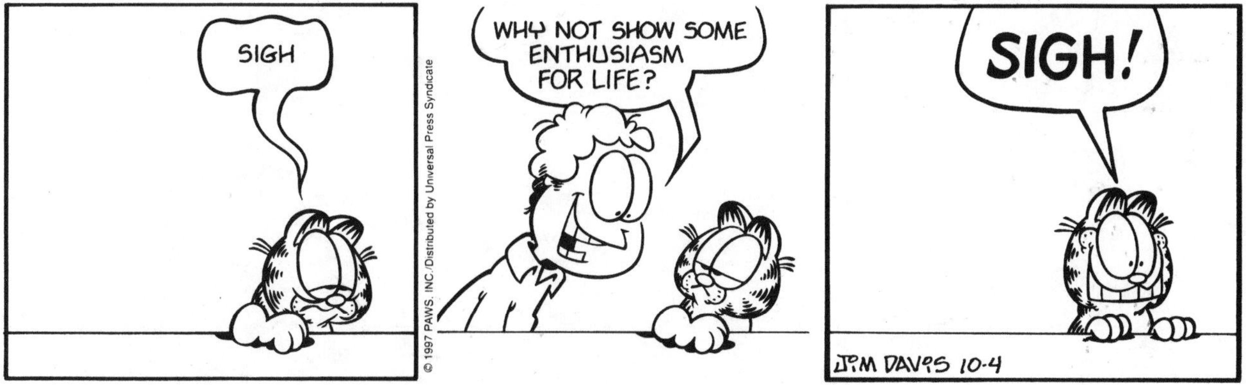
SIGH
WHY NOT SHOW SOME ENTHUSIASM FOR LIFE?
SIGH!
JIM DAVIS 10-4

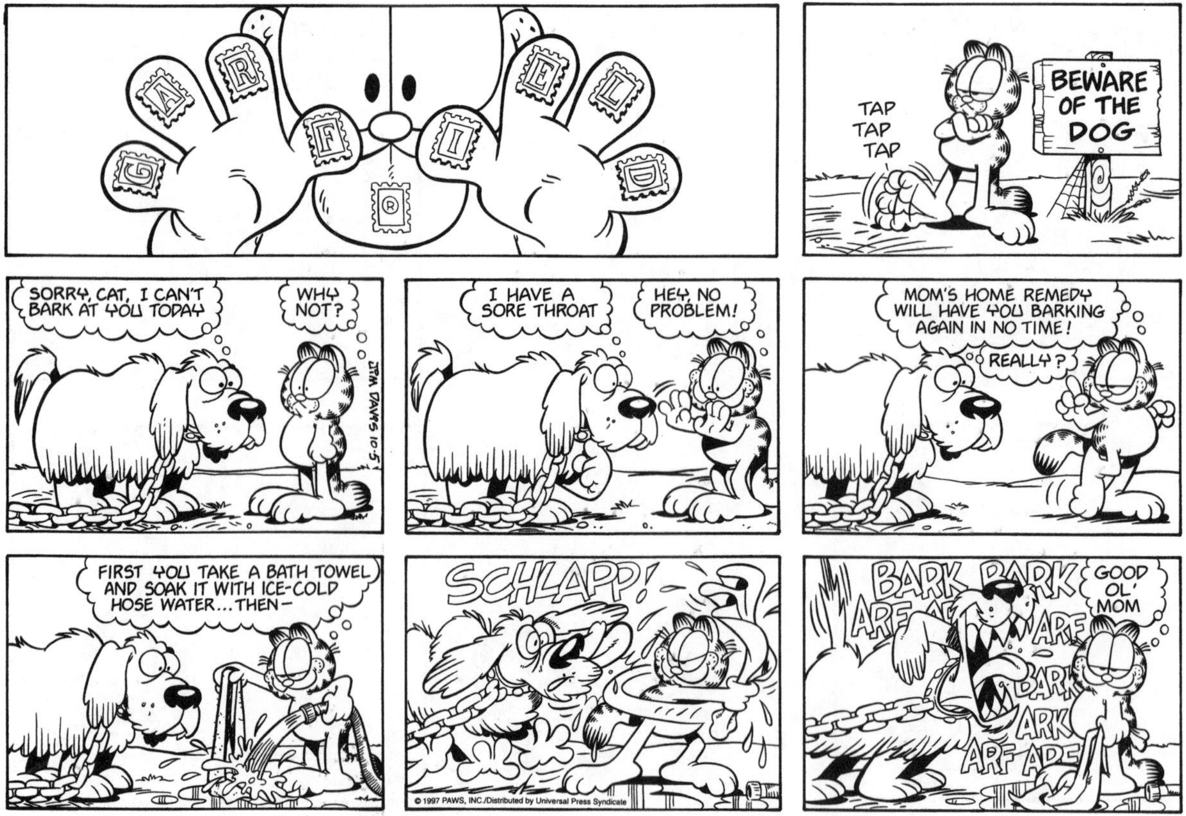
GARFIELD ®
TAP
TAP
TAP
BEWARE OF THE DOG
SORRY, CAT, I CAN'T BARK AT YOU TODAY
WHY NOT?
JPM DAVIS 10-5
I HAVE A SORE THROAT
HEY, NO PROBLEM!
MOM'S HOME REMEDY WILL HAVE YOU BARKING AGAIN IN NO TIME!
REALLY?
FIRST YOU TAKE A BATH TOWEL AND SOAK IT WITH ICE-COLD HOSE WATER... THEN–
SCHLAPP!
© 1997 PAWS, INC./Distributed by Universal Press Syndicate
BARK BARK
ARF
ARF
BARK
ARK
ARF ARF
GOOD OL' MOM

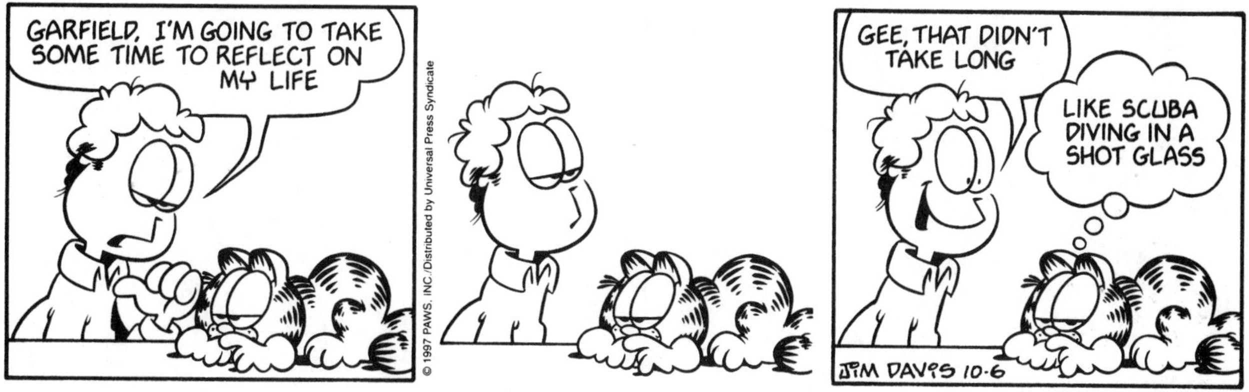
GARFIELD, I'M GOING TO TAKE SOME TIME TO REFLECT ON MY LIFE
GEE, THAT DIDN'T TAKE LONG
LIKE SCUBA DIVING IN A SHOT GLASS
© 1997 PAWS, INC./Distributed by Universal Press Syndicate
JIM DAVIS 10-6

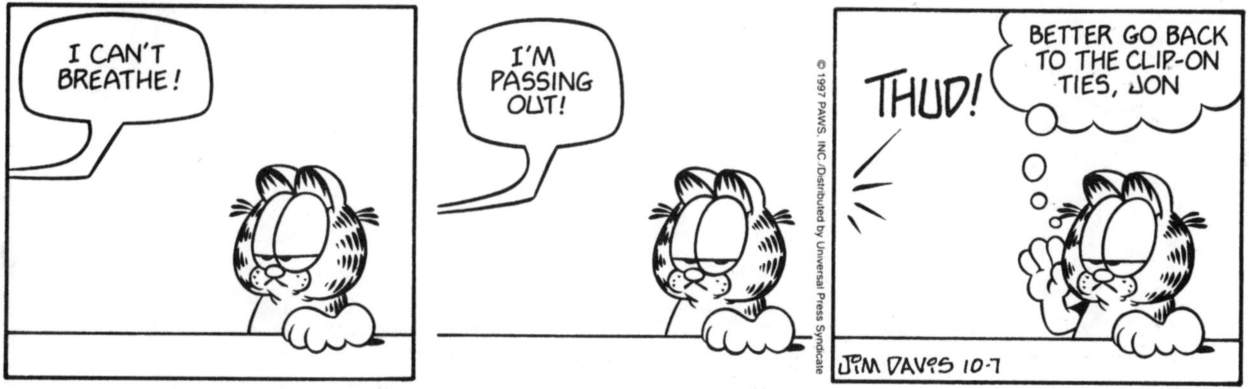
I CAN'T BREATHE!
I'M PASSING OUT!
THUD!
BETTER GO BACK TO THE CLIP-ON TIES, JON
© 1997 PAWS, INC./Distributed by Universal Press Syndicate
JIM DAVIS 10-7

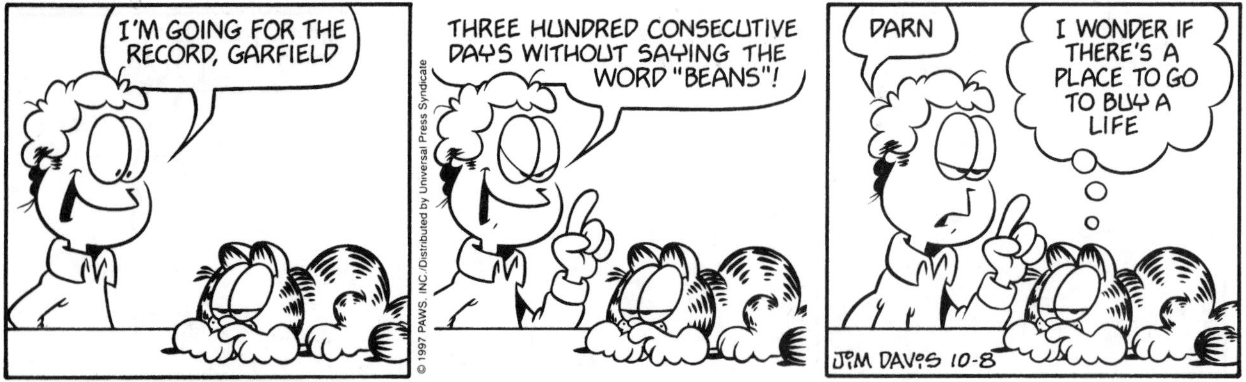
I'M GOING FOR THE RECORD, GARFIELD
THREE HUNDRED CONSECUTIVE DAYS WITHOUT SAYING THE WORD "BEANS"!
DARN
I WONDER IF THERE'S A PLACE TO GO TO BUY A LIFE
JIM DAVIS 10-8
© 1997 PAWS, INC./Distributed by Universal Press Syndicate

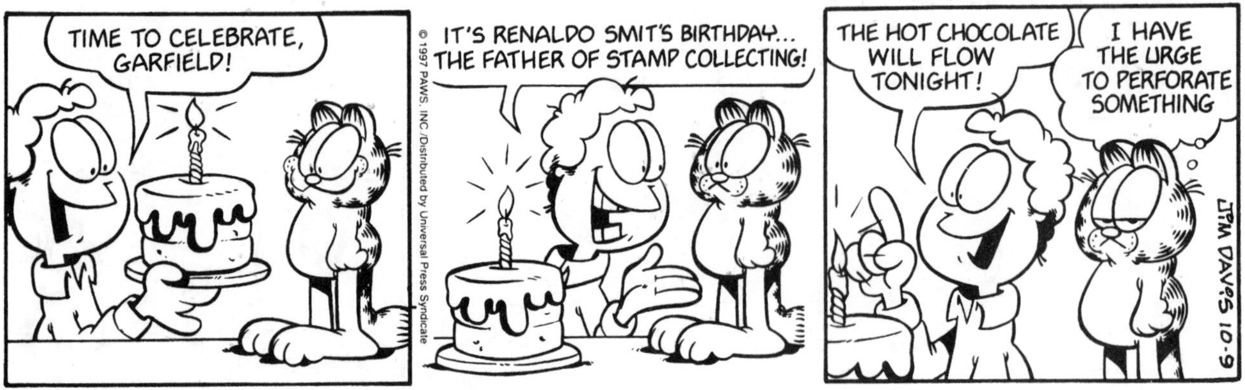
TIME TO CELEBRATE, GARFIELD!
IT'S RENALDO SMIT'S BIRTHDAY... THE FATHER OF STAMP COLLECTING!
THE HOT CHOCOLATE WILL FLOW TONIGHT!
I HAVE THE URGE TO PERFORATE SOMETHING
JIM DAVIS 10-9
© 1997 PAWS, INC./Distributed by Universal Press Syndicate

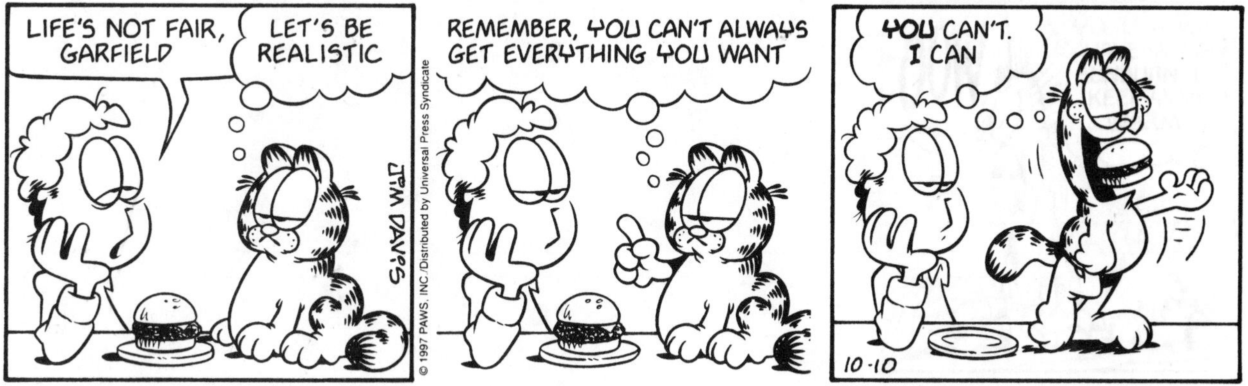
LIFE'S NOT FAIR, GARFIELD
LET'S BE REALISTIC
JIM DAVIS
© 1997 PAWS, INC./Distributed by Universal Press Syndicate
REMEMBER, YOU CAN'T ALWAYS GET EVERYTHING YOU WANT
YOU CAN'T. I CAN
10-10

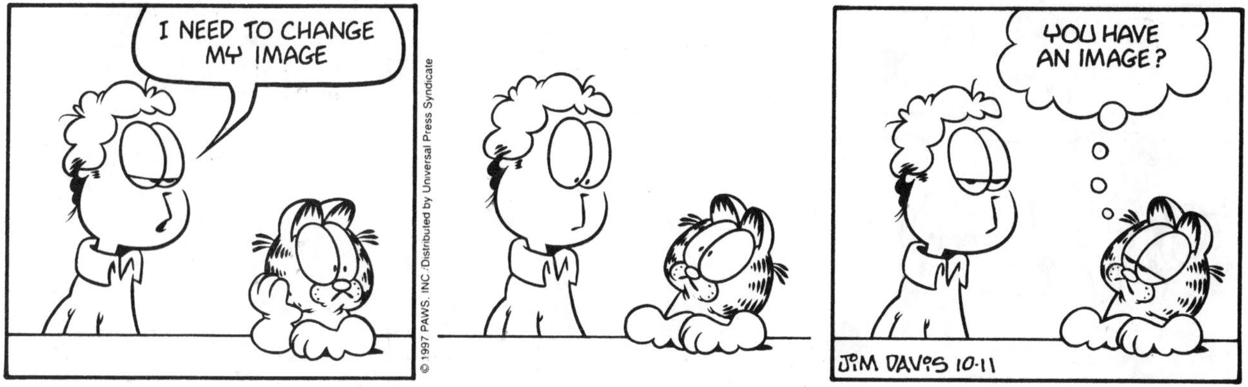
I NEED TO CHANGE MY IMAGE
© 1997 PAWS, INC./Distributed by Universal Press Syndicate
YOU HAVE AN IMAGE?
JIM DAVIS 10-11

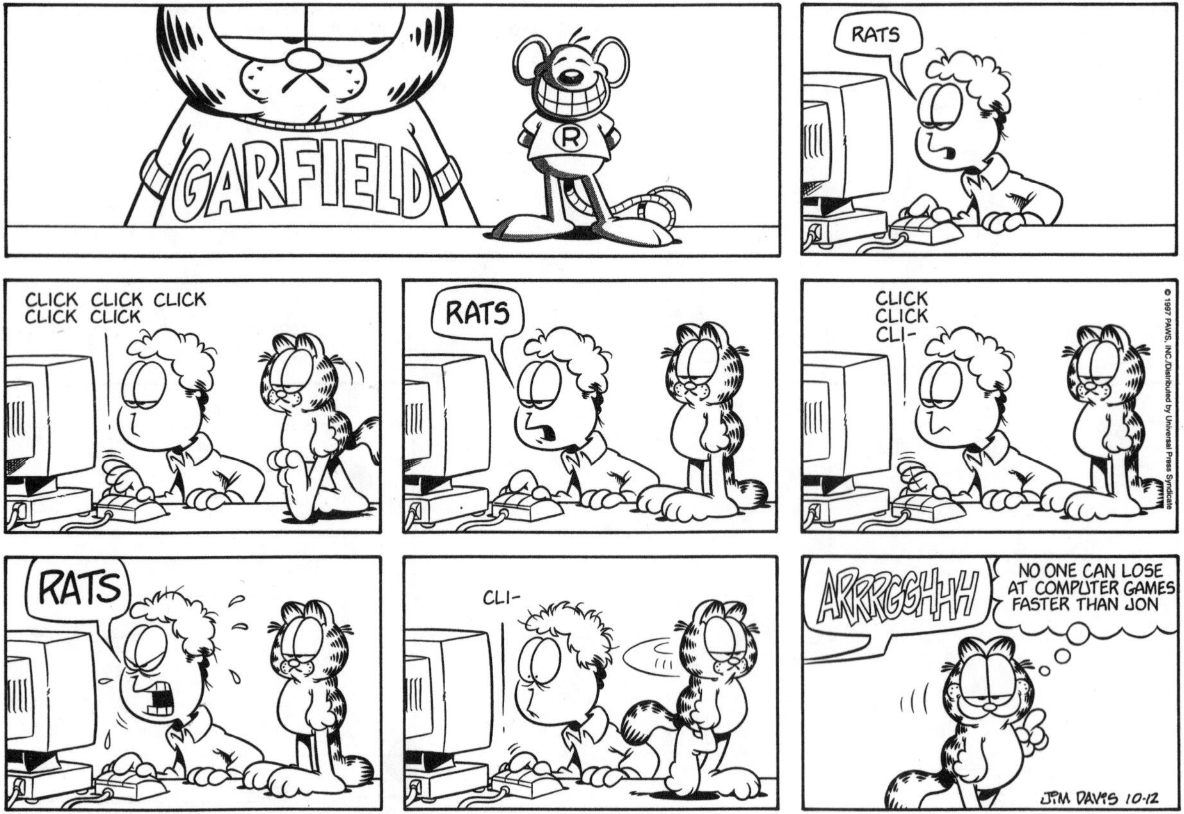
GARFIELD
R
RATS
CLICK CLICK CLICK CLICK CLICK
RATS
CLICK CLICK CLI-
© 1997 PAWS, INC./Distributed by Universal Press Syndicate
RATS
CLI-
ARRRGGHHH
NO ONE CAN LOSE AT COMPUTER GAMES FASTER THAN JON
JIM DAVIS 10-12

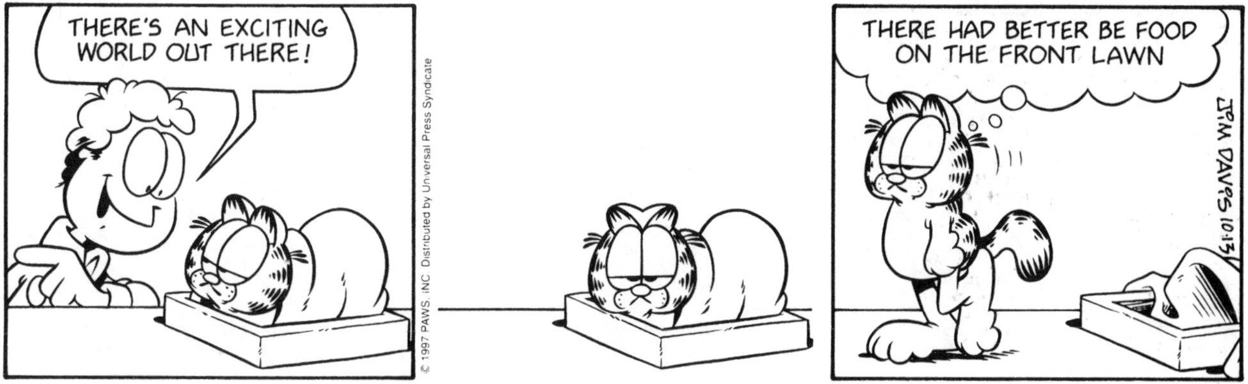
THERE'S AN EXCITING WORLD OUT THERE!
THERE HAD BETTER BE FOOD ON THE FRONT LAWN
JIM DAVIS 10-13

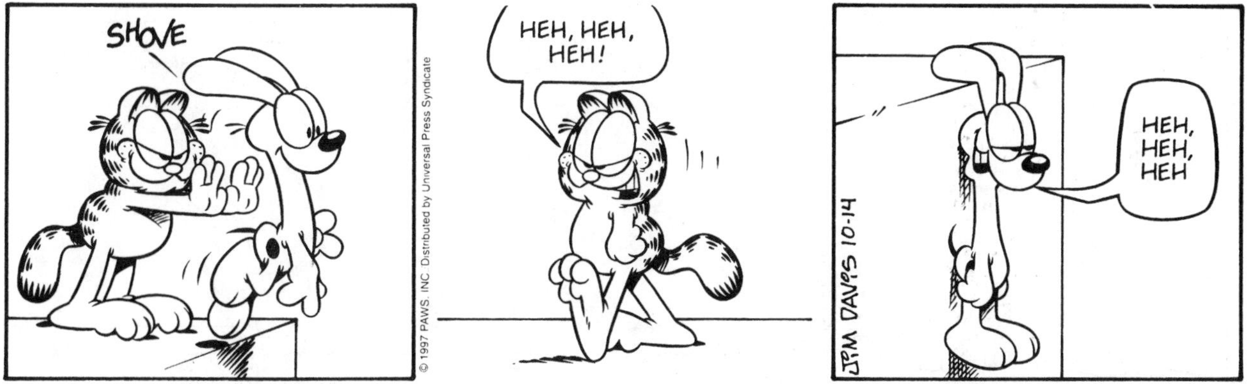
SHOVE
HEH, HEH, HEH!
HEH, HEH, HEH
JIM DAVIS 10-14

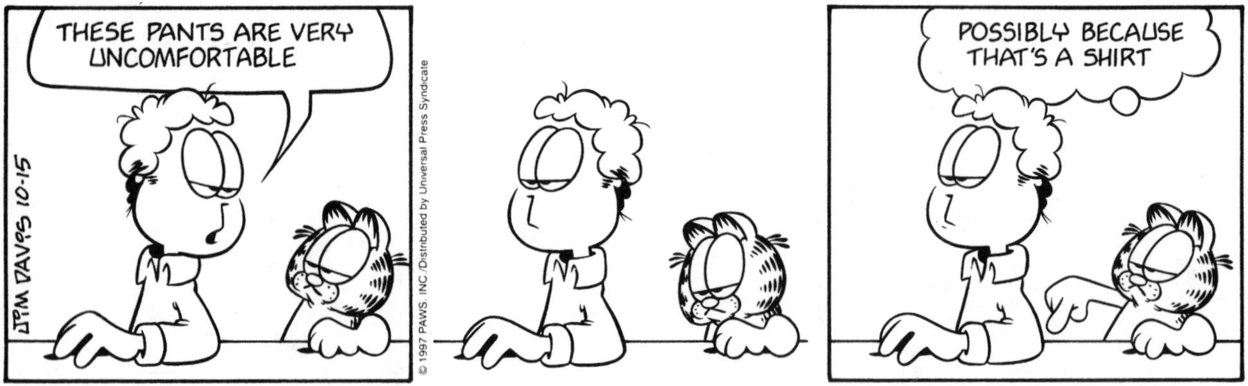
JIM DAVIS 10-15
THESE PANTS ARE VERY UNCOMFORTABLE
POSSIBLY BECAUSE THAT'S A SHIRT
© 1997 PAWS, INC./Distributed by Universal Press Syndicate

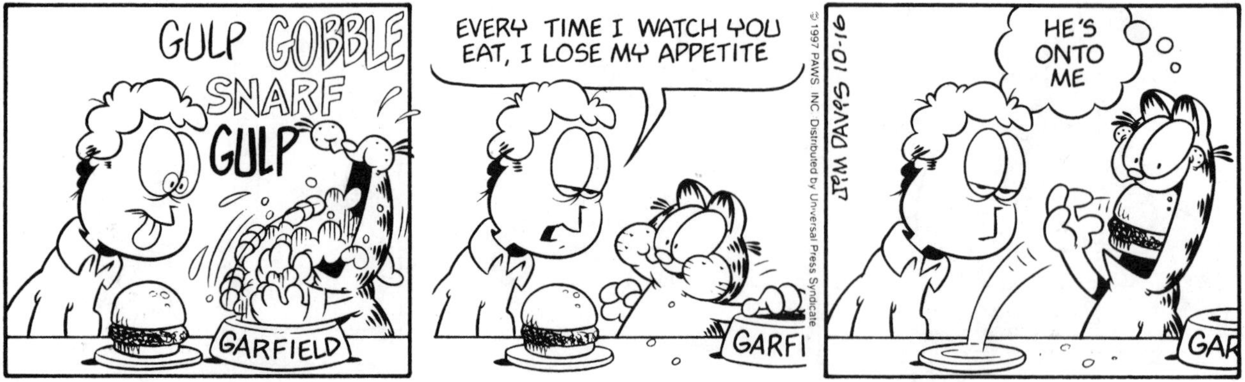
GULP GOBBLE
SNARF
GULP
GARFIELD
EVERY TIME I WATCH YOU EAT, I LOSE MY APPETITE
GARFI
© 1997 PAWS, INC./Distributed by Universal Press Syndicate
JIM DAVIS 10-16
HE'S ONTO ME
GAR

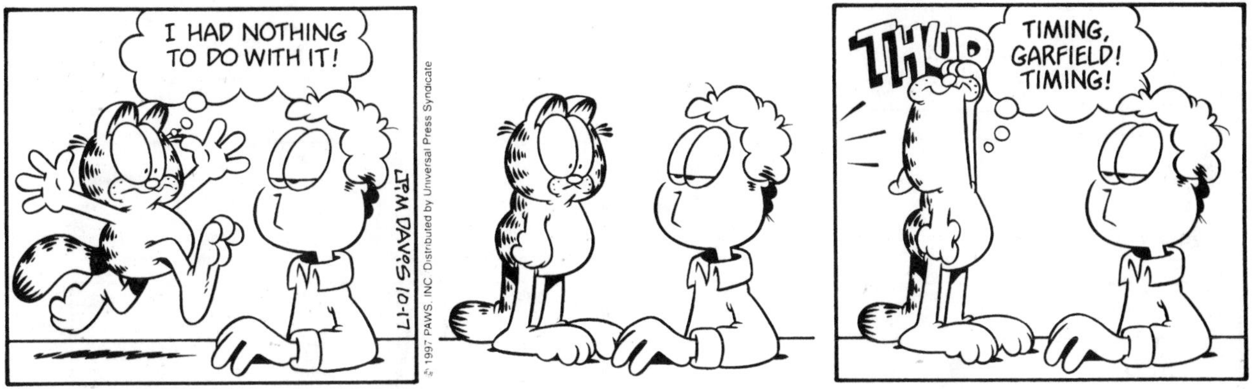
I HAD NOTHING TO DO WITH IT!
JIM DAVIS 10-17
THUD
TIMING, GARFIELD! TIMING!

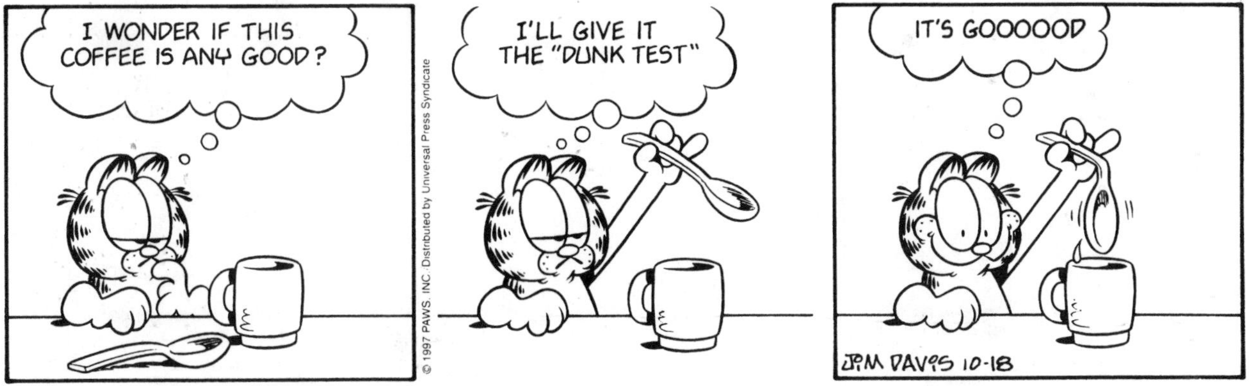
I WONDER IF THIS COFFEE IS ANY GOOD?
I'LL GIVE IT THE "DUNK TEST"
IT'S GOOOOOD
JIM DAVIS 10-18

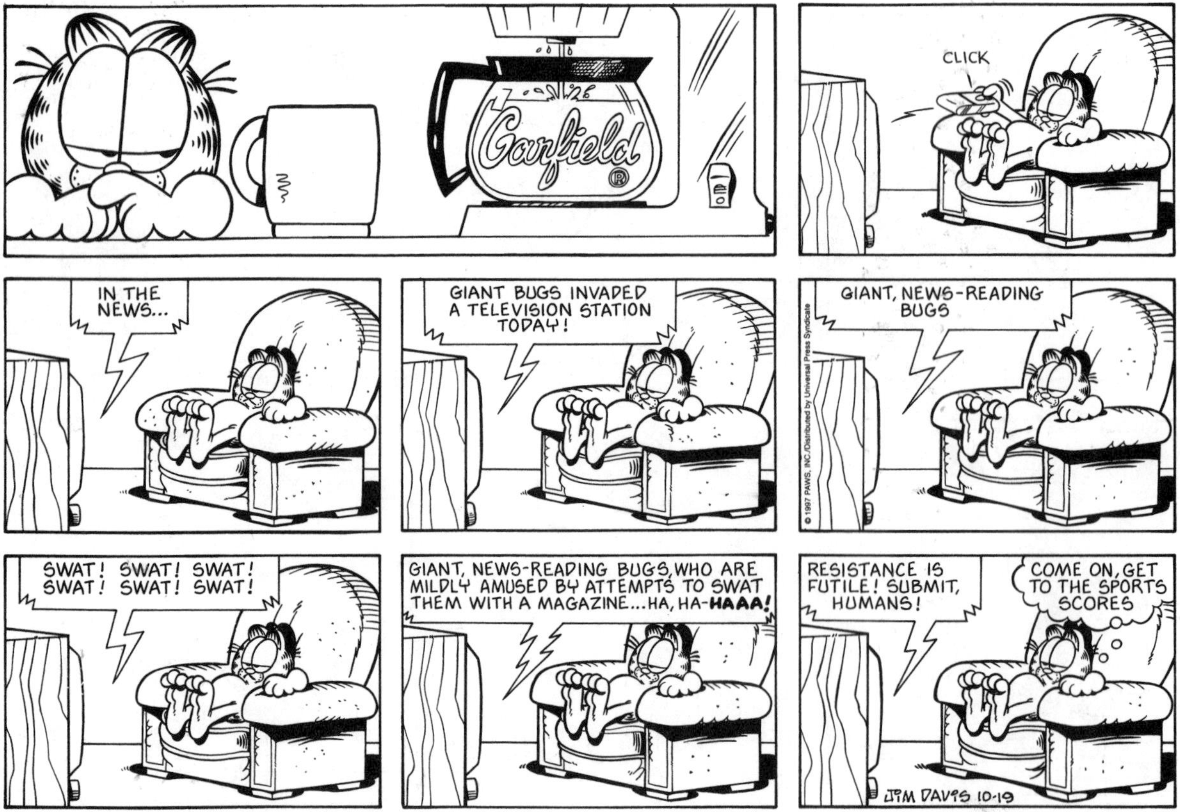

Garfield
CLICK
IN THE NEWS...
GIANT BUGS INVADED A TELEVISION STATION TODAY!
GIANT, NEWS-READING BUGS
© 1997 PAWS, INC./Distributed by Universal Press Syndicate
SWAT! SWAT! SWAT! SWAT! SWAT! SWAT!
GIANT, NEWS-READING BUGS, WHO ARE MILDLY AMUSED BY ATTEMPTS TO SWAT THEM WITH A MAGAZINE...HA, HA-HAAA!
RESISTANCE IS FUTILE! SUBMIT, HUMANS!
COME ON, GET TO THE SPORTS SCORES
JIM DAVIS 10-19

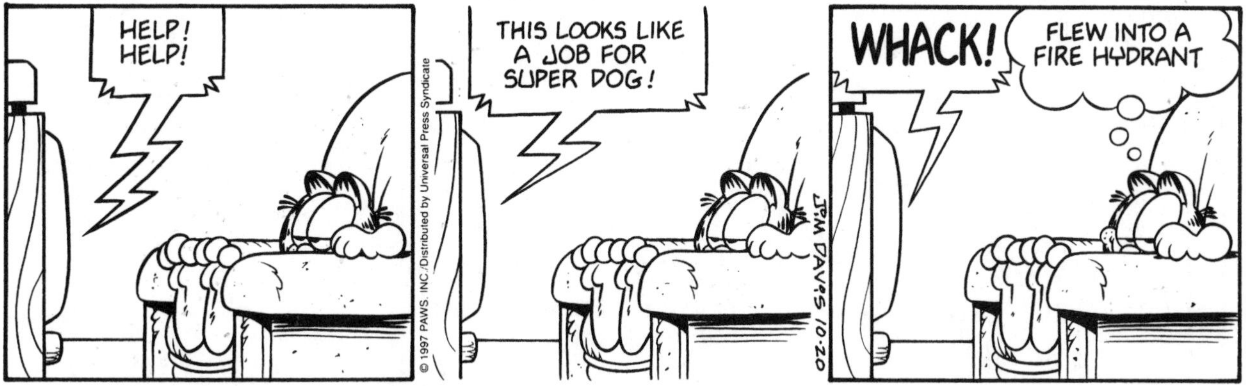
HELP! HELP!
THIS LOOKS LIKE A JOB FOR SUPER DOG!
WHACK!
FLEW INTO A FIRE HYDRANT
© 1997 PAWS. INC./Distributed by Universal Press Syndicate
JIM DAVIS 10-20

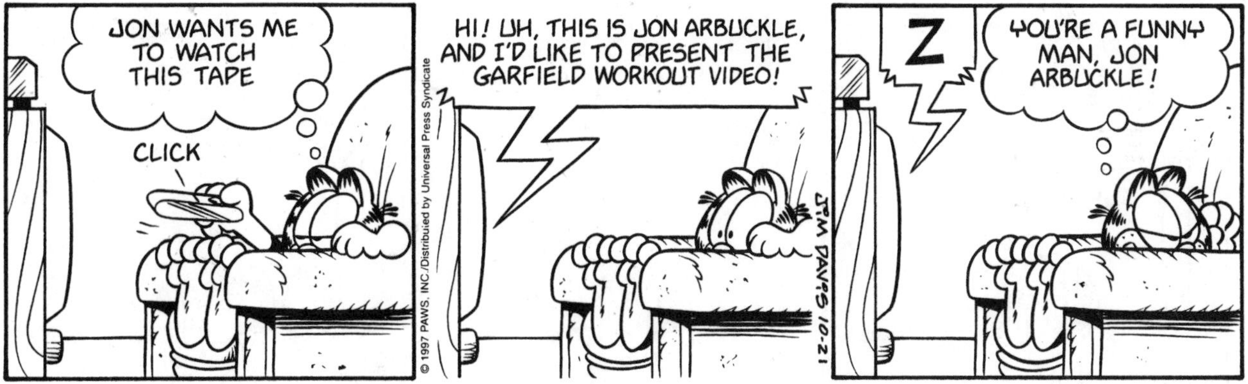
JON WANTS ME TO WATCH THIS TAPE
CLICK
HI! UH, THIS IS JON ARBUCKLE, AND I'D LIKE TO PRESENT THE GARFIELD WORKOUT VIDEO!
Z
YOU'RE A FUNNY MAN, JON ARBUCKLE!
© 1997 PAWS. INC./Distribuied by Universal Press Syndicate
JIM DAVIS 10-21

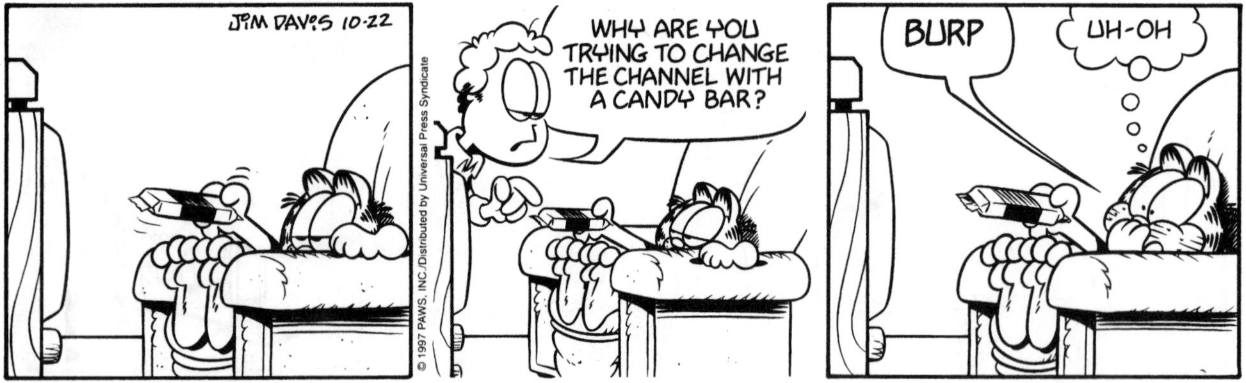
JIM DAVIS 10-22
© 1997 PAWS, INC./Distributed by Universal Press Syndicate
WHY ARE YOU TRYING TO CHANGE THE CHANNEL WITH A CANDY BAR?
BURP
UH-OH

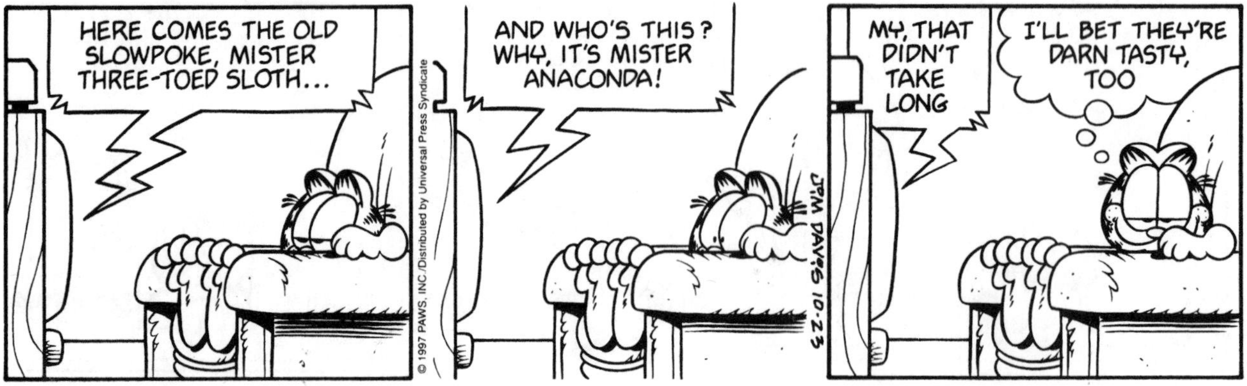
HERE COMES THE OLD SLOWPOKE, MISTER THREE-TOED SLOTH...
© 1997 PAWS, INC./Distributed by Universal Press Syndicate
AND WHO'S THIS? WHY, IT'S MISTER ANACONDA!
JIM DAVIS 10-23
MY, THAT DIDN'T TAKE LONG
I'LL BET THEY'RE DARN TASTY, TOO

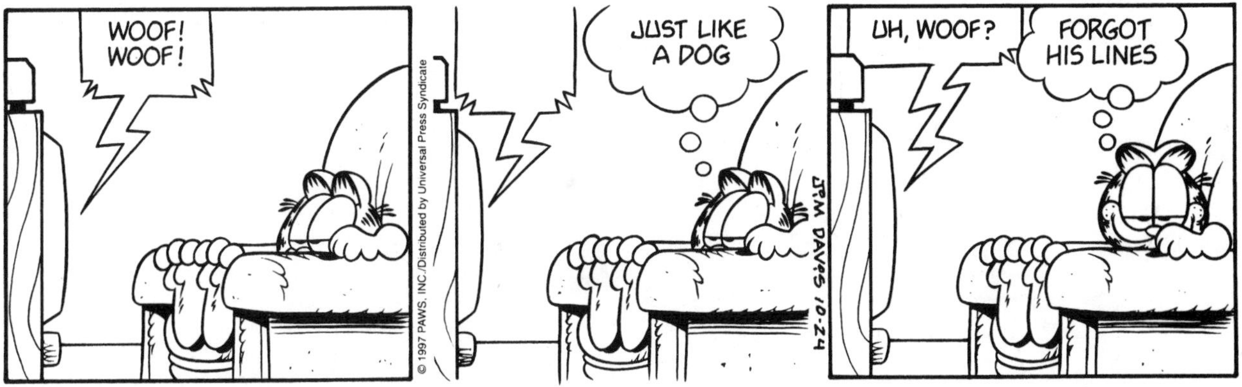
WOOF! WOOF!
© 1997 PAWS, INC./Distributed by Universal Press Syndicate
JUST LIKE A DOG
JIM DAVIS 10-24
UH, WOOF?
FORGOT HIS LINES

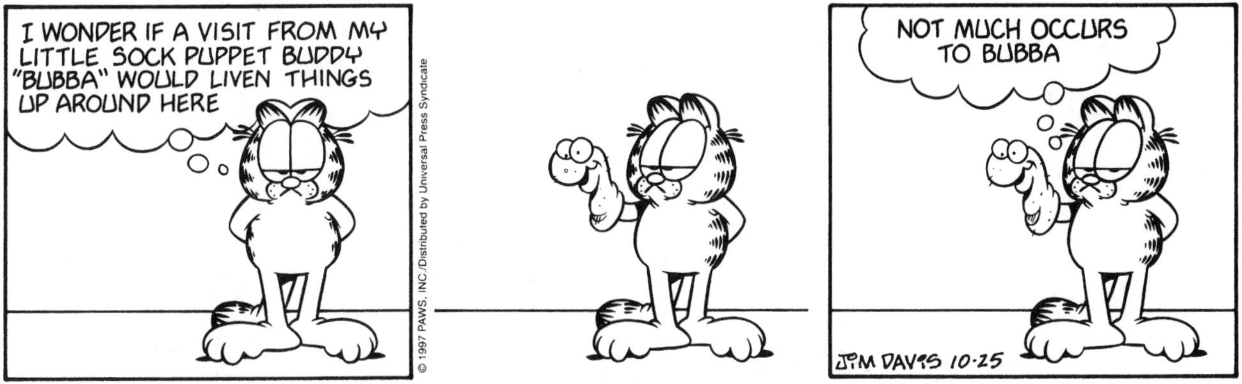
I WONDER IF A VISIT FROM MY LITTLE SOCK PUPPET BUDDY "BUBBA" WOULD LIVEN THINGS UP AROUND HERE
© 1997 PAWS, INC./Distributed by Universal Press Syndicate
NOT MUCH OCCURS TO BUBBA
JIM DAVIS 10-25

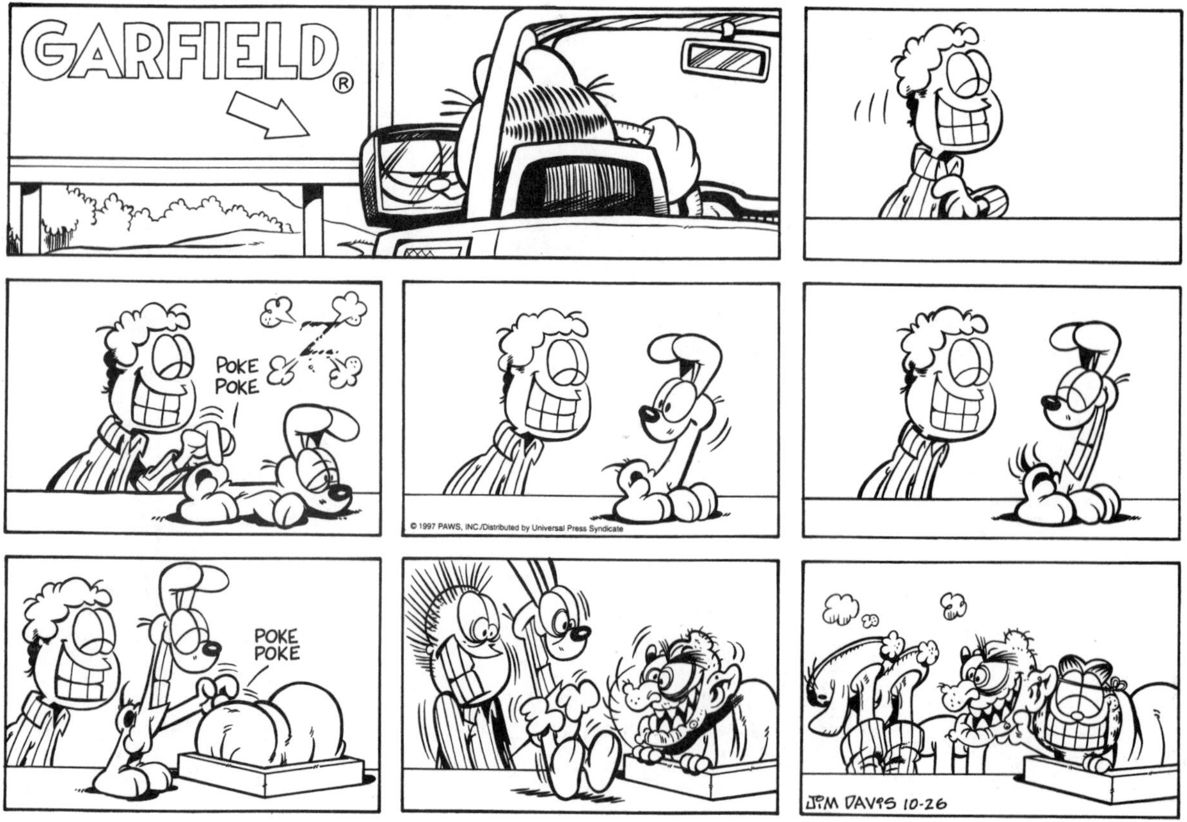
GARFIELD®
POKE POKE
© 1997 PAWS, INC./Distributed by Universal Press Syndicate
POKE POKE
JIM DAVIS 10-26

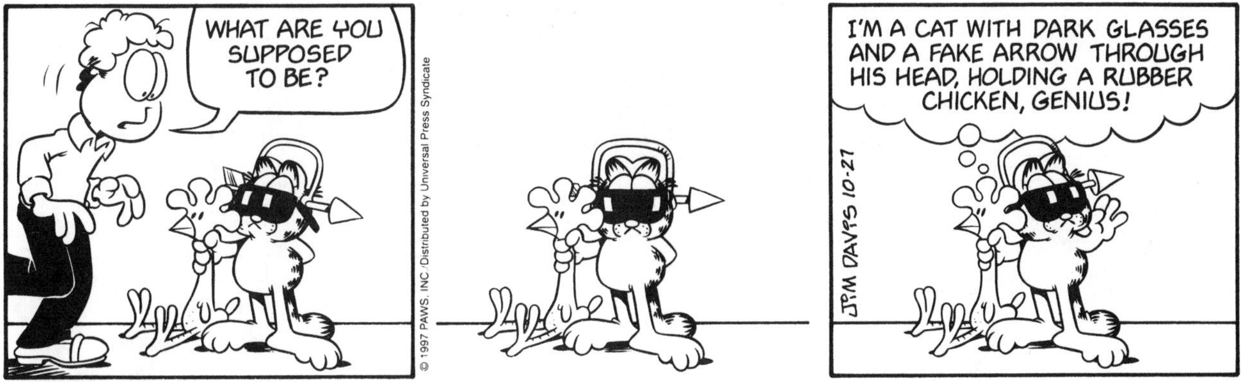
WHAT ARE YOU SUPPOSED TO BE?
I'M A CAT WITH DARK GLASSES AND A FAKE ARROW THROUGH HIS HEAD, HOLDING A RUBBER CHICKEN, GENIUS!
JIM DAVIS 10-27

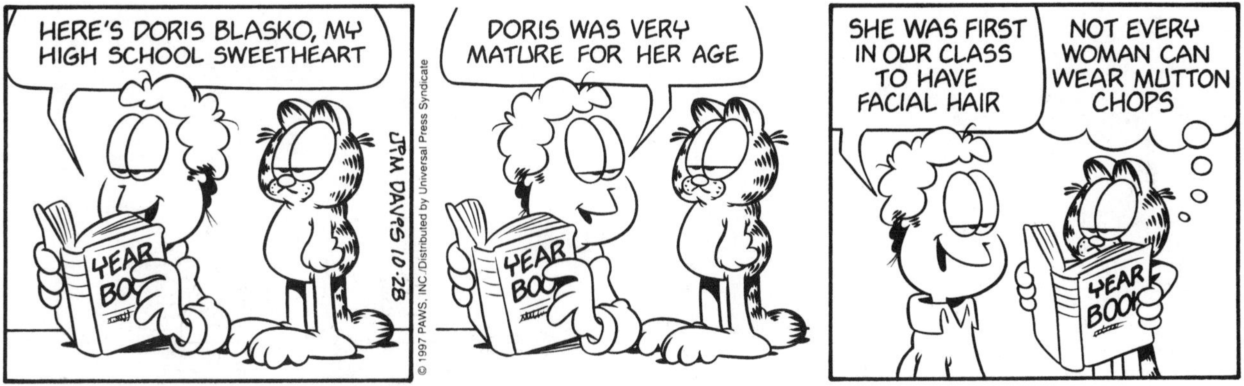
HERE'S DORIS BLASKO, MY HIGH SCHOOL SWEETHEART
YEAR BOO
JIM DAVIS 10-28
DORIS WAS VERY MATURE FOR HER AGE
YEAR BOO
SHE WAS FIRST IN OUR CLASS TO HAVE FACIAL HAIR
NOT EVERY WOMAN CAN WEAR MUTTON CHOPS
YEAR BOOK

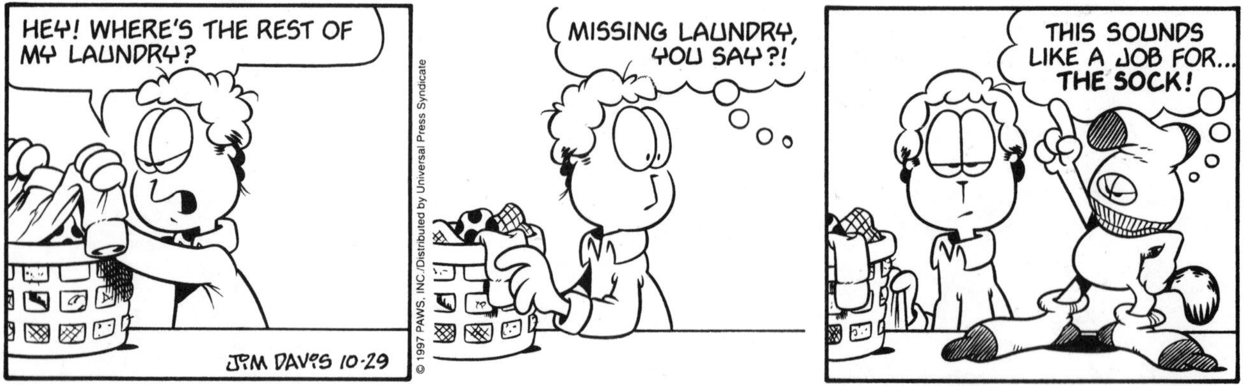
HEY! WHERE'S THE REST OF MY LAUNDRY?
JIM DAVIS 10-29
© 1997 PAWS, INC./Distributed by Universal Press Syndicate
MISSING LAUNDRY, YOU SAY?!
THIS SOUNDS LIKE A JOB FOR... **THE SOCK!**

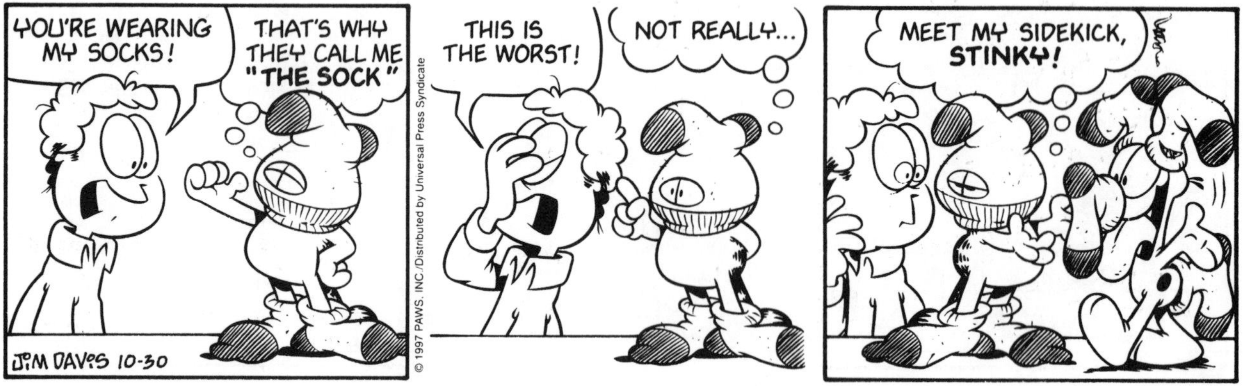
YOU'RE WEARING MY SOCKS!
THAT'S WHY THEY CALL ME **"THE SOCK"**
JIM DAVIS 10-30
© 1997 PAWS, INC./Distributed by Universal Press Syndicate
THIS IS THE WORST!
NOT REALLY...
MEET MY SIDEKICK, **STINKY!**

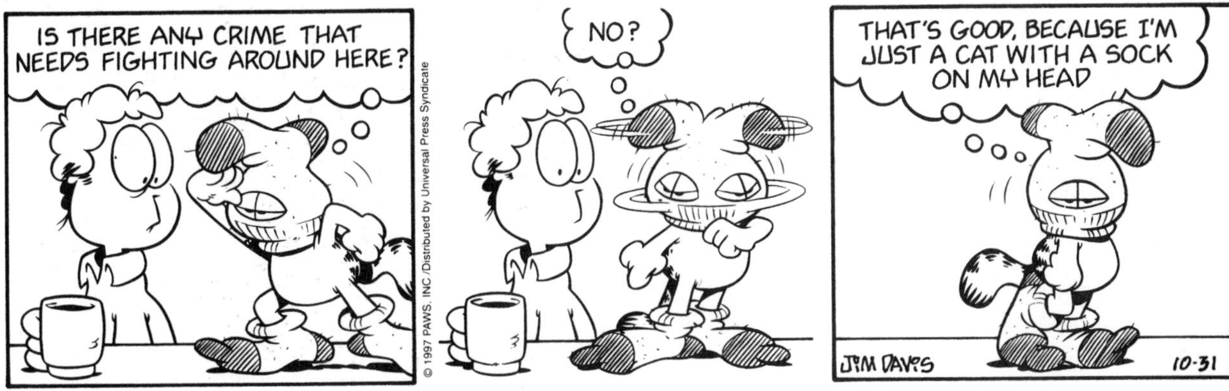
IS THERE ANY CRIME THAT NEEDS FIGHTING AROUND HERE?
© 1997 PAWS, INC./Distributed by Universal Press Syndicate
NO?
THAT'S GOOD, BECAUSE I'M JUST A CAT WITH A SOCK ON MY HEAD
JIM DAVIS
10-31

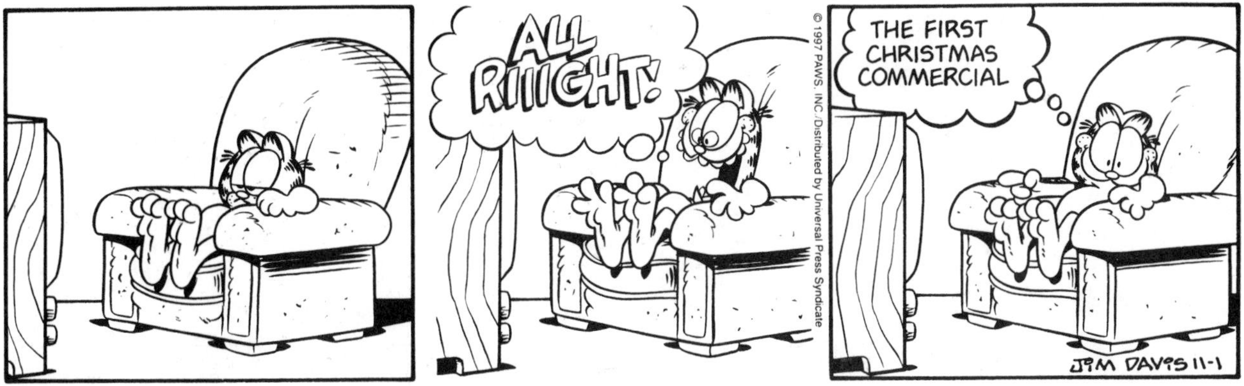
ALL RIIIGHT!
© 1997 PAWS, INC./Distributed by Universal Press Syndicate
THE FIRST CHRISTMAS COMMERCIAL
JIM DAVIS 11-1

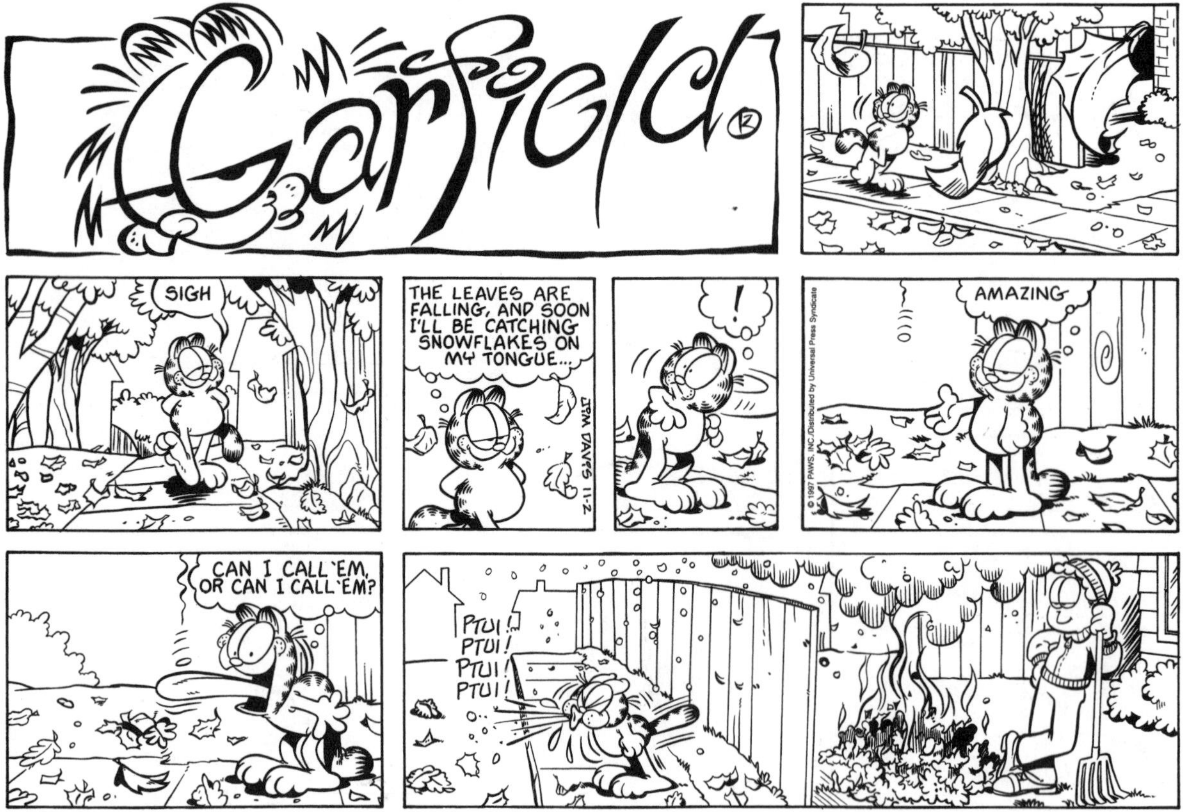
Garfield®
SIGH
THE LEAVES ARE FALLING, AND SOON I'LL BE CATCHING SNOWFLAKES ON MY TONGUE...
JIM DAVIS 11-2
!
AMAZING
© 1997 PAWS, INC./Distributed by Universal Press Syndicate
CAN I CALL 'EM, OR CAN I CALL 'EM?
PTUI! PTUI! PTUI! PTUI!

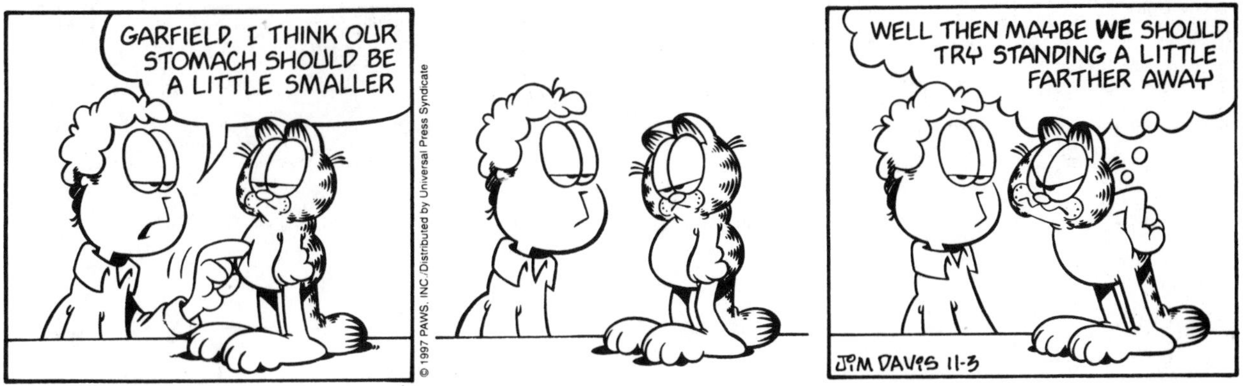
GARFIELD, I THINK OUR STOMACH SHOULD BE A LITTLE SMALLER
WELL THEN MAYBE **WE** SHOULD TRY STANDING A LITTLE FARTHER AWAY
JIM DAVIS 11-3
© 1997 PAWS, INC./Distributed by Universal Press Syndicate

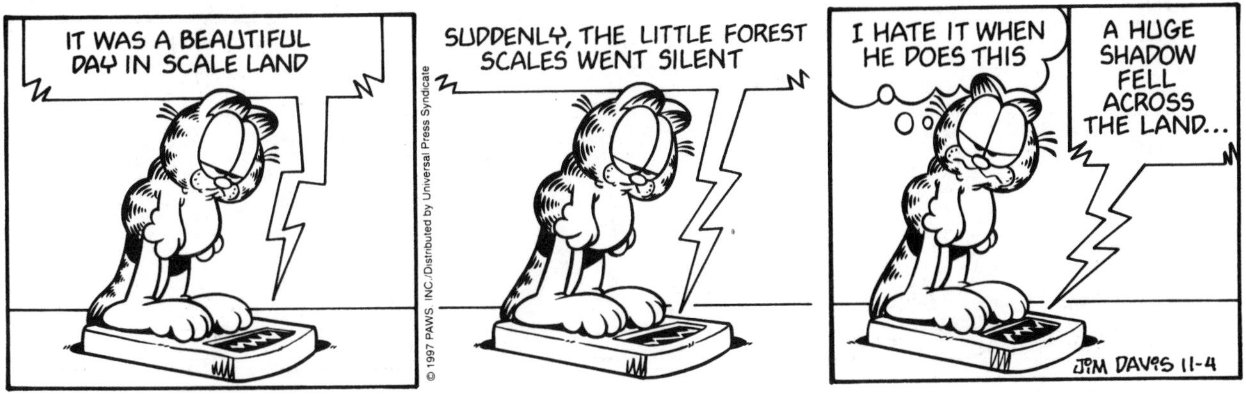
IT WAS A BEAUTIFUL DAY IN SCALE LAND
SUDDENLY, THE LITTLE FOREST SCALES WENT SILENT
I HATE IT WHEN HE DOES THIS
A HUGE SHADOW FELL ACROSS THE LAND...
JIM DAVIS 11-4
© 1997 PAWS, INC./Distributed by Universal Press Syndicate

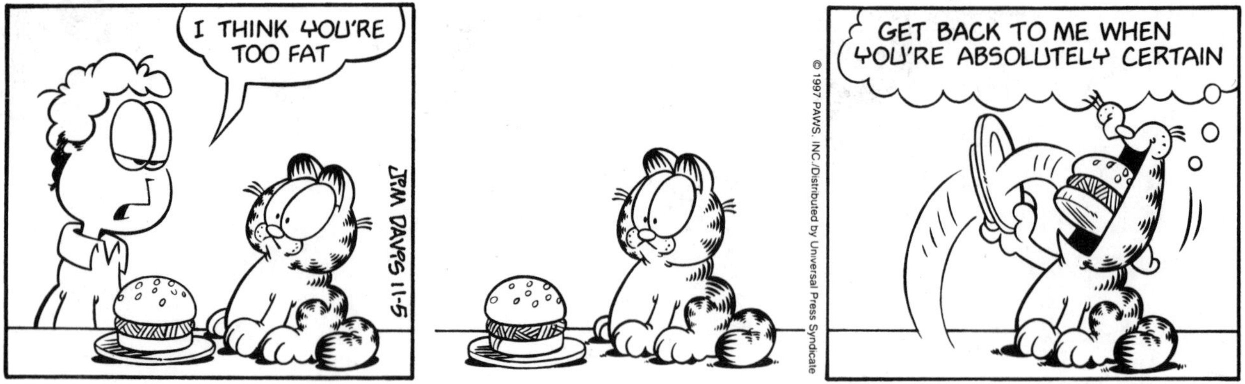
I THINK YOU'RE TOO FAT
JIM DAVIS 11-5
GET BACK TO ME WHEN YOU'RE ABSOLUTELY CERTAIN
© 1997 PAWS, INC./Distributed by Universal Press Syndicate

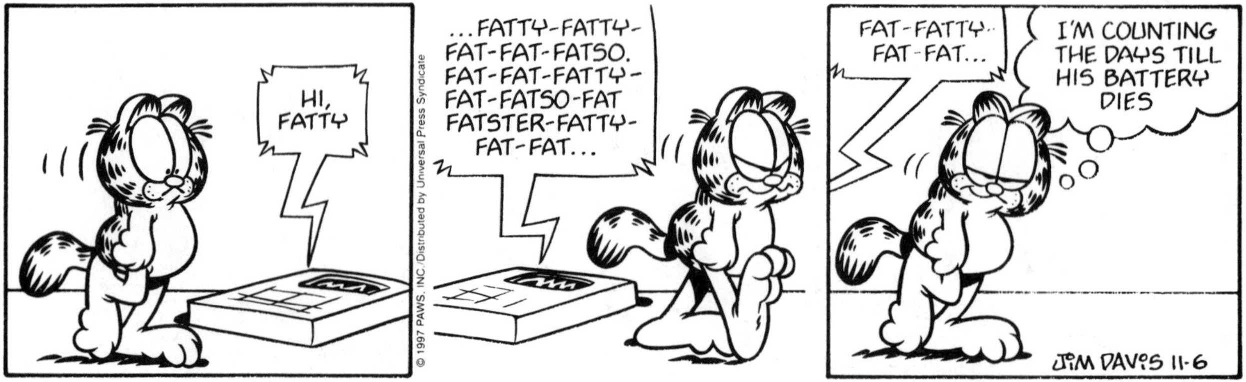
HI, FATTY
...FATTY-FATTY-FAT-FAT-FATSO. FAT-FAT-FATTY-FAT-FATSO-FAT FATSTER-FATTY-FAT-FAT...
FAT-FATTY.. FAT-FAT...
I'M COUNTING THE DAYS TILL HIS BATTERY DIES
JIM DAVIS 11-6
© 1997 PAWS, INC./Distributed by Universal Press Syndicate

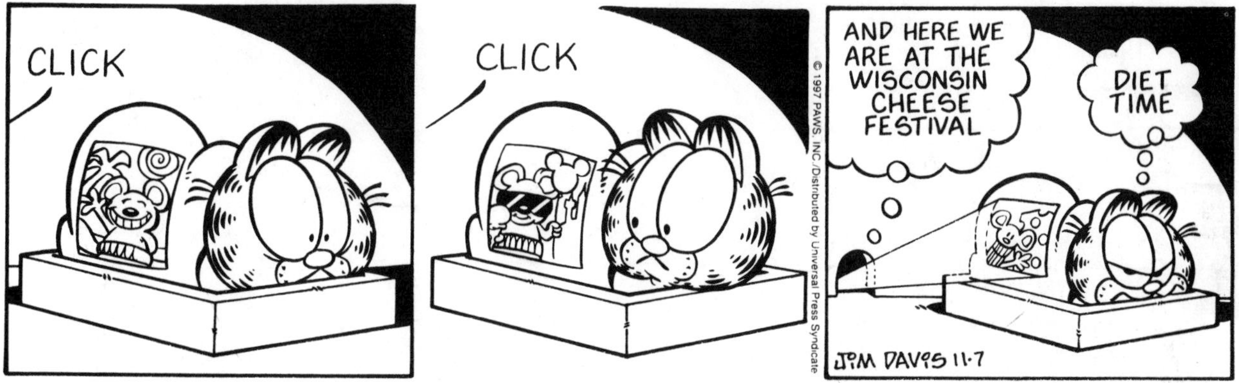
CLICK
CLICK
© 1997 PAWS, INC./Distributed by Universal Press Syndicate
AND HERE WE ARE AT THE WISCONSIN CHEESE FESTIVAL
DIET TIME
JIM DAVIS 11-7

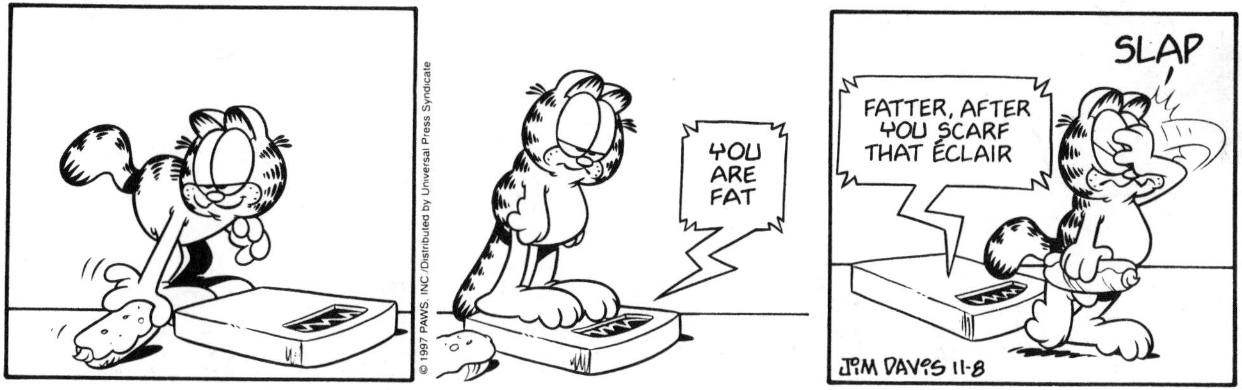
© 1997 PAWS, INC./Distributed by Universal Press Syndicate
YOU ARE FAT
SLAP
FATTER, AFTER YOU SCARF THAT ÉCLAIR
JIM DAVIS 11-8

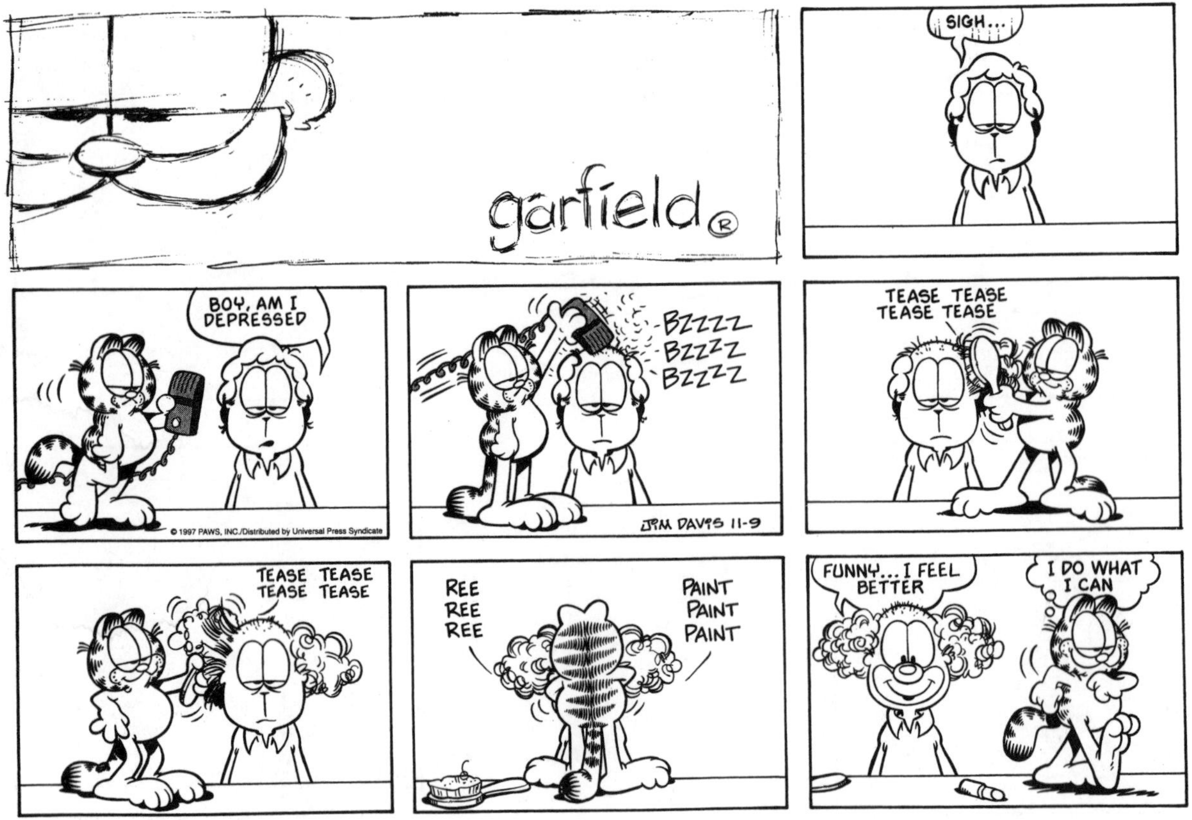
garfield ®
SIGH...
BOY, AM I DEPRESSED
BZZZZ BZZZZ BZZZZ
JIM DAVIS 11-9
TEASE TEASE TEASE TEASE
TEASE TEASE TEASE TEASE
REE REE REE
PAINT PAINT PAINT
FUNNY... I FEEL BETTER
I DO WHAT I CAN

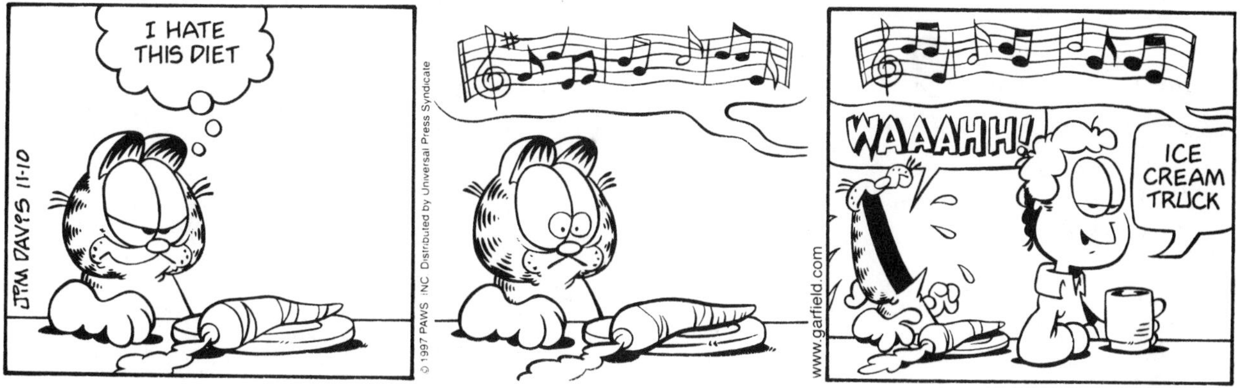
JIM DAVIS 11-10
I HATE THIS DIET
© 1997 PAWS, INC. Distributed by Universal Press Syndicate
www.garfield.com
WAAAHH!
ICE CREAM TRUCK

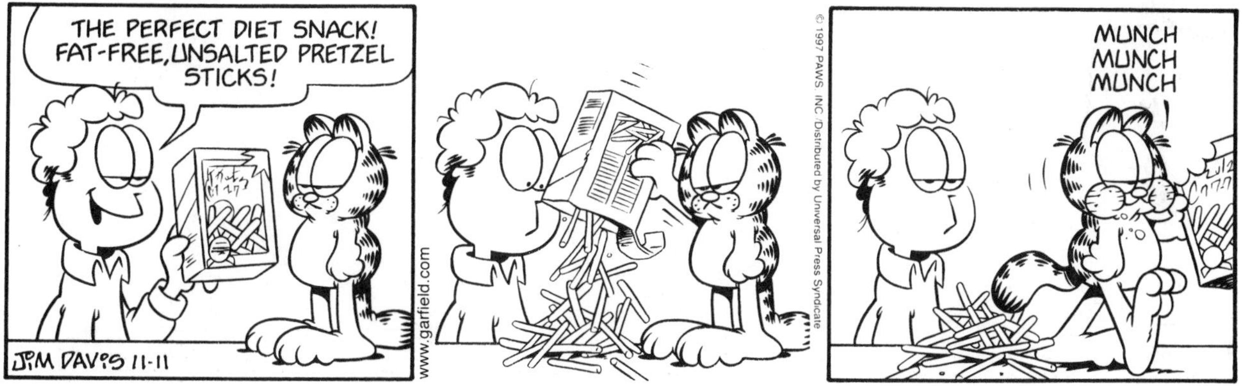
THE PERFECT DIET SNACK! FAT-FREE, UNSALTED PRETZEL STICKS!
JIM DAVIS 11-11
www.garfield.com
© 1997 PAWS, INC. Distributed by Universal Press Syndicate
MUNCH MUNCH MUNCH

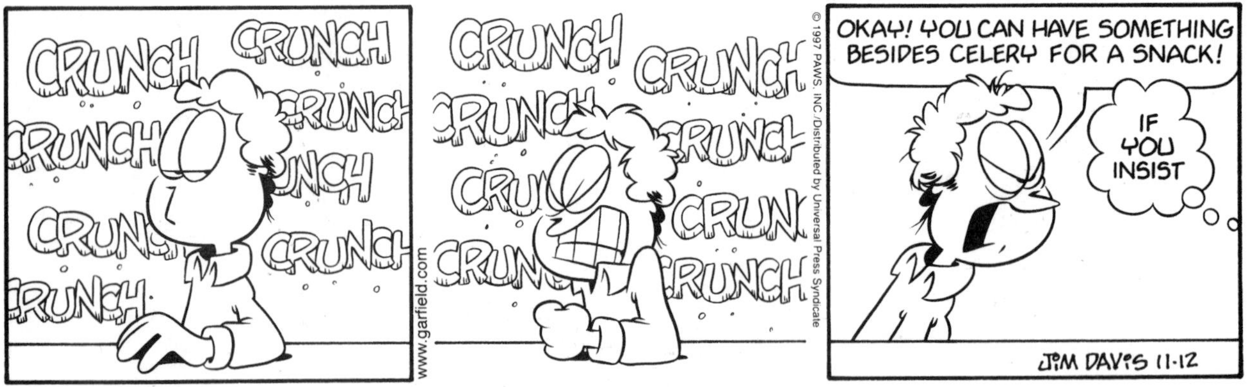
CRUNCH
CRUNCH
CRUNCH
CRUNCH
CRUNCH
CRUNCH
CRUNCH
CRUNCH
CRUNCH
CRUNCH
CRUNCH
CRUNCH
CRUNCH
CRUNCH
CRUNCH
OKAY! YOU CAN HAVE SOMETHING BESIDES CELERY FOR A SNACK!
IF YOU INSIST
JIM DAVIS 11-12
www.garfield.com
© 1997 PAWS, INC./Distributed by Universal Press Syndicate

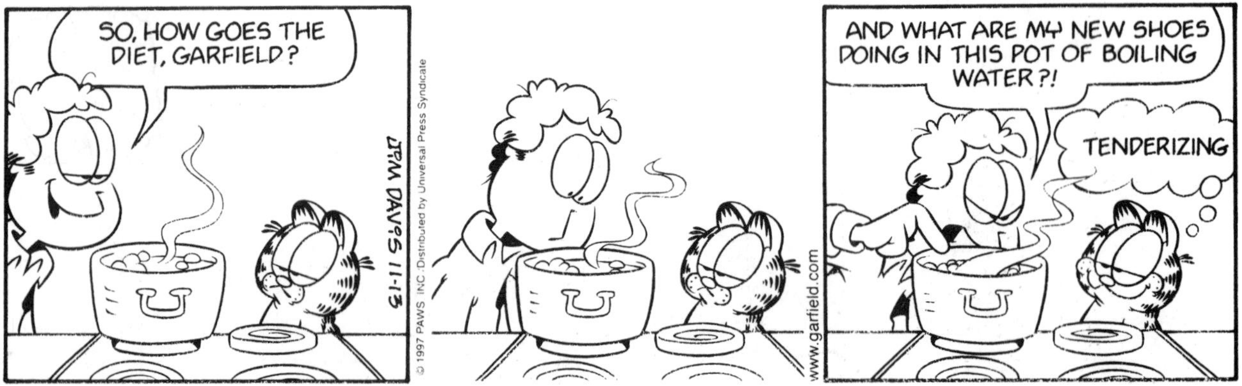
SO, HOW GOES THE DIET, GARFIELD?
JIM DAVIS 11-13
© 1997 PAWS, INC./Distributed by Universal Press Syndicate
www.garfield.com
AND WHAT ARE MY NEW SHOES DOING IN THIS POT OF BOILING WATER?!
TENDERIZING

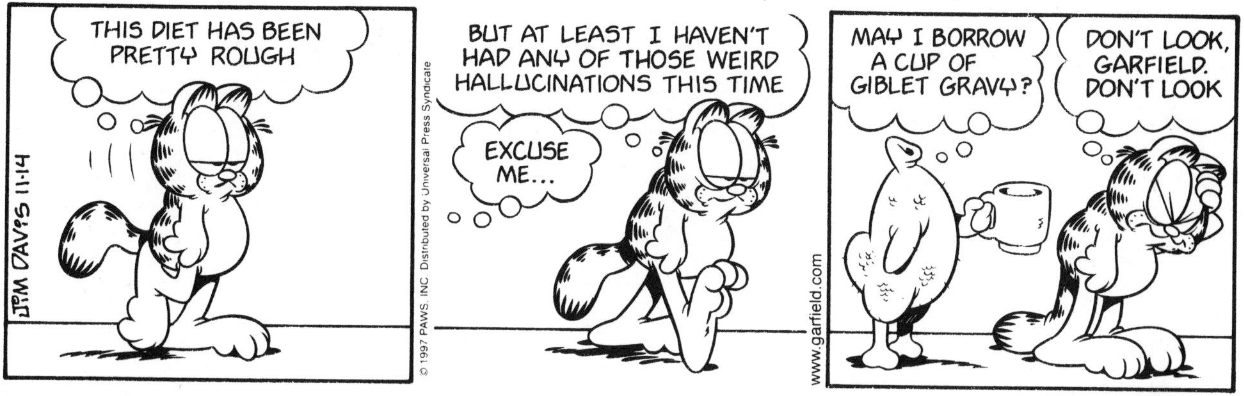
THIS DIET HAS BEEN PRETTY ROUGH
JIM DAVIS 11-14
BUT AT LEAST I HAVEN'T HAD ANY OF THOSE WEIRD HALLUCINATIONS THIS TIME
EXCUSE ME...
MAY I BORROW A CUP OF GIBLET GRAVY?
DON'T LOOK, GARFIELD. DON'T LOOK

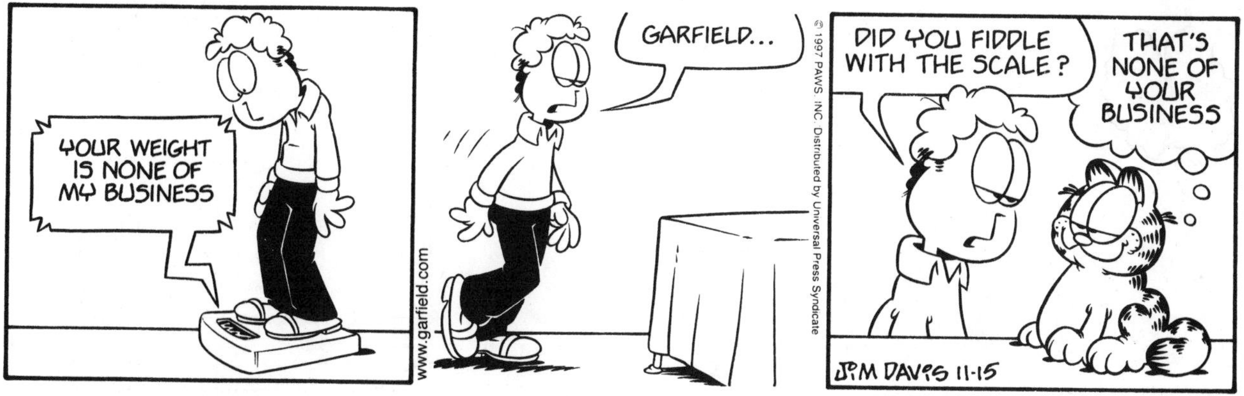
YOUR WEIGHT IS NONE OF MY BUSINESS
GARFIELD...
DID YOU FIDDLE WITH THE SCALE?
THAT'S NONE OF YOUR BUSINESS
JIM DAVIS 11-15

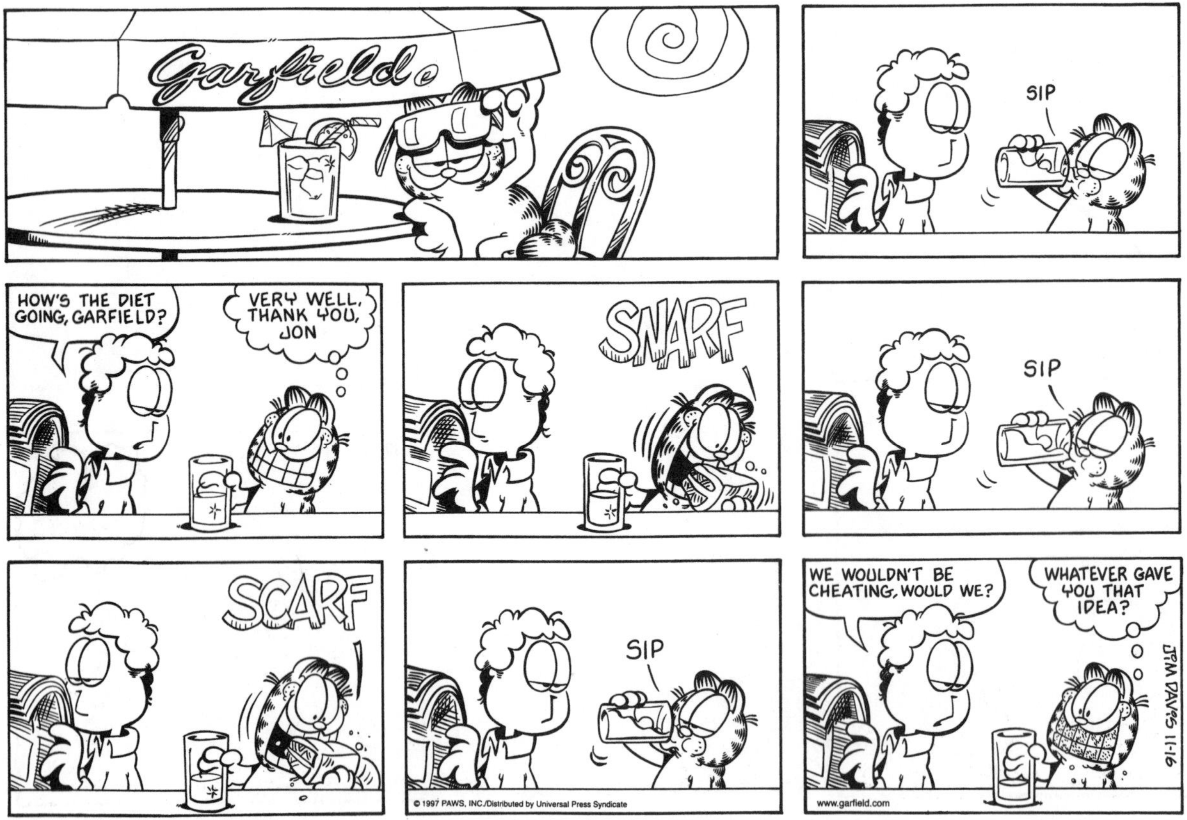
Garfield
SIP
HOW'S THE DIET GOING, GARFIELD?
VERY WELL, THANK YOU, JON
SNARF
SIP
SCARF
SIP
WE WOULDN'T BE CHEATING, WOULD WE?
WHATEVER GAVE YOU THAT IDEA?
JPM DAVIS 11-16
© 1997 PAWS, INC./Distributed by Universal Press Syndicate
www.garfield.com

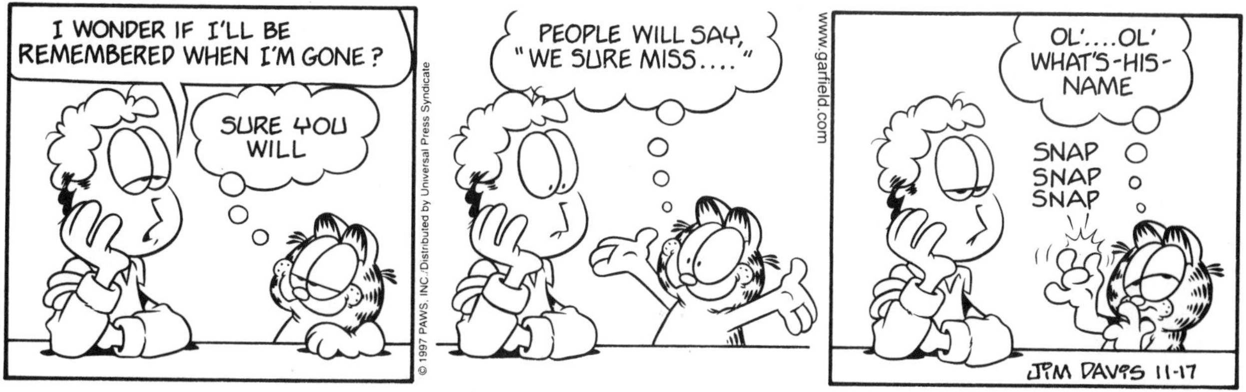
I WONDER IF I'LL BE REMEMBERED WHEN I'M GONE?
SURE YOU WILL
© 1997 PAWS, INC./Distributed by Universal Press Syndicate
PEOPLE WILL SAY, "WE SURE MISS...."
www.garfield.com
OL'....OL' WHAT'S-HIS-NAME
SNAP SNAP SNAP
JIM DAVIS 11-17

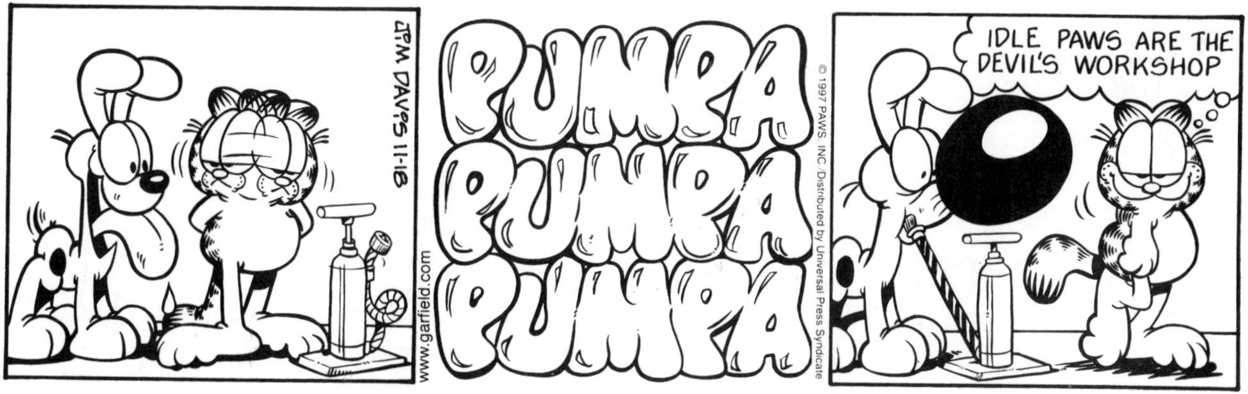
JIM DAVIS 11-18
www.garfield.com
PUMPA PUMPA PUMPA
© 1997 PAWS, INC./Distributed by Universal Press Syndicate
IDLE PAWS ARE THE DEVIL'S WORKSHOP

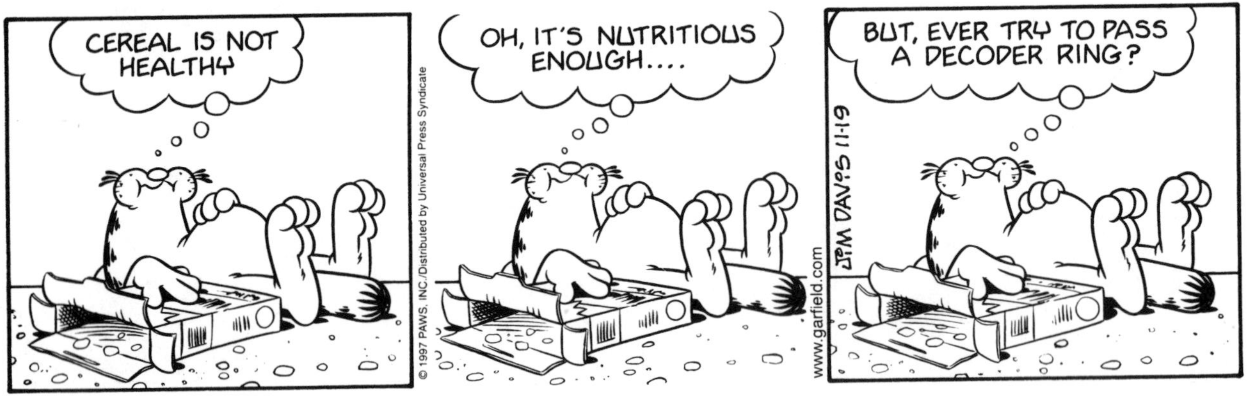
CEREAL IS NOT HEALTHY
OH, IT'S NUTRITIOUS ENOUGH....
BUT, EVER TRY TO PASS A DECODER RING?
JIM DAVIS 11-19
© 1997 PAWS, INC./Distributed by Universal Press Syndicate
www.garfield.com

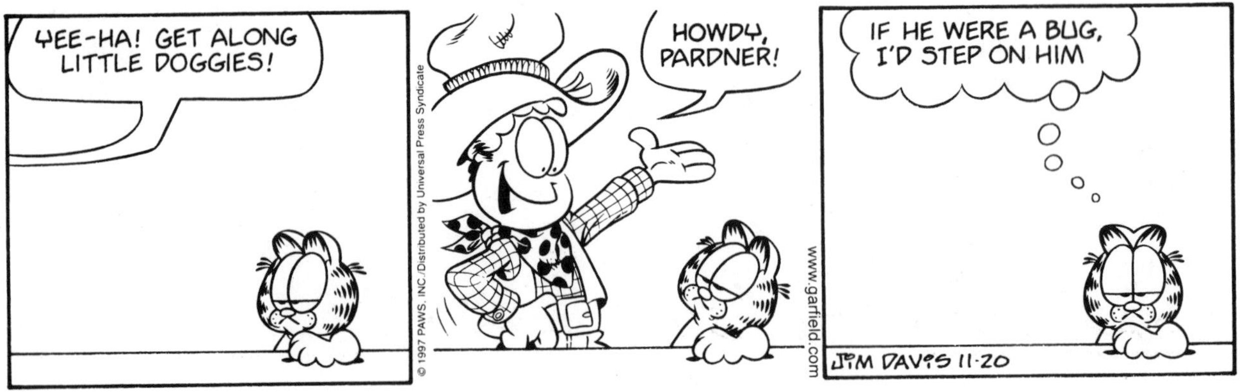
YEE-HA! GET ALONG LITTLE DOGGIES!
HOWDY, PARDNER!
IF HE WERE A BUG, I'D STEP ON HIM
JIM DAVIS 11-20
© 1997 PAWS, INC./Distributed by Universal Press Syndicate
www.garfield.com

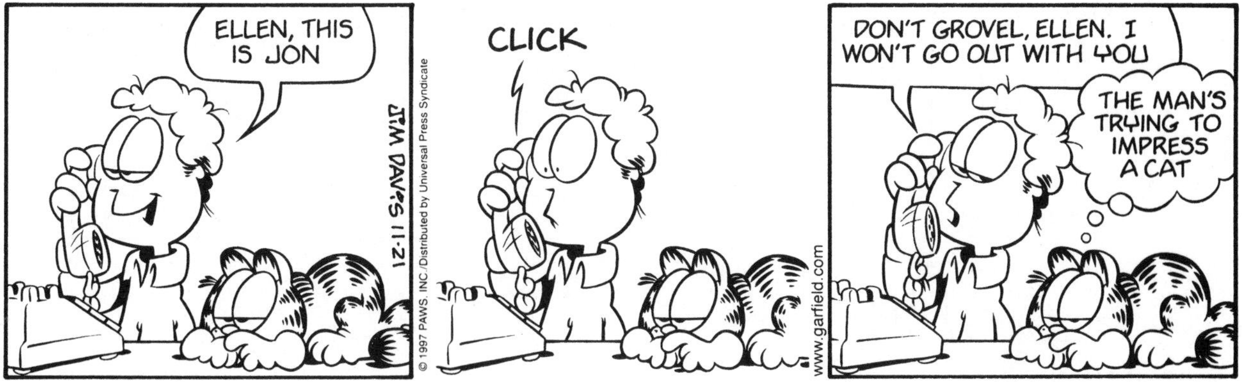
ELLEN, THIS IS JON
JIM DAVIS 11-21
© 1997 PAWS. INC./Distributed by Universal Press Syndicate
CLICK
www.garfield.com
DON'T GROVEL, ELLEN. I WON'T GO OUT WITH YOU
THE MAN'S TRYING TO IMPRESS A CAT

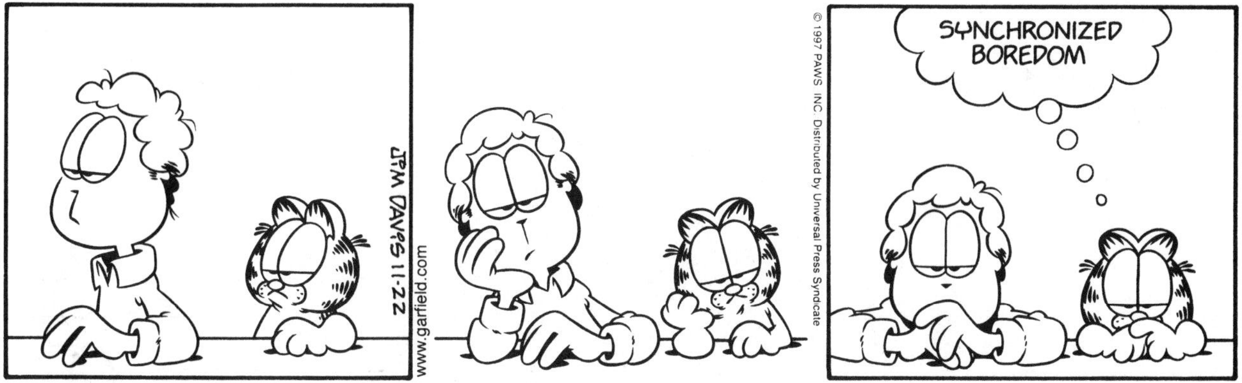
JIM DAVIS 11-22
www.garfield.com
© 1997 PAWS. INC. Distributed by Universal Press Syndicate
SYNCHRONIZED BOREDOM

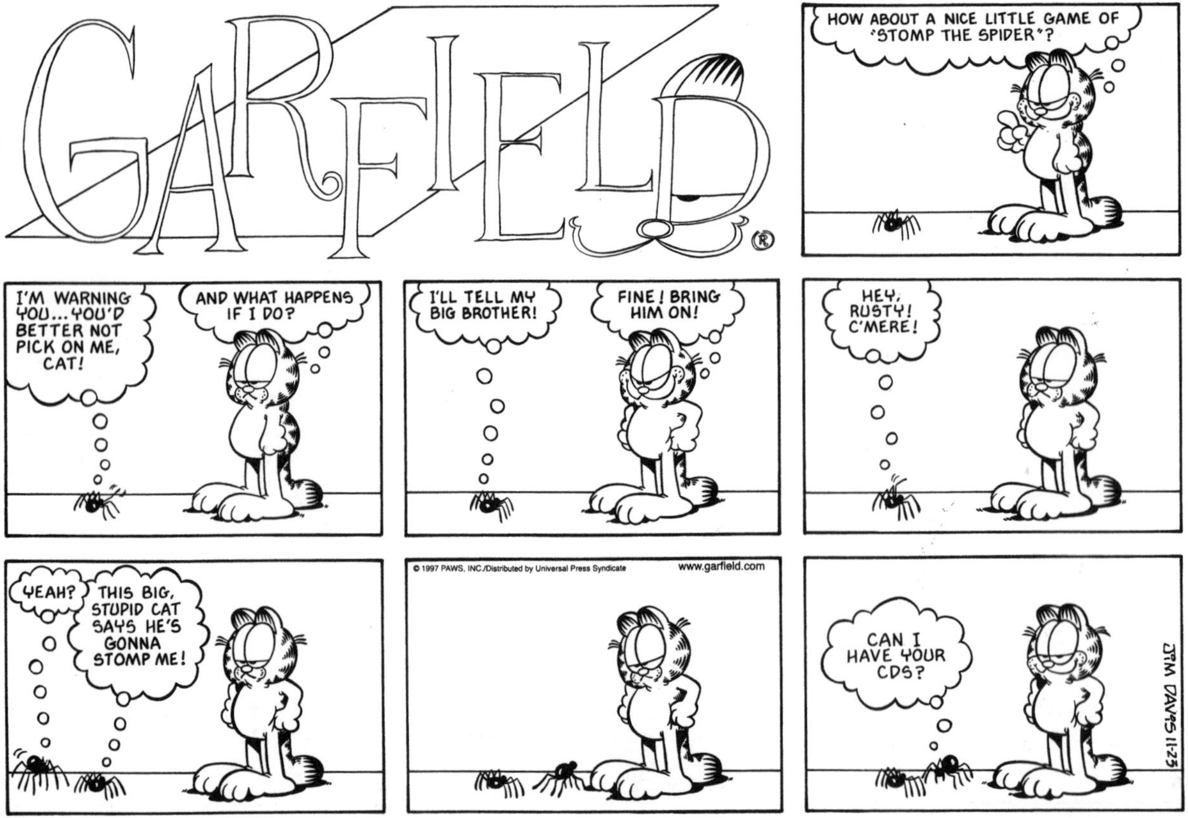
GARFIELD®
HOW ABOUT A NICE LITTLE GAME OF "STOMP THE SPIDER"?
I'M WARNING YOU... YOU'D BETTER NOT PICK ON ME, CAT!
AND WHAT HAPPENS IF I DO?
I'LL TELL MY BIG BROTHER!
FINE! BRING HIM ON!
HEY, RUSTY! C'MERE!
YEAH?
THIS BIG, STUPID CAT SAYS HE'S GONNA STOMP ME!
© 1997 PAWS, INC./Distributed by Universal Press Syndicate
www.garfield.com
CAN I HAVE YOUR CDS?
JIM DAVIS 11-23

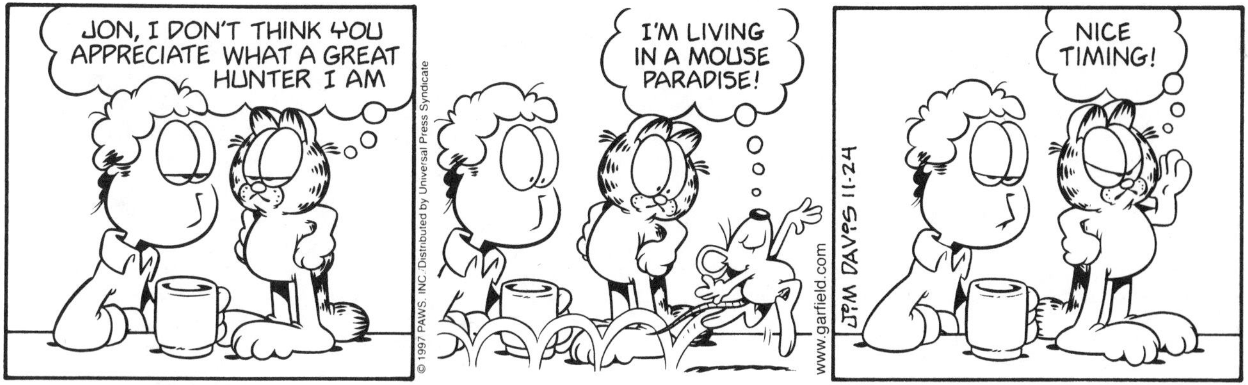
JON, I DON'T THINK YOU APPRECIATE WHAT A GREAT HUNTER I AM
I'M LIVING IN A MOUSE PARADISE!
NICE TIMING!
JIM DAVIS 11-24
© 1997 PAWS, INC./Distributed by Universal Press Syndicate
www.garfield.com

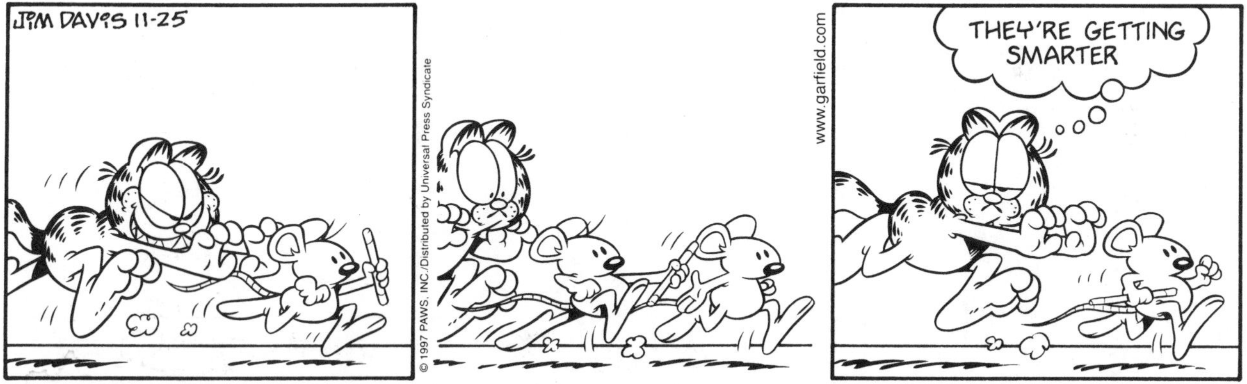
JIM DAVIS 11-25
THEY'RE GETTING SMARTER
© 1997 PAWS, INC./Distributed by Universal Press Syndicate
www.garfield.com

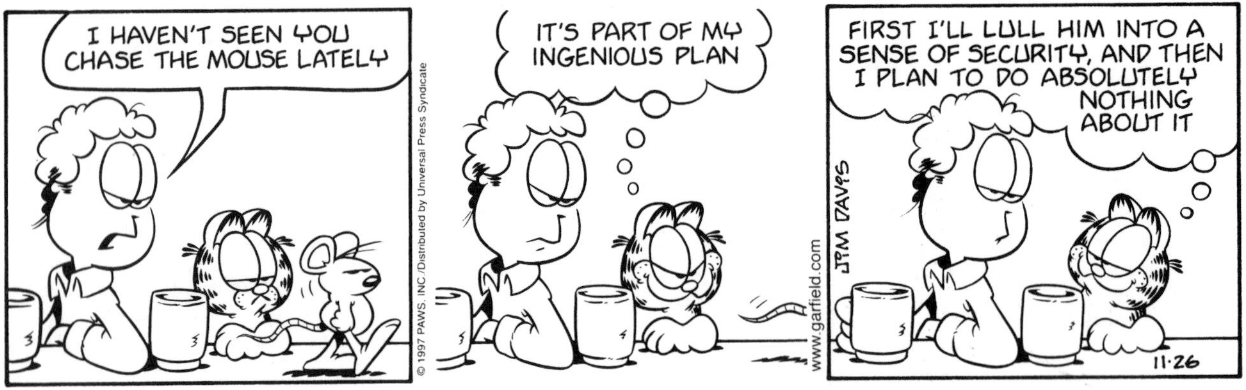
I HAVEN'T SEEN YOU CHASE THE MOUSE LATELY
IT'S PART OF MY INGENIOUS PLAN
FIRST I'LL LULL HIM INTO A SENSE OF SECURITY, AND THEN I PLAN TO DO ABSOLUTELY NOTHING ABOUT IT
JIM DAVIS
11·26

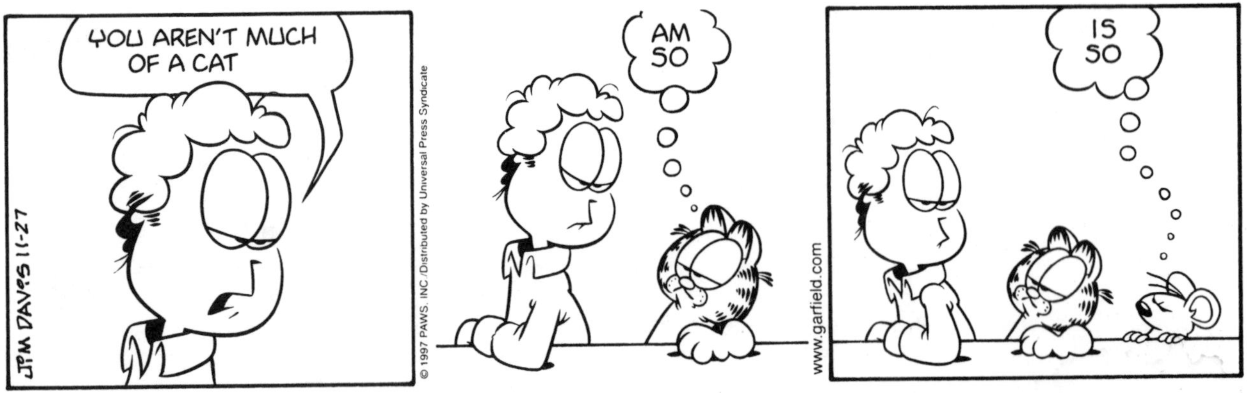
JIM DAVIS 11-27
YOU AREN'T MUCH OF A CAT
AM SO
IS SO

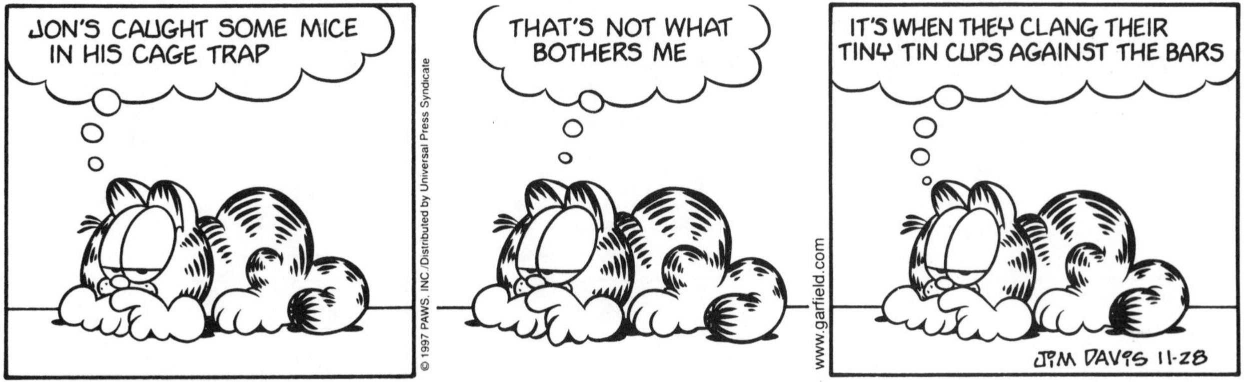

JON'S CAUGHT SOME MICE IN HIS CAGE TRAP
THAT'S NOT WHAT BOTHERS ME
IT'S WHEN THEY CLANG THEIR TINY TIN CUPS AGAINST THE BARS
JIM DAVIS 11-28
© 1997 PAWS, INC./Distributed by Universal Press Syndicate
www.garfield.com

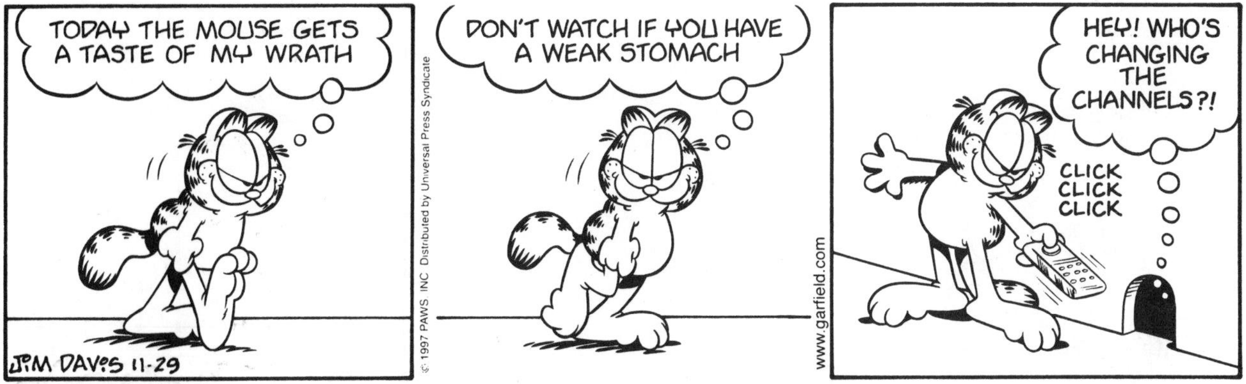

TODAY THE MOUSE GETS A TASTE OF MY WRATH
DON'T WATCH IF YOU HAVE A WEAK STOMACH
HEY! WHO'S CHANGING THE CHANNELS?!
CLICK CLICK CLICK
JIM DAVIS 11-29
© 1997 PAWS, INC Distributed by Universal Press Syndicate
www.garfield.com

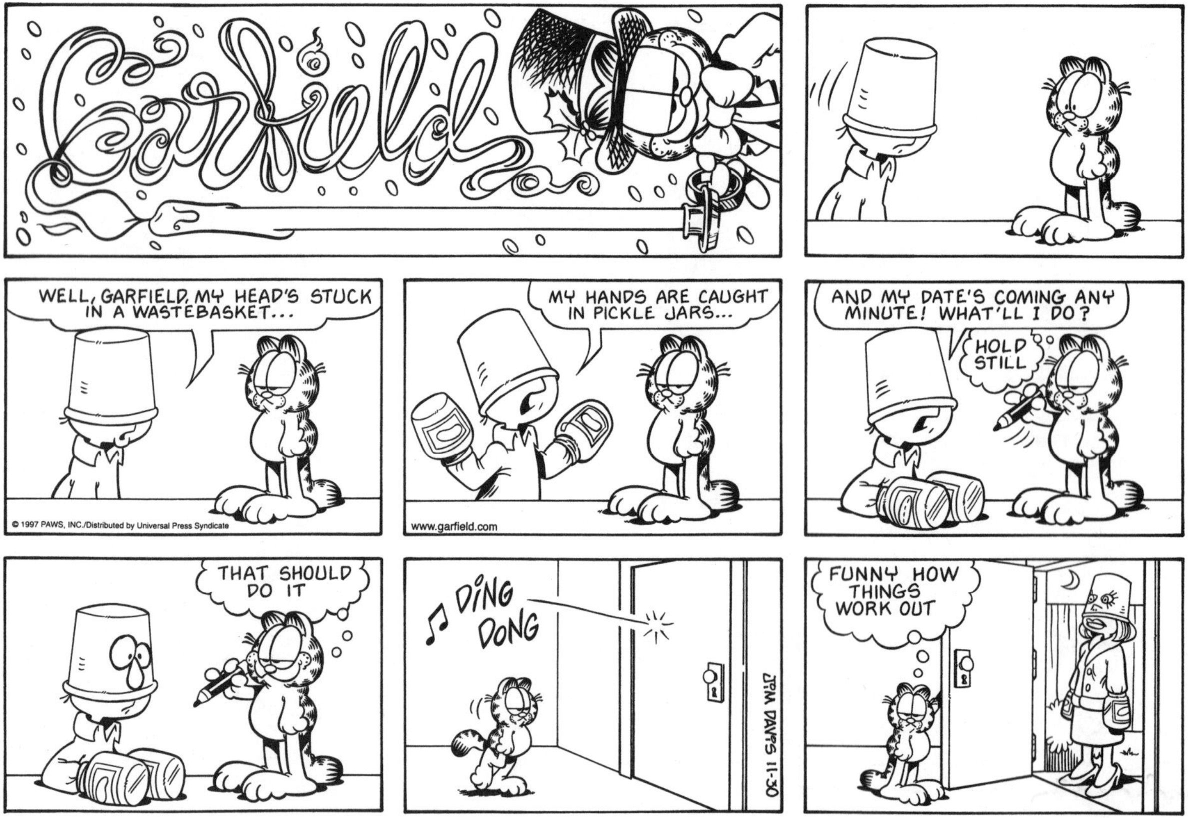
Garfield
WELL, GARFIELD, MY HEAD'S STUCK IN A WASTEBASKET...
© 1997 PAWS, INC./Distributed by Universal Press Syndicate
MY HANDS ARE CAUGHT IN PICKLE JARS...
www.garfield.com
AND MY DATE'S COMING ANY MINUTE! WHAT'LL I DO?
HOLD STILL
THAT SHOULD DO IT
DING DONG
JPM DAVPS 11-30
FUNNY HOW THINGS WORK OUT

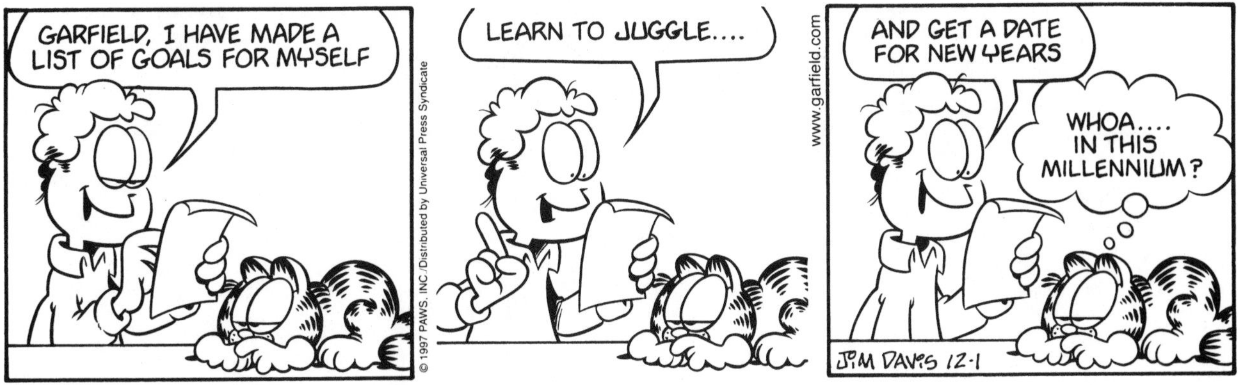
GARFIELD, I HAVE MADE A LIST OF GOALS FOR MYSELF
© 1997 PAWS, INC./Distributed by Universal Press Syndicate
LEARN TO JUGGLE....
www.garfield.com
AND GET A DATE FOR NEW YEARS
WHOA.... IN THIS MILLENNIUM?
JIM DAVIS 12-1

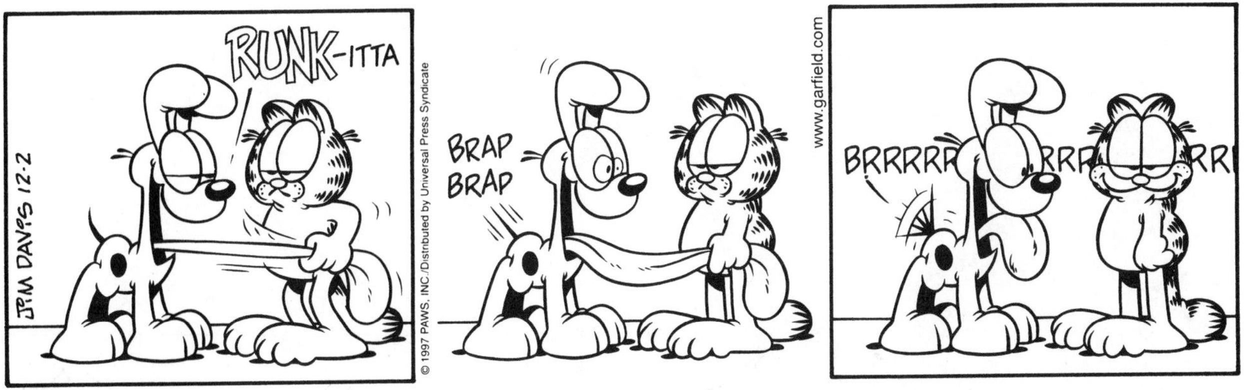
JIM DAVIS 12-2
RUNK-ITTA
© 1997 PAWS, INC./Distributed by Universal Press Syndicate
BRAP
BRAP
www.garfield.com
BRRRRR

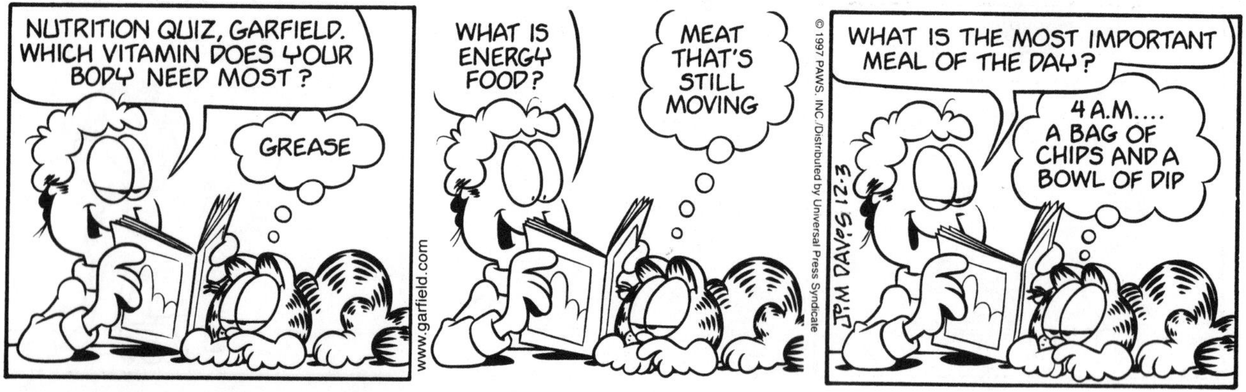
NUTRITION QUIZ, GARFIELD. WHICH VITAMIN DOES YOUR BODY NEED MOST?
GREASE
WHAT IS ENERGY FOOD?
MEAT THAT'S STILL MOVING
WHAT IS THE MOST IMPORTANT MEAL OF THE DAY?
4 A.M.... A BAG OF CHIPS AND A BOWL OF DIP
JPM DAVIS 12-3

25

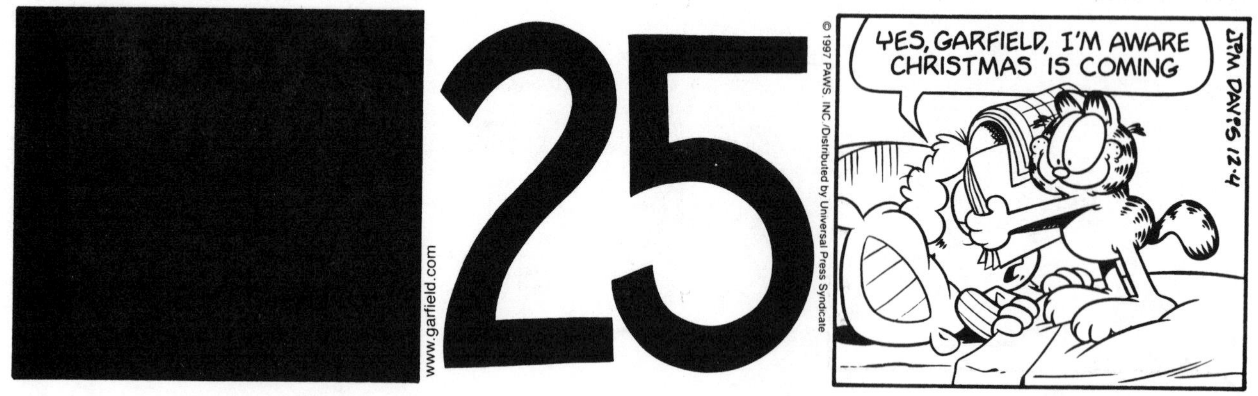
YES, GARFIELD, I'M AWARE CHRISTMAS IS COMING
JPM DAVIS 12-4

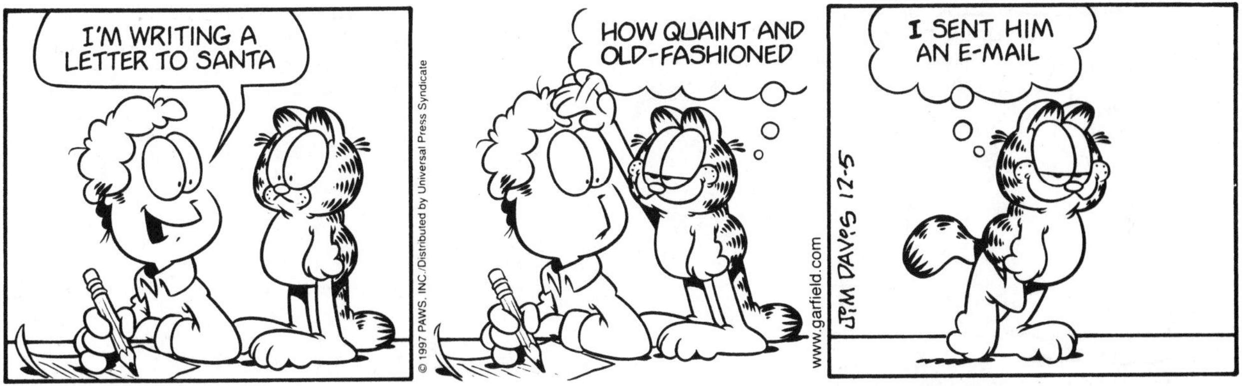
I'M WRITING A LETTER TO SANTA
HOW QUAINT AND OLD-FASHIONED
I SENT HIM AN E-MAIL
© 1997 PAWS, INC./Distributed by Universal Press Syndicate
JIM DAVIS 12-5
www.garfield.com

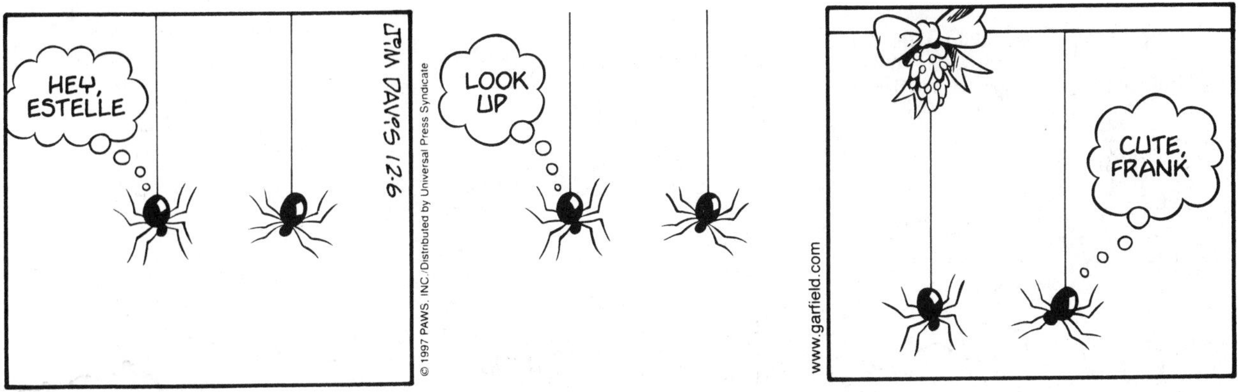
HEY, ESTELLE
LOOK UP
CUTE, FRANK
JIM DAVIS 12-6
© 1997 PAWS, INC./Distributed by Universal Press Syndicate
www.garfield.com

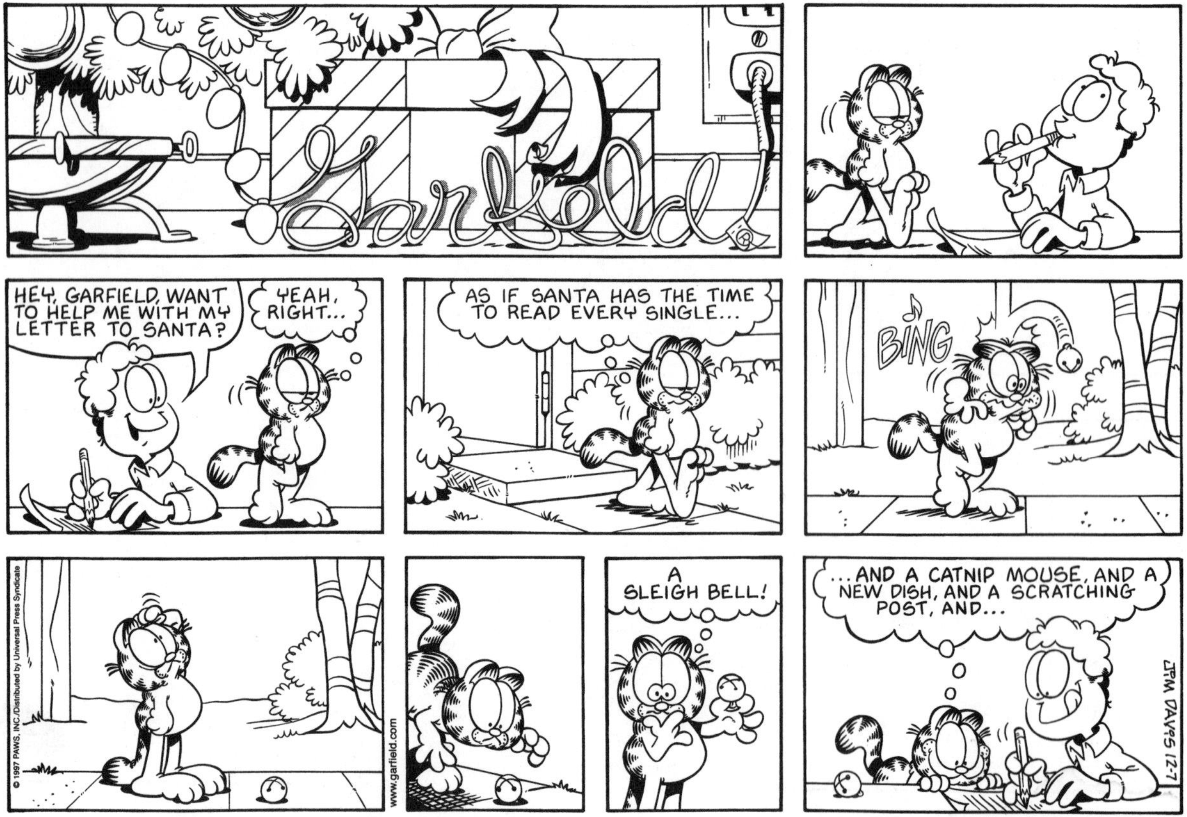
Garfield®
HEY, GARFIELD, WANT TO HELP ME WITH MY LETTER TO SANTA?
YEAH, RIGHT...
AS IF SANTA HAS THE TIME TO READ EVERY SINGLE...
BING
© 1997 PAWS, INC./Distributed by Universal Press Syndicate
www.garfield.com
A SLEIGH BELL!
...AND A CATNIP MOUSE, AND A NEW DISH, AND A SCRATCHING POST, AND...
JPM DAVIS 12-7

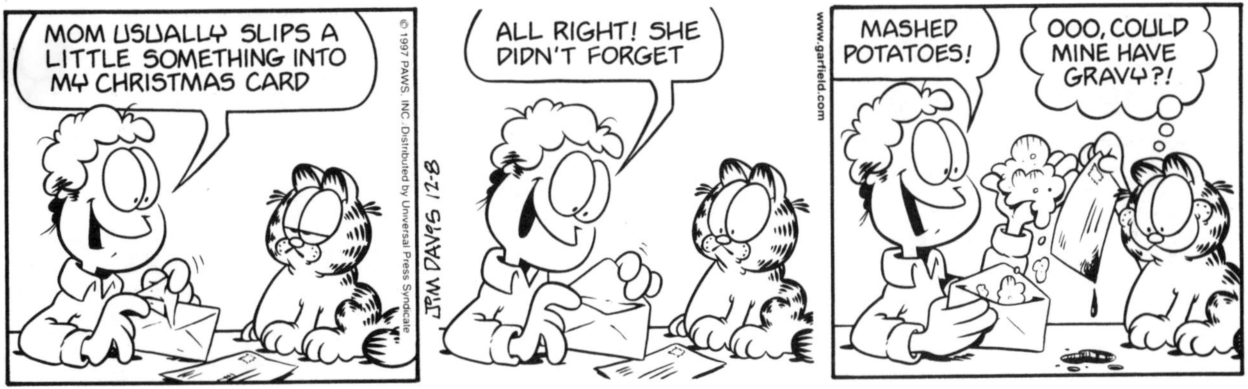
MOM USUALLY SLIPS A LITTLE SOMETHING INTO MY CHRISTMAS CARD
© 1997 PAWS, INC./Distributed by Universal Press Syndicate
JIM DAVIS 12-8
ALL RIGHT! SHE DIDN'T FORGET
www.garfield.com
MASHED POTATOES!
OOO, COULD MINE HAVE GRAVY?!

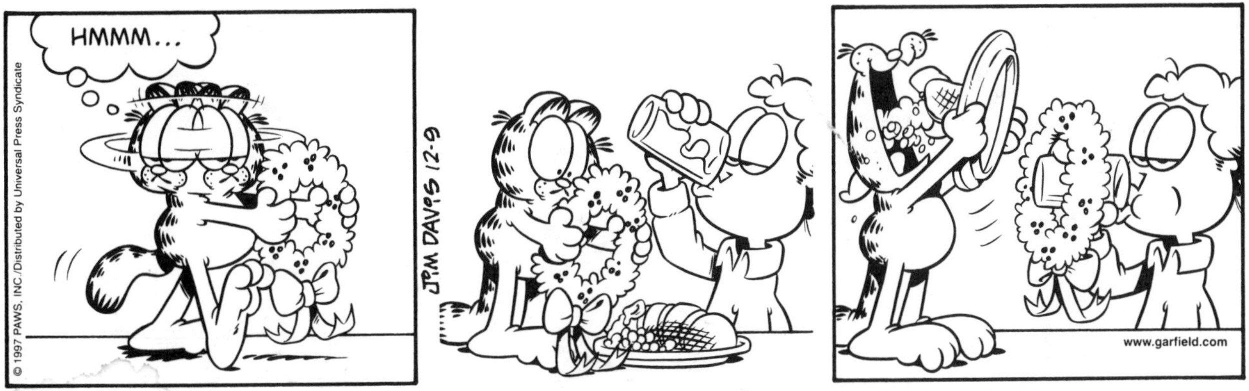
HMMM...
© 1997 PAWS, INC./Distributed by Universal Press Syndicate
JIM DAVIS 12-9
www.garfield.com

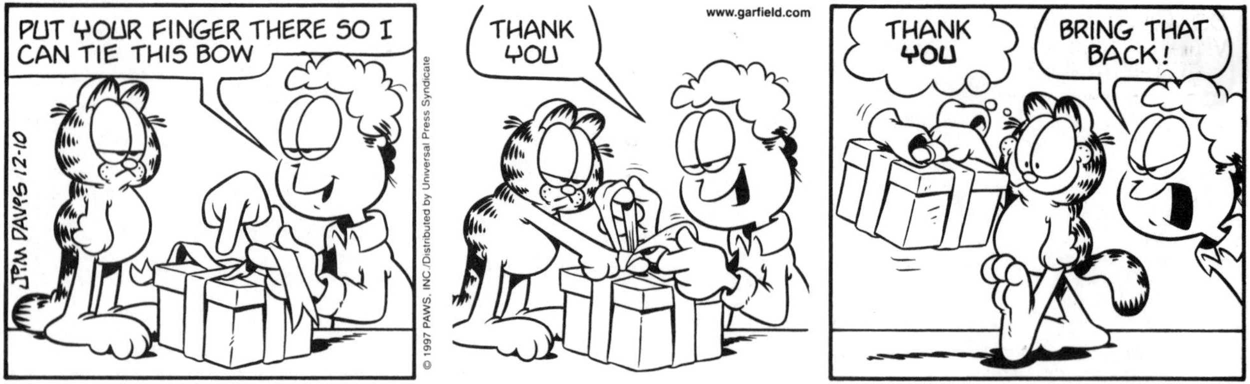
PUT YOUR FINGER THERE SO I CAN TIE THIS BOW
JIM DAVIS 12-10
© 1997 PAWS, INC./Distributed by Universal Press Syndicate
THANK YOU
www.garfield.com
THANK YOU
BRING THAT BACK!

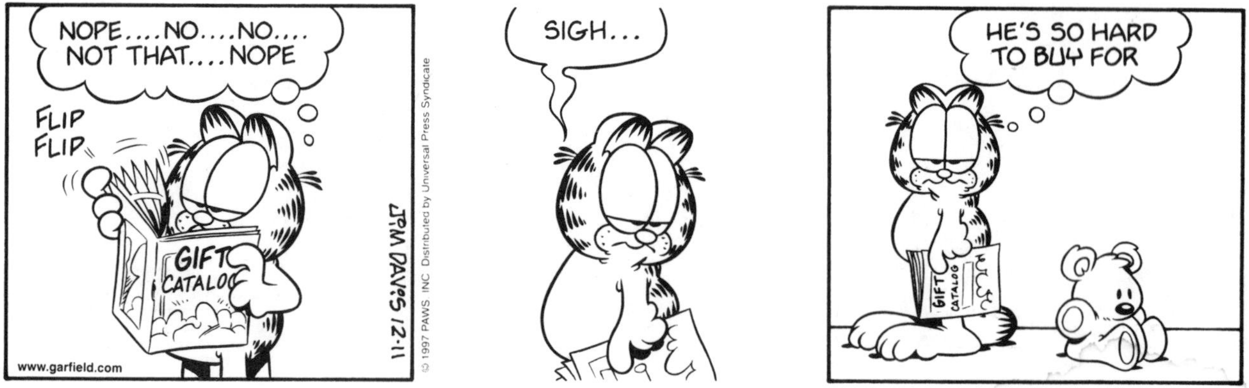
NOPE....NO....NO.... NOT THAT....NOPE
FLIP FLIP
GIFT CATALOG
www.garfield.com
JIM DAVIS 12-11
© 1997 PAWS, INC Distributed by Universal Press Syndicate
SIGH...
HE'S SO HARD TO BUY FOR
GIFT CATALOG

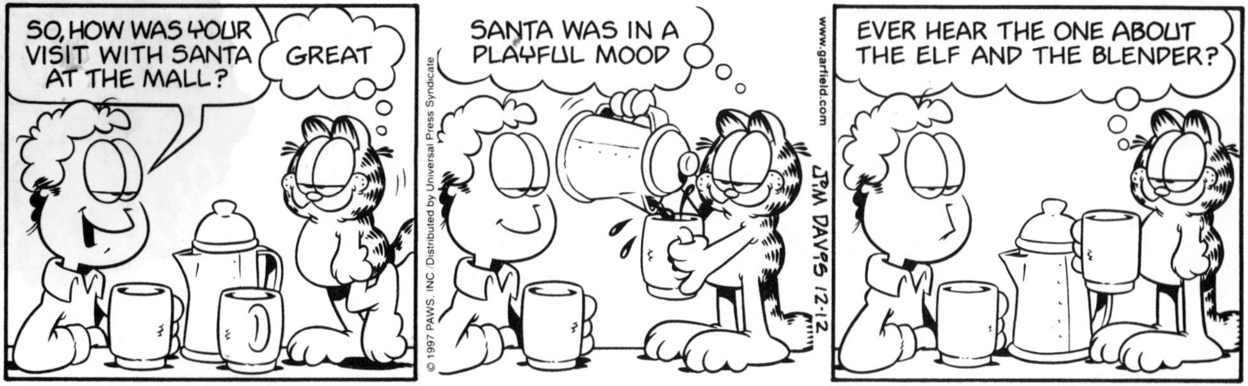
SO, HOW WAS YOUR VISIT WITH SANTA AT THE MALL?
GREAT
SANTA WAS IN A PLAYFUL MOOD
EVER HEAR THE ONE ABOUT THE ELF AND THE BLENDER?
© 1997 PAWS, INC./Distributed by Universal Press Syndicate
JIM DAVIS 12-12
www.garfield.com

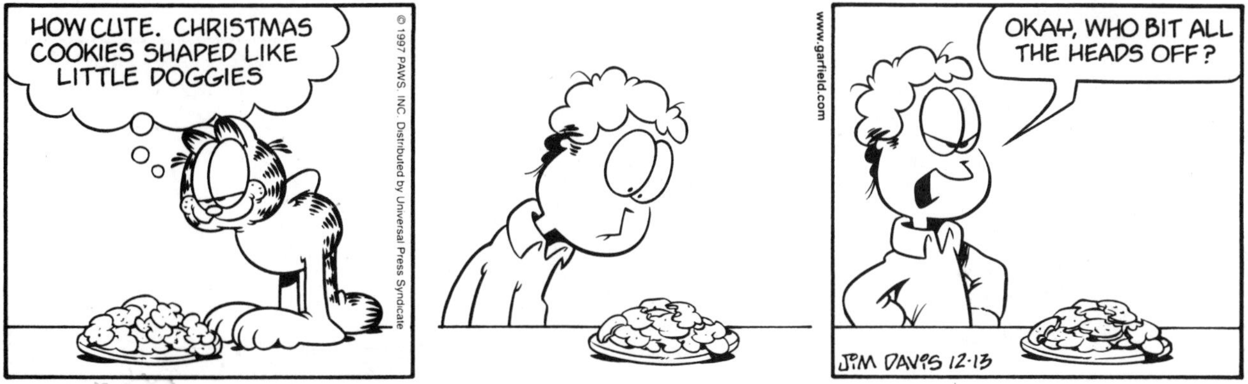
HOW CUTE. CHRISTMAS COOKIES SHAPED LIKE LITTLE DOGGIES
© 1997 PAWS, INC. Distributed by Universal Press Syndicate
OKAY, WHO BIT ALL THE HEADS OFF?
www.garfield.com
JIM DAVIS 12-13

GARFIELD'S PAST LIVES

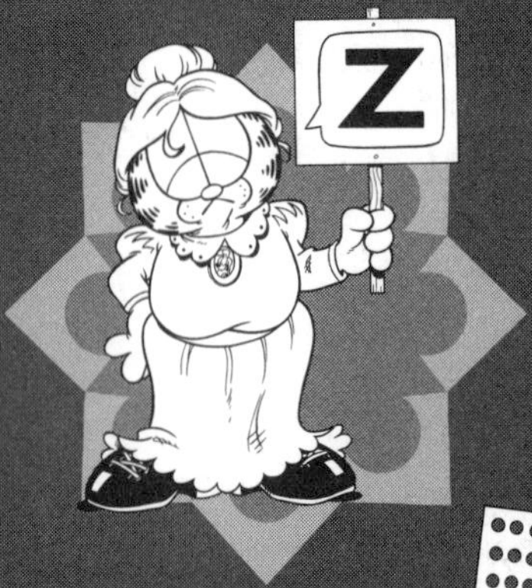
Z

SNOOZIN' B. ANTHONY

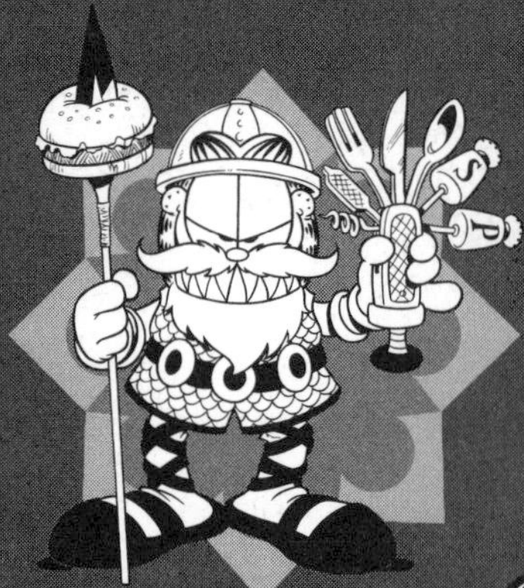

ATTILA THE HUNGRY

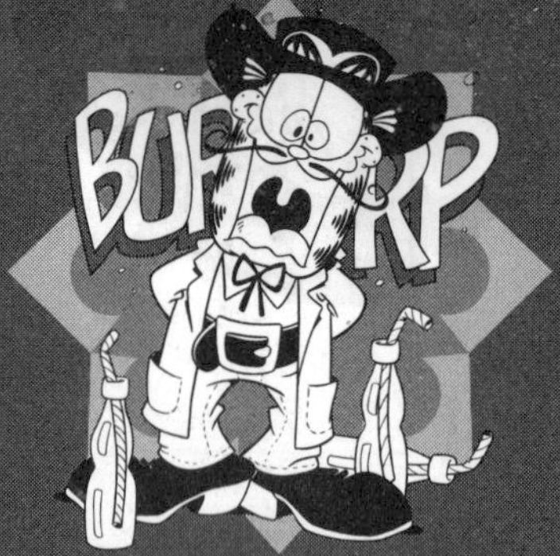

WYATT BURP

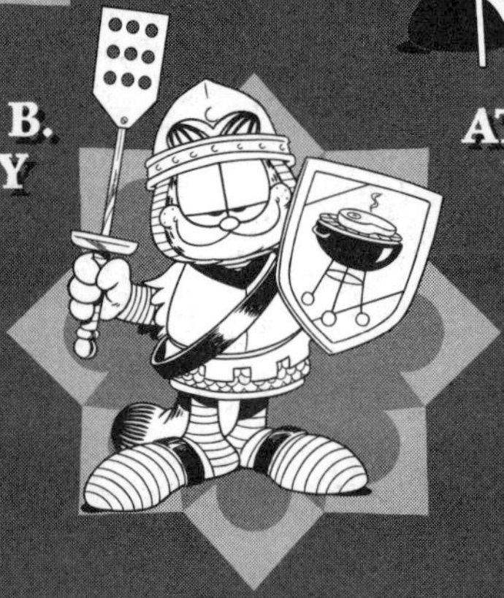

SIR LUNCHALOT

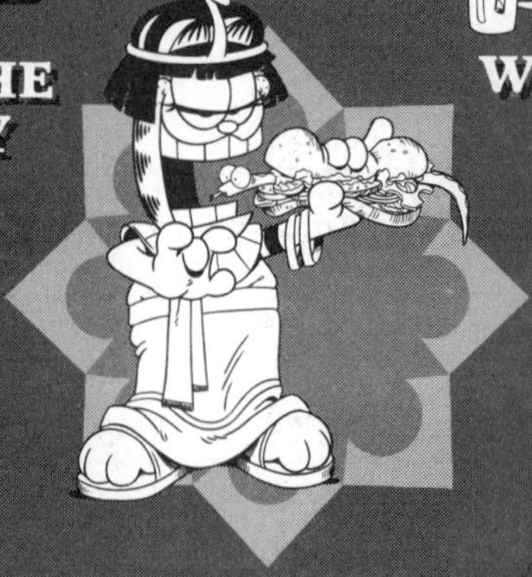

CLEOFATRA

Like to get a **COOL CAT**alog stuffed with great **GARFIELD** products? Then just write down the information below, stuff it in an envelope and mail it back to us...or you can fill in the card on our website - HTTP://www.GARFIELD.com. We'll get one out to you in two shakes of a cat's tail!

Name:
Address:
City:
State:
Zip:
Phone:
Date of Birth:
Sex:

Please mail your information to:

Garfield Stuff Catalog
Dept.2BB38A
5804 Churchman By-Pass
Indianapolis, IN 46203-6109

© PAWS

STRIPS, SPECIALS, OR BESTSELLING BOOKS . . .
GARFIELD'S ON EVERYONE'S MENU
Don't miss even one episode in the Tubby Tabby's hilarious series!

__GARFIELD AT LARGE (#1)   32013/$6.95
__GARFIELD GAINS WEIGHT (#2)   32008/$6.95
__GARFIELD BIGGER THAN LIFE (#3)   32007/$6.95
__GARFIELD WEIGHS IN (#4)   32010/$6.95
__GARFIELD TAKES THE CAKE (#5)   32009/$6.95
__GARFIELD EATS HIS HEART OUT (#6)   32018/$6.95
__GARFIELD SITS AROUND THE HOUSE (#7)   32011/$6.95
__GARFIELD TIPS THE SCALES (#8)   33580/$6.95
__GARFIELD LOSES HIS FEET (#9)   31805/$6.95
__GARFIELD MAKES IT BIG (#10)   31928/$6.95
__GARFIELD ROLLS ON (#11)   32634/$6.95
__GARFIELD OUT TO LUNCH (#12)   33118/$6.95
__GARFIELD FOOD FOR THOUGHT (#13)   34129/$6.95
__GARFIELD SWALLOWS HIS PRIDE (#14)   34725/$6.95
__GARFIELD WORLDWIDE (#15)   35158/$6.95
__GARFIELD ROUNDS OUT (#16)   35388/$6.95
__GARFIELD CHEWS THE FAT (#17)   35956/$6.95
__GARFIELD GOES TO WAIST (#18)   36430/$6.95
__GARFIELD HANGS OUT (#19)   36835/$6.95
__GARFIELD TAKES UP SPACE (#20)   37029/$6.95
__GARFIELD SAYS A MOUTHFUL (#21)   37368/$6.95

__GARFIELD BY THE POUND (#22)   37579/$6.95
__GARFIELD KEEPS HIS CHINS UP (#23)   37959/$6.95
__GARFIELD TAKES HIS LICKS (#24)   38170/$6.95
__GARFIELD HITS THE BIG TIME (#25)   38332/$6.95
__GARFIELD PULLS HIS WEIGHT (#26)   38666/$6.95
__GARFIELD DISHES IT OUT (#27)   39287/$6.95
__GARFIELD LIFE IN THE FAT LANE (#28)   39776/$6.95
__GARFIELD TONS OF FUN (#29)   40386/$6.95
__GARFIELD BIGGER AND BETTER (#30)   40770/$6.95
__GARFIELD HAMS IT UP (#31)   41241/$6.95
__GARFIELD THINKS BIG (#32)   41671/$6.95

GARFIELD AT HIS SUNDAY BEST!
__GARFIELD TREASURY   32106/$11.95
__THE SECOND GARFIELD TREASURY   33276/$10.95
__THE THIRD GARFIELD TREASURY   32635/$11.00
__THE FOURTH GARFIELD TREASURY   34726/$10.95
__THE FIFTH GARFIELD TREASURY   36268/$12.00
__THE SIXTH GARFIELD TREASURY   37367/$10.95
__THE SEVENTH GARFIELD TREASURY   38427/$10.95
__THE EIGHTH GARFIELD TREASURY   39778/$12.00
__THE NINTH GARFIELD TREASURY   41670/$12.50

AND DON'T MISS...
GARFIELD'S TWENTIETH ANNIVERSARY COLLECTION!   42126/$14.95

Please send me the BALLANTINE BOOKS I have checked above. I am enclosing $_____. (Please add $2.00 for the first book and $.50 for each additional book for postage and handling and include the appropriate state sales tax.) Send check or money order (no cash or C.O.D.'s) to Ballantine Mail Sales Dept. TA, 400 Hahn Road, Westminster, MD 21157.

To order by phone, call 1-800-733-3000 and use your major credit card.

Prices and numbers are subject to change without notice. Valid in the U.S. only. All orders are subject to availability.

Name_____

Address_____

City_____ State_____ Zip_____